Disability and World Religions

SRTD
STUDIES IN RELIGION, THEOLOGY, AND DISABILITY

SERIES EDITORS

Sarah J. Melcher
Xavier University (Cincinnati, Ohio)

and

Amos Yong
Fuller Theological Seminary (Pasadena, California)

Disability and World Religions

An Introduction

Darla Y. Schumm and Michael Stoltzfus

Editors

BAYLOR UNIVERSITY PRESS

Jacket design by Adam Bohannon
Cover image: *This Breathing World* by Rachel Gadsden, www.rachelgadsden.com, London, UK

Library of Congress Cataloging-in-Publication Data

Names: Schumm, Darla Y. (Darla Yvonne), editor. | Stoltzfus, Michael, 1965–
editor.
Title: Disability and world religions : an introduction / Darla Y. Schumm and
Michael Stoltzfus, Editors.
Description: Waco, Texas : Baylor University Press, 2016. | Series: Studies
in religion, theology, and disability | Includes bibliographical
references and index.
Identifiers: LCCN 2016003891| ISBN 9781481305211 (hardback : alk. paper) |
ISBN 9781481305228 (ebook-mobi/kindle) | ISBN 9781481305235 (web pdf)
Subjects: LCSH: Disabilities—Religious aspects. | Religions.
Classification: LCC BL65.B63 D573 2016 | DDC 200.87—dc23
LC record available at http://lccn.loc.gov/2016003891

Printed in the United States of America on acid-free paper with a minimum of 30 percent post-consumer waste.

Series Introduction

Studies in Religion, Theology, and Disability brings newly established and emerging scholars together to explore issues at the intersection of religion, theology, and disability. The series editors encourage theoretical engagement with secular disability studies while supporting the reexamination of established religious doctrine and practice. The series fosters research that takes account of the voices of people with disabilities and the voices of their family and friends.

The volumes in the series address issues and concerns of the global religious studies/theological studies academy. Authors come from a variety of religious traditions with diverse perspectives to reflect on the intersection of the study of religion/theology and the human experience of disability. This series is intentional about seeking out and publishing books that engage with disability in dialogue with Jewish, Christian, Buddhist, or other religious and philosophical perspectives.

Themes explored include religious life, ethics, doctrine, proclamation, liturgical practices, physical space, spirituality, or the interpretation of sacred texts through the lens of disability. Authors in the series are aware of conversation in the field of disability studies and bring that discussion to bear methodologically and theoretically in their analyses at the intersection of religion and disability.

Studies in Religion, Theology, and Disability reflects the following developments in the field: First, the emergence of disability studies as an interdisciplinary endeavor that has impacted theological studies, broadly defined. More and more scholars are deploying disability perspectives in their work, and this applies also to those working in the theological academy. Second, there is a growing need for critical reflection on disability in world religions. While books from a Christian standpoint have dominated the discussion at the interface of religion and disability so far, Jewish, Muslim, Buddhist, and Hindu scholars, among those from other religious traditions, have begun to resource their own religious traditions to rethink disability in the twenty-first century. Third, passage of the Americans with Disabilities Act in the United States has raised the consciousness of the general public about the importance of critical reflection on disability in religious communities. General and intelligent lay readers are looking for scholarly discussions of religion and disability as these bring together and address two of the most important existential aspects of human lives. Fourth, the work of activists in the disability rights movement has mandated fresh critical reflection by religious practitioners and theologians. Persons with disabilities remain the most disaffected group from religious organizations. Fifth, government representatives in several countries have prioritized the greater social inclusion of persons with disabilities. Disability policy often proceeds based on core cultural and worldview assumptions that are religiously informed. Work at the interface of religion and disability thus could have much broader purchase—that is, in social, economic, political, and legal domains.

Under the general topic of thoughtful reflection on the religious understanding of disability, Studies in Religion, Theology, and Disability includes shorter, crisply argued volumes that articulate a bold vision within a field; longer scholarly monographs, more fully developed and meticulously documented, with the same goal of engaging wider conversations; textbooks that provide a state of the discussion at this intersection and chart constructive ways forward; and select edited volumes that achieve one or more of the preceding goals.

Contents

Acknowledgments

Editing a text is one of the most challenging yet satisfying forms of scholarly collaboration. Many people contributed their time and expertise to bring this book to fruition. We are deeply grateful to the authors of the chapters for their scholarly insights, their careful research, and, most of all, their patience with our deadline and revision requests. This book would not have been possible without the generosity of spirit, time, and talent of Julia Watts Belser, Amy Donahue, Stephen Harris, Mary Jo Iozzio, Andrew Lambert, Lavonna Lovern, Benjamin Lukey, Thomas Reynolds, and Vardit Rispler-Chaim.

We thank Amos Yong and Sarah J. Melcher, the editors of the Studies in Religion, Theology, and Disability series at Baylor University Press, for showing confidence in our editing abilities by inviting us to engage this project and for their guidance and support throughout the process. We are equally grateful to Baylor University Press for demonstrating a strong commitment to exploring the important intersections between religion, theology, and disability through this series. We offer our thanks to the Baylor University Press editorial staff for deftly guiding us through the manuscript preparation and publication maze.

Most of what we do would not be possible without the love and support of our families. We thank our parents, Clare and Katie Ann Schumm and Glenn and Geneva Stoltzfus, for their constant care, encouragement, and nurture. Our spouses and children—Rebecca Green, William Stoltzfus, Jonathan Harris, and Henry Schumm—provide daily inspiration and encouragement and receive our deep gratitude for sustaining us from the beginning to the end of the project.

There are too many people to name individually who offered support and encouragement to this project, but Rebecca Seipp and Brian Heart deserve special recognition and thanks. Rebecca and Brian spent countless hours proofreading, copy editing, formatting, and helping us prepare the manuscript for submission. Their meticulous attention to detail is the sort of work that often goes unrecognized but is at the core of what makes a text truly accessible and user friendly. Thank-you does not seem adequate to convey the depth of our gratitude to those specifically mentioned here, and to many we have not mentioned, but we extend our heartfelt thanks to all who helped us bring this text into existence.

Preface

This book presents a unique collection of chapters that introduce readers to the rich diversity of some of the world's religions through the lens of disability studies. Contributors examine how particular religious traditions tend to represent, theologize, theorize, and respond to people living with physical and mental differences and disabilities. It is widely recognized that religious teachings and practices across the globe help establish cultural representations for what is deemed normal human physical and mental behavior and typical standards for measuring conventional health and well-being. In its many manifestations, religion plays a critical role in determining how disability is understood and how persons with disabilities are treated in a given cultural context. Each chapter introduces a specific religious tradition in a manner that offers innovative approaches to familiar themes in contemporary debates about religion and disability, including personhood, autonomy, community, ability, transcendence, morality, practice, interpretation of texts, and conditioned claims regarding the normal human body or mind.

Editing a textbook with multiple contributors involves striking a balance between maintaining chapter consistency and granting the author latitude to present the unique elements of particular religious traditions in creative and flexible formats. To this end, authors were asked to construct their respective chapters in a manner that would appeal to a broad readership of scholars and students from the disciplines of religious studies, disability studies, and cultural studies, as well as everyday religious practitioners from multiple traditions. Generally speaking, each chapter functions in four specific ways. First, each chapter describes the specific religious tradition to an audience that may not be familiar with its central themes, teachings, and worldviews. Second, each chapter introduces the relevance of religious studies and religious themes to people who are grounded in the field of disability studies and who are interested in the social experience of disability. Third, each chapter introduces the interdisciplinary nature of the field of disability studies to people who are rooted in religious studies or a specific religious tradition. The fields of disability studies and religious studies are both multidisciplinary at their core. Both incorporate dynamic connections across many fields of analysis, including health-care, psychological, economic, historical, social, artistic, legal, and other perspectives. Fourth, each chapter critically engages a specific religious tradition from the perspective of strengths, weaknesses, and constructive suggestions for how contemporary religious communities might be transformed in order to be more hospitable to and informed by the voices and experiences of people with disabilities or chronic illnesses. Each author, however, addresses these issues in his or her own way, resulting in a format that mimics the rich diversity of many of the world's religions.

As an introduction to both world religions and disability studies, this book can be utilized in a variety of educational contexts. For example, in a disability studies course, this book will reveal how religion is one component of the cultural, social, anthropological, and historical representations of disability. Each contributor describes and contextualizes the nature and scope of religion and religious experience from the unique contours of a specific tradition. Contributors were not asked to structure their approach or analysis into any preordained definitional categories or methodological frameworks. In a world religions course, this book will not only expose students to the key elements of specific religious traditions but will also allow them to explore how religious teachings and practices affect the daily lives of people living with disabilities or chronic illnesses. This book was designed to be accessible to a multicultural audience, to be helpful as a tool for learning from our near and distant religious and cultural neighbors, to highlight the many forms of human embodiment, and to create a resource for investigating issues in disability studies from the perspective of religious pluralism. Although composed of chapters focusing on specific religious traditions, this book, when taken as a whole, facilitates examination of the relationship between disability, religion, culture, and ongoing personal and social transformation from multicultural and interreligious perspectives.

The very notion of disability as a concept, comprising a wide range of cognitive, physical, sensory, and psychological states of being, is understood quite differently among various cultural and religious communities and even within those communities. Several contributors note that some languages do not have a word for disability and that speakers of those languages find such a cultural construct strange as all human beings have different levels of ability for sight, hearing, movement, and memory. The limiting and fragmented ways that religious and cultural traditions conceptualize disability—and the struggle to critically engage such conceptualization—is a major theme addressed throughout this book.

Each contributor, in his or her own unique way and style, recognizes that narrow concepts of natural or normal are often barriers to overcome rather than outcomes to aspire toward. Emerging trends in the connections between religion, culture, and living with some form of disability raise the issue of how to realize a meaningful life as a whole person in a personal, medical, social, cultural, and spiritual context. This type of an approach to religion and transformation, rooted in a willingness to live with flexibility, uncertainty, and vulnerability, can help to transform everybody, from individuals living with disabilities to those with narrower cultural, medical, or religious approaches to health, ability, normality, and human community.

An important step toward expanding narrower perspectives and cultivating flexible horizons of awareness involves acknowledging that neither religious experience nor disability experience can be categorized in universal or static terms. Pluralism, not homogeneity, is the mark of both religious and disability experience. One reason why the field of disability studies is so dynamic and multidimensional is that disability defies simple categorization. According to the "Factsheet on Persons with Disabilities" presented by United Nations Enable (the official website of the Secretariat for the Convention on the Rights of Persons with Disabilities), people with disabilities are the largest minority group in the world, comprising 15 percent of the world's population, or about one billion people (UN Enable). Moreover, the World Health Organization (WHO) notes that these numbers have continued to increase as a result of medical advances, population aging, and population growth (UN Enable). Additionally, disability cuts across all races, classes, genders, ethnicities, nationalities, religions, and generations, and all human beings are likely to experience some form of disability if they live long enough. Disability experiences are varied and unique, not uniform and homogenous.

People with disabilities have more differences than similarities. Disabling conditions can include intellectual, physical, and psychological issues that are remittent or persistent, acquired or genetic, progressive or static. For example, the challenges and opportunities a person who is blind encounters differ widely from those encountered by a person who uses a wheelchair. There may be some shared general concerns regarding issues of accessibility and accommodation, but the specific details of those concerns may have little to no common ground. People who use wheelchairs may have no trouble finding the entrance to an unfamiliar building, but once they get to the door, they may find that the opening is not wide enough to accommodate their chair, or that there are only steps into the building and no ramp. A person who is blind, by contrast, may experience great difficulty in locating the entrance to an unfamiliar building, but once the entrance has been found, going through the door or up steps may be no problem. Each of these individuals needs different types of assistance and/or accommodation and experiences barriers and challenges in very different ways. Even people with the same disability may have varying needs and challenges. A person who is blind and uses a cane will not have the same challenges being stuck in an airport for eight hours due to weather delays as will a person who uses guide dogs. People who use canes do not have to worry about whether or not their dogs will be able to wait to relieve themselves until the travel day is complete. These examples only scratch the surface in illustrating the wide diversity of challenges, opportunities, barriers, and gifts that people with disabilities face. These dissimilarities make a broad definition of people with disabilities difficult, if not impossible.

As with disability, religious practices, texts, symbols, rituals, prayers, meditations, meanings, and traditions are beyond simplistic summation or description. Religious practices are ever changing, and great diversity and variation exists within each religious tradition, making definitive answers to specific questions such as "What is the explanation or response to disability within a specific religious community?" impossible. Indeed, such broad questions are misleading as they tend to cultivate static theoretical responses to pluralistic practical issues. While the themes of disability as punishment for sin or moral failure, disability as a lesson for learning or growth, or disability as a gift or test from God do appear in diverse religious traditions, it is not accurate to suggest that religious traditions fit a uniform model for defining or responding to disability. None of the contributors to this book claim to speak with an authoritative voice for the religious traditions that they describe. Readers should approach this text with the understanding that what is learned about any given religion is simply one individual's interpretation. There are undoubtedly other ways of understanding the tradition.

Most of the contributors in this book explicitly or implicitly draw on scholarship from the expanding field of disability studies. In particular, many of the contributors highlight the ongoing struggle for full social and religious access for people with disabilities from around the globe. Accessibility has become a rallying cry among people with disabilities, and the body is often the focal point for addressing issues of political and social access. In challenging society's definitions of disabled bodies as flawed and incapable, people with disabilities have refused to tolerate discrimination in employment, restriction from public buildings, isolation from educational opportunities, and lack of access to medical care or legal protection. However, several contributors make the important point that full participation goes beyond issues of institutional accommodation and physical modification to include issues of attitudinal orientation and participatory availability. There is a notable difference between physical accessibility and socioreligious integration, between formal protection under the law and the advent of community, friendships, and a sense of belonging. When religious and social affiliations treat the disabled as they treat the abled—as multidimensional people with diverse spiritual and dispositional needs—then these affiliations extend a gesture of accessibility that is as important as architectural accommodation.

The growing field of disability studies developed, in part, as a response to prior culturally prescribed meanings or models of disability and disability issues. A brief overview of some of the typical categories used to contextualize disability may help to integrate the diverse perspectives on religion and disability presented in this book. In particular, some contributors refer to impairment, medical, and social models of disability. Numerous disability studies theorists and activists observe that in spite of the vast diversity associated with disabling human conditions, socio-scientific models continue to label individual bodies with dualistic descriptive terms such as sick or healthy, abnormal or normal, disabled or abled (see Davis, *Enforcing Normalcy*; Wendell, *Rejected Body*; Linton, *Claiming Disability*).

Impairment, medical, and social models are common examples used as conceptual categories. The impairment model tends to label individual bodies based on functional deficits, views impairment as a lack of wholeness, and associates health, normality, and ability with living without the presence of impairment.

Medical models of disability also tend to emphasize individual deficits or impairments but incorporate a narrative focusing on diagnosis, treatment, and cure. People are not whole, not really able, unless they are cured or restored to health. Normal human bodies eventually get better—the bone mends, the pain subsides, the scar heals. Disability studies scholar Rosemarie Garland-Thomson describes disability according to the medical model as "an inherent inferiority, pathology to cure, or undesirable trait to eliminate" ("Feminist Disability Studies," 1558). This approach often fails to incorporate issues associated with social exclusion or social accommodation while perpetuating the misnomer that the root problem often lies in the disabled, individual body rather than in the social, political, medical, and economic forces that may marginalize and stigmatize persons with disabilities. In addition, acute-care medical models tend to ignore important issues associated with chronic conditions that often have no established medical protocols for their cure. Chronic disabilities do not fit the typical pattern of a health crisis and resolution but last for a long period, often for life. For people living with a chronic illness or disability, the condition is an intrinsic element of being alive, a permanent feature of living in which people must learn to integrate their conditions constructively into their sense of personal, social, medical, and spiritual self-identity. In many cases, the ongoing task is holistic healing rather than curing a specific, individual disease state. This task requires an explicit focus on the human experience of disability in all its multifaceted dynamics, corresponding flexibility in coping responses, and learning to live well in the presence, rather than the absence, of physical or mental incapacity while recognizing vulnerability as a way of life.

In contrast to the impairment and medical models, which tend to associate disability with individual impairment that requires treatment or cure, the social model of disability tries to normalize impaired bodies and minds in order to contextualize oppressive social and historical conditions. Many in the disabled population suggest that economic hardships, inaccessible environments, and social prejudice pose greater difficulty than the actual disability, although this is certainly not always the case (see Linton, *Claiming Disability*; Wendell, *Rejected Body*; Davis, *Enforcing Normalcy*). Nonetheless, the integration of disability as a natural form of embodiment and a normal element of social awareness empowers disability activists and theorists to destabilize oppressive interpretations and rethink inflexible categories. As physical and/ or psychological outsiders, people with disabilities offer a valuable critique of a world that others may take for granted, thereby opening new vistas for creative transformation in the interpersonal and social dimensions of our collective lives.

While the social model challenges discriminatory attitudes and social structures, some disability studies scholars also warn that there is a danger in glossing over the all-too-real challenges that accompany both physical and mental disabilities (see Morris 1991). Alexa Schriempf illustrates these dangers when she writes: "The social model, in focusing on the social construction of disability, has amputated disabled (especially women's) bodies from their impairments and their biological and social needs" (60). Despite important critiques and a variety of interpretive approaches, some form of the social model of disability continues to be endorsed by many leading scholars in the field of disability studies.

Most of the contributors in this text incorporate discussions about models of disability in their respective chapters. In some chapters, authors explicitly refer to the models mentioned above, while in other cases these characterizations of disability are more implicit. Either way, as readers undertake their own critical review of the material in this book, it may be helpful to ask the following questions: Is a particular model of disability being critiqued and/ or promoted? How are the various models of disability reflected through the author's analysis, or how are the various models of disability reflected in this religious tradition's understanding of and/or response to disability? None of these models of disability tell the whole story about what it means to live with some form of disability, but they can help reveal how disability is interpreted within a particular religious, historical, cultural, or social context.

Given the pervasive roles that disability and religion play in human experience, the chapters included in this volume portray varied and complex perspectives that are by no means exhaustive or uniform. Consensus regarding the experience of religion and disability or the understanding of how religious traditions and practices should conceptualize and respond to disability is not the objective of this project. Rather, we hope this textbook helps to foster an exploration of world religions through the lens of disability studies and to cultivate creative ways to respond to the fields of both religious studies and disability studies.

—Darla Y. Schumm and Michael Stoltzfus

1

Hinduism and Disability

Amy Donahue

INTRODUCTION

Hinduism's pluralism distinguishes it from other contemporary religious traditions. While other religions are diverse, Hinduism is, as Wendy Doniger stresses, *polylithic*—in other words, the very antithesis of monolithic. "Pluralism and diversity," she writes, "are deeply ingrained in polylithic Hinduism, the Ellis Island of religions; the lines between different beliefs and practices are permeable membranes. . . . The texts wrestle with competing truths, rather than offer pat answers" (*Hindus*, 43–44). Doniger offers an image to help us imagine this polylithic character. Picture a Venn diagram of practices and commitments that different scholars and practitioners might say are essential to a tradition. Every Hindu would adhere to some combination of representative customs and concepts, while non-Hindus would not. Few Hindus, however, would adhere to the same combination. While common threads wend across representations of Hinduism, none are clearly essential or even properly central. This pluralism contrasts with religious traditions that presume their members share foundational commitments or practices (e.g., belief that the sole path to salvation is through Jesus Christ or that there is no God but Allah). Instead, members of the Hindu tradition resemble one another more like members of a family; practices and commitments recur, but none are indubitably central (28). "The configuration of the clusters of Hinduism's defining characteristics changes through time, through space, and through each individual," Doniger writes. Hinduism is a polylithic (rather than monolithic) fabric; therefore, whatever one might consider central to Hinduism, such as the Vedas, karma, dharma, or the *Mahabharata* (we will discuss these texts and concepts below), can only be an imaginary center in a fabric that has no center (29).

Before looking at particular texts and practices, we should note two methodological implications of Hinduism's polylithic character. First, because Hinduism is polylithic, this chapter's discussion of Hinduism and disability is not authoritative. It should serve as an invitation to further study, reflection, and discussion rather than a source of fixed answers. Second, as Doniger observes, since Hinduism is a fabric lacking any uncontested center, the tradition must also be a fabric with no uncontested margins (*Hindus*, 29). We should therefore be alert to a potential benefit of studying disability through the lens of world religions and through a Hindu lens in particular. Asking questions cross-culturally sometimes requires that we contest apparently universal, but actually provincial, "master images," as Arjun Appadurai calls them (93). Master images are taken-for-granted assumptions that circumstances or arrangements are natural, timeless, or somehow central to human experience. For example, contemporary disability studies theorists who adopt cultural models challenge ableist master images of universal, "normal" human subjectivity, physiology, and ability. By engaging diverse Hindu narratives of subjectivity, embodiment, and social identity, we may similarly, as Appadurai advises, discover that taken-for-granted assumptions of disability that circulate not only in the West but now also globally are parochial and not universal. Our second general methodological conclusion, then, is this: while we should not expect the polylithic Hindu tradition to univocally affirm specific perspectives about disability—and surely should not expect to encounter only perspectives that contemporary disability theorists would favor—we may expect to find resources in the Hindu religious tradition which challenge global disability-related assumptions. By examining disability within Hindu contexts, we may discover that master images create locally interested and imaginary centers on a polylithic fabric—humanity— that has no center and, hence, can have no peripheries.

SOME CONCEPTUAL AND TEXTUAL BACKGROUND

The word "Hinduism" derives from a Sanskrit name for the Indus River (*sindhu*). It was first coined by outsiders to refer to the cultures and peoples around the Indus River valley region.[1] Only in the past several centuries have South Asians begun using the term to designate a seemingly unified religion that the majority population of present-day India shares; even today, many Hindus often prefer more specific terms, such as "Golkonda Vyaparis," to describe their religious identities, practices, and commitments (Doniger, *Hindus*, 30).

Although the notion of Hinduism as a unified religion is to some extent modern and colonially inflected, the tradition also draws on practices, texts, and concepts that are ancient. Certain of these ancient elements, such as the Vedas, karma, dharma, and the *Mahabharata*, recur in contemporary discussions of disability in India. Therefore, before proceeding further, it will help to develop some background familiarity with these texts and concepts.

The Vedas

The Vedas are anthologies of Sanskrit hymns or incantations (*sūktas*) that are associated with the performance of ritual sacrifices (*yajña*). Some, but not all, Hindus regard the Vedas as an infallible source of knowledge or wisdom. (The word *veda* comes from the Sanskrit verb root *vid*, "to know.") Scholars date the oldest of these anthologies, the Rig Veda, to approximately the sixteenth century BCE (Doniger, *Hindus*, 86). Other Vedas include the Sama Veda, the Yajur Veda, and, depending on one's perspective, a fourth collection, the Atharva Veda. Scholars date these latter collections to between the thirteenth and tenth centuries BCE (693).

Vedic sūktas consist of metered mantras that are to be voiced within ritual practices. For most of their history, the Vedas were transmitted orally. They continued to be transmitted orally even when other kinds of texts circulated in writing (Doniger, *Textual Sources*, 1). Their history of oral transmission partially reflects the special power that they were, and for many still are, believed to possess. A Sanskrit word that is used for the Vedas (and select other texts) reflects both their perceived special power and their history of oral transmission: they are *shruti*—a kind of authoritative and inerrant knowledge that is heard. As we will see, there has been much debate and discussion in Hindu traditions about who should be allowed to hear, speak, and know the Vedas.

The oldest anthology, the Rig Veda (Knowledge of praise/hymns), like all the Vedas, is varied. It consists of more than one thousand sūktas, many lauding various gods, goddesses, and other divine agents. Some tell stories about deities. Some entreat divinities for assistance, both in grand matters (e.g., deliverance of rain, preparation for war, and protection from harm), and in more mundane projects (e.g., accumulating riches, warding off sexual rivals, and overcoming gambling compulsions). Some sūktas speculate about death and the creation of the universe. Even when they address unitary topics, different accounts are typically given, often in the same incantation. For example, consider the following Rig Veda creation sūkta:

10.129 *Creation Hymn (Nāsadīya)*

1. There was neither non-existence nor existence then; there was neither the realm of space nor the sky which is beyond. What stirred? Where? In whose protection? Was there water, bottomlessly deep?

2. There was neither death nor immortality then. There was no distinguishing sign of night nor of day. That one breathed, windless, by its own impulse. Other than that there was nothing beyond.

3. Darkness was hidden by darkness in the beginning; with no distinguishing sign, all this was water. The life force that was covered with emptiness, that one arose through the power of heat [*tapas*].

4. Desire came upon that one in the beginning; that was the first seed of mind. Poets seeking in their heart with wisdom found the bond of existence in non-existence.

5. Their cord was extended across. Was there below? Was there above? There were seed-placers; there were powers. There was impulse beneath; there was giving-forth above.

6. Who really knows? Who will here proclaim it? Whence was it produced? Whence is this creation? The gods came afterwards, with the creation of this universe. Who then knows whence it has arisen?

7. Whence this creation has arisen—perhaps it formed itself, or perhaps it did not—the one who looks down on it, in the highest heaven, only he knows—or perhaps he does not know. (Doniger, *Rig Veda*, 25–26)

The closing words of this sūkta and the use of paradox throughout foreground the mystery of creation. In contrast, elsewhere in the incantation, one can discern a chronology of the universe's unfolding. Pure, still darkness first concealed undifferentiated reality. Then heat emerged, and with heat desire, and with desire differentiation (i.e., creation). The closing lines then throw this chronology into doubt.

Other Rig Veda sūktas describe creation differently and with apparently different motivations. The following sūkta pictures the totality of reality as a primordial person, *purusha*, and explains how the ritual sacrifice of purusha carved the undifferentiated entirety of everything into an ordered cosmos. Instead of emphasizing mystery (though such themes surely remain present, especially in vv. 1-5), this hymn seems to stress (and to prescribe) divisions:

10.90 *The Hymn of Man (Puruṣa-Sūkta)*

1. The Man [Purusha] has a thousand heads, a thousand eyes, a thousand feet. He pervaded the earth on all sides and extended beyond it as far as ten fingers.

2. It is the Man who is all this, whatever has been and whatever is to be. He is the ruler of immortality, when he grows beyond everything through food.

3. Such is his greatness, and the Man is yet more than this. All creatures are a quarter of him; three quarters are what is immortal in heaven.

4. With three quarters the Man arose upwards, and one quarter of him still remains here. From this, he spread out in all directions, into that which eats and that which does not eat.

5. From him Virāj was born, and from Virāj came the Man [Purusha]. When he was born, he ranged beyond the earth behind and before.

6. When the gods spread the sacrifice with the Man as the offering, spring was the clarified butter, summer the fuel, autumn the oblation.

7. They anointed the Man, the sacrifice born at the beginning, upon the sacred grass. With him the gods, Sādhyas, and sages sacrificed.

8. From that sacrifice in which everything was offered, the melted fat was collected, and he made it into those beasts who live in the air, in the forest, and in villages.

9. From that sacrifice in which everything was offered, the verses and chants were born, the metres were born from it, and from it the formulas [for Vedic sacrifices] were born.

10. Horses were born from it, and those other animals that have two rows of teeth; cows were born from it, and from it goats and sheep were born.

11. When they divided the Man, into how many parts did they apportion him? What do they call his mouth, his two arms and thighs and feet?

12. His mouth became the Brahmin; his arms were made into the Warrior [*rājanya*; i.e., Kshatriya], his thighs the People [Vaishya], and from his feet the Servants [Shudra] were born.

13. The moon was born from his mind; from his eye the sun was born. Indra and Agni came from his mouth, and from his vital breath the Wind was born.

14. From his navel the middle realm of space arose; from his head the sky evolved. From his two feet came the earth, and the quarters of the sky from his ear. Thus they set the worlds in order.

15. There were seven enclosing sticks for him, and thrice seven fuel-sticks, when the gods, spreading the sacrifice, bound the Man as the sacrificial beast.

16. With the sacrifice the gods sacrificed to the sacrifice. These were the first ritual laws. These very powers reached the dome of the sky where dwell the Sādhyas, the ancient gods. (Doniger, *Rig Veda*, 30–31)

The first creation sūkta examined above foregrounds the mystery of creation, while this second seems primarily to delineate and rank natural kinds. Line twelve, for example, carves humanity into four categories or *varna*s. A priestly or "Brahmin" varna emerges from the mouth. Elsewhere, the mouth and breath are associated with purity—in this incantation, too, Indra, lord of the gods, and Agni, god of the sacrificial flame, emerge from Purusha's mouth. The Shudra varna, a natural class of servants, is said to emerge from Purusha's feet, and feet, as we will see, are elsewhere associated with impurity. Hence, this creation sūkta prescribes a fourfold system of human categorization, consisting of Brahmin, Kshatriya, Vaishya, and Shudra varnas. This system of categorization informs later Hindu conceptions of caste and serves as an important backdrop in later theories and practices related to disability.

Later texts are also often counted among the Vedic textual corpus and therefore as *shruti*. The Brahmanas are collections of prose commentaries on the Vedas. In general, these offer guidelines for the proper performance of Vedic ritual sacrifices and, according to scholars, were composed between the ninth and seventh centuries BCE (Doniger, *Hindus*, 693). The Aranyakas, like the Brahmanas, are collections of prose commentaries on the Vedas. Dated by scholars to the seventh and sixth centuries BCE (693), their name means "forest related." Whereas the Brahmanas tend to offer prescriptions for the performance of Vedic sacrifices, commentaries on the Vedas in the Aranyakas tend to be more speculative and fond of paradox. They serve as something of a textual bridge to the Upanishads. In the Upanishads, which scholars date to between the sixth and second centuries BCE, we find sustained and diverse philosophical inquiries into the meaning of the Vedas. The Upanishads address topics such as the nature of the self and the universe, the consequences of moral and immoral action, the fate of the self after death, the causes of ignorance and suffering on earth, and worthwhile life pursuits.

Some Hindus think of the Upanishads as elaborating and bringing to a close the meaning of the Vedas. Hence the Upanishads are sometimes called Vedanta (i.e., the conclusion or end, *anta*, of the Vedas). Others, however, favor elements of the tradition of the sort emphasized in the Brahmanas and the Purusha Sūkta. Both esoteric (arcane) and exoteric (householder, *grihastha*) approaches, although contrary, are equally present in the Vedic tradition and in contemporary Hinduism.

Karma

Few concepts are as widely associated with Hinduism in Western popular imagination as karma. Understandings in the West, however, often caricature Hindu conceptions by disassociating them from their background contexts. The first clear appearance in the Vedic textual corpus of theories positing moral causation and the transmigration of souls, key elements of contemporary, popular Hindu notions of karma, is in the Upanishads. Theories of moral causation claim that actions with specific moral qualities produce effects with specific moral qualities. For instance, one who believes in moral causality could hold that morally good actions lead to morally superior states and morally bad actions lead to morally inferior states. A theory of the transmigration of souls, on the other hand, posits that souls or identities migrate to other forms and bodies after death. When coupled, these ideas align with something like contemporary Hindu ideas of karma—morally good actions lead to morally superior rebirths, and morally bad actions lead to morally inferior rebirths. Etymologically, however, karma simply means "action" (from the Sanskrit verb root *kr*, "to do").

In the Rig Veda, karma is most obviously used with this simple etymological meaning. Consider these mantras from Rig Veda 10.117:

2. The man with food who hardens his heart against the poor man who comes to him suffering and searching for nourishment—though in the past he had made use of him—he surely finds no sympathy.

3. The man who is truly generous gives to the beggar who approaches him thin and in search of food. He puts himself at the service of the man who calls to him from the road, and makes him a friend for times to come.

   . . . .

5. Let the stronger man give to the man whose need is greater; let him gaze upon the lengthening path. For riches roll like the wheels of a chariot, turning from one to another.

   . . . .

7. The plough that works the soil makes a man well-fed; the legs that walk put the road behind them. The priest who speaks is better than the one who does not speak. The friend who gives freely surpasses the one who does not. (Doniger, *Rig Veda*, 68–69)

While these mantras are not inconsistent with a theory of moral causation, they do not necessitate such a theory. Mantra seven could be read as teaching that, if people want to be well fed, then they must act to be well fed—they must work, for example, by pushing the plow. And if people want to excel as friends or priests, then they must act as friends or priests—for example, they must give freely and chant the Vedas. Because being well fed, well liked, and a successful priest are not necessarily morally superior states, karma here can be read simply as "action," without commitment to moral causality or transmigration, and this remains the case throughout the Vedas. It is possible, of course, to read later Hindu theories of moral causation and transmigration back into the Vedas, and many sects do this.

In the Upanishads, which were composed approximately a millennium after the Rig Veda, the term *karma* begins to be linked to theories of moral causality and the transmigration of souls. We first clearly encounter this intersection of concepts in the Chandogya Upanishad. Consider the following:

> Those who know this, and those who worship in the forest, concentrating on faith and asceticism, they are born into the flame, and from the flame into the day, and from the day into the fortnight of the waxing moon, and from the fortnight of the waxing moon into the six months during which the sun moves north; from these months, into the year; from the year, into the sun; from the sun into the moon; from the moon into the lightening. There a Person [Purusha] who is not a human leads them to the ultimate reality. This is the path that the gods go on.
>
> But those who worship in the village, concentrating on sacrifices and good works and charity, they are born [after death] into smoke, and from the smoke into the night, and from the night into the other fortnight, and from the other fortnight into the six months when the sun moves south. They do not reach the year. From these months they go to the world of the fathers, and from the world of the fathers to space, and from space to the moon. That is king Soma. That is the food of the gods. The gods eat that.
>
> When they have dwelt there for as long as there is a remnant (of their merit), then they return along that very same road that they came along, back into space; but from space they go to wind, and when one has become wind, he becomes smoke, and when he has become smoke he becomes mist; when he has become mist, he becomes a cloud, and when he has become a cloud, he rains. These are then born here as rice, barley, plants, trees, sesame plants, and beans. It is difficult to move forth out of this condition; for only if someone eats him as food and then emits him as semen, he becomes that creature's semen and is born.
>
> And so those who behave nicely here will, in general, find a nice womb, the womb of a Brahmin or the womb of a Kshatriya or the womb of a Vaishya. But those whose behavior is stinking will, in general, find a stinking womb, the womb of a dog or the womb of a pig or the womb of an Untouchable. (Doniger, *Textual Sources*, 36–37)

Doniger translates *Chandala* in the closing paragraph of this excerpt as "Untouchable." Classical Sanskrit texts often use the term to signify an especially depraved category of persons outside of the fourfold varna system.[2] Chandalas are people who were believed to be neither Brahmins, Kshatriyas, Vaishyas, nor Shudras, and, as can be seen, the text associates them with a kind of moral stench. In contrast, the text claims, the life-fires of householders who behave well and are reborn generally reemerge as more cosmically sweet-smelling Brahmins, Kshatriyas, or Vaishyas. Shudras are assumed here to be more polluted than members of the other varnas and are not included among the three sweet-smelling groups, which the Vedic textual corpus calls the varnas of those who are "twice-born."

The notion of purity that undergirds the Chandogya Upanishad's theory of karma is linked to a metaphysics that describes manifest reality as constituted by three intertwined threads or *gunas*—*sattva, rajas,* and *tamas.* Sattva is purity and clarity; rajas is activity and passion; and tamas is inertia, ignorance, impurity, and darkness. These three threads are said to intertwine in all manifest existence—that is, in the whole realm of karma—and are color coded in Hindu texts as white, red, and black, respectively. (One meaning of the Sanskrit term *varna* is "color.") In the Chandogya Upanishad, before the excerpt presented above, manifest reality is explained as a progressive unfolding of what is maximally pure and sweet, the sound ॐ (Oṃ, associated with breath), into relatively less pure, less sattvic states. Manifest realities that are allegedly more sweet-smelling, such as Brahmin, Kshatriya, and Vaishya persons, are supposed to be characterized more by sattva and less by tamas and rajas. And manifest realities that are allegedly more pungent, such as wombs of dogs, pigs, and Chandalas, are supposed to be characterized more by tamas and rajas and less by sattva.

The Chandogya Upanishad's theory of karma assumes that, as a birthright (albeit a birthright contingent to one life), categories of persons bear different moral ranks. It attributes people's social positions, embodiments, and challenges to activities in unwitnessed previous existences. Further, it rationalizes the Purusha Sūkta's hierarchy of persons and prescribes a system of cosmic carrots and sticks to incentivize adherence to this ideal. Note, however, that the excerpt also includes an alternative. The first paragraph indicates that people who retreat from society as ascetics and master esoteric Upanishadic knowledge transmigrate along a different path. Rather than rising as smoke, spending time on the moon as food for the gods, and returning to earth as food to be eaten once more, those who retreat to the forest to practice austerities may attain release (*moksha*) from the karmic cycle of rebirth, the realm of the three gunas, and the division of humanity into the four varnas. This distinction between a forest path of flame and a village path of smoke echoes the distinction between the esoteric Aranyakas and the exoteric Brahmanas. Again, in Hinduism, rather than receiving pat answers, we find competing accounts, often in the same source material, presented as potentially valid paths (Doniger, *Hindus*, 173–75).

Dharma

According to the Chandogya Upanishad and other Upanishads, people's karmic trajectories depend on actions in unwitnessed past lives and on the performance of their current duties. Beings who fulfill their present duties tend
toward more morally fragrant rebirths, while beings who neglect their duties
tend toward more morally polluted states—unless, that is, they retreat to the
forest, literally or metaphorically, to perform appropriate austerities.

The Sanskrit term for "duty" is *dharma*. Unlike duties in Western liberal
discourse, which tend to be tied to human beings in general, duties in Hinduism are, for the most part, thought to vary according to the ends that persons
seek and their social positions and personal tendencies. Although there are
some dharmas that all persons are thought to share, Hinduism shows relatively scant interest in establishing universal narratives of duty.

Classical Hindu texts tend to recognize, and variously rank, four basic
ends or aims (*arthas*): wealth (*artha*, a homonym that shares some connotations), pleasure (*kama*, not to be confused with *karma*), righteousness (*dharma*),
and release from the karmic cycle of rebirth (*moksha*). From approximately
the fourth century BCE to the fourth century CE, an abundance of technical manuals (*shastras*) prescribed rules for the proper pursuit of each basic
end. Some texts synthesized these ends by linking them and their corresponding duties, first to different personal tendencies and, later, to different
stages of human life (*ashramas*). This latter association is more influential in
contemporary popular Hinduism (Doniger, *Hindus*, 207). Representations
of duties appropriate to life stages vary and are represented differently in
texts. According to the *Kama-Sutra*, children should primarily seek knowledge and other kinds of artha (wealth). After attaining these, young adults
should primarily seek kama (pleasure). After attaining kama, middle-aged
persons should primarily pursue dharma (righteousness), and, after pursuing
dharma, the elderly should retreat from mundane society (i.e., go to "the forest") and eventually seek moksha (release from rebirth) (208). Standards of
appropriate action (i.e., duties and norms) vary with each life stage.

The duties appropriate to different life stages are further complicated by
accounts of duties that are said to be appropriate to one's varna and gender. A
relatively late technical manual establishing rules for the pursuit of dharma,
the approximately second century CE *Manusmriti* (translated by Doniger
as *The Laws of Manu*), differentiates people's (presumed to be men's) duties
according to the fourfold varna system. Consider the following:

> 31) Then, so that the worlds and people would prosper and increase,
> from his mouth he created the priest [Brahmin], from his arms the

ruler [Kshatriya], from his thighs the commoner [Vaishya], and from his feet the servant [Shudra].

. . . .

87) But to protect this whole creation, the lustrous one made separate innate activities for those born of his mouth, arms, thighs, and feet.

88) For priests, he ordained teaching and learning, sacrificing for themselves and sacrificing for others, giving and receiving.

89) Protecting his subjects, giving, having sacrifices performed, studying, and remaining unaddicted to the sensory objects are, in summary, for a ruler.

90) Protecting his livestock, giving, having sacrifices performed, studying, trading, lending money, and farming the land are for a commoner.

91) The Lord assigned only one activity to a servant: serving these (other) classes [*varnas*] without resentment.

92) A man is said to be purer above the navel; therefore the Self-existent one said that his mouth was the purest part of him. (Doniger, *Laws*, 11; ch. 1)

These excerpts prescribe separate duties for people of each varna. According to this text, only Brahmins should perform sacrifices and recite the Vedas. Only Brahmins, Kshatriyas, and Vaishyas should observe sacrificial rituals and hear the Vedas recited. Meanwhile, the text bars Shudras, as well as those who are placed outside of the varna system, from participating in or hearing Vedic sacrificial rituals.

The audience of the *Manusmriti* is assumed to be male, and this assumption, along with the text's broader patriarchal commitments, leaves women in a weird place in the shastra. Although women are also categorized by varna, the text addresses women's duties separately, *en masse* and through the gaze of men (Doniger, *Laws*, ch. 9). Besides gender, further complications to the *Manusmriti* emerge from the text's recognition that, even then, people were not neatly categorized into four varnas. Much of the text tries to explain how, despite the Purusha Sūkta's division of humanity into the fourfold varna system, other kinds of persons (*jātis*) are present.[3] The existence of persons outside of the varna system, such as Chandalas, is attributed to the universe's cyclical departure from dharma, which has resulted in miscegenation between members of different varnas and in people failing to abide by their dharma (ch. 10). Suffice it to say, the text's division of duties according to the fourfold varna system is complicated by this abundance of *jātis*.[4] With different dharmas associated with different varnas, *jātis*, genders, life stages, and dispositions, the prospects for overarching theories of duty for humanity as such, or for global theories of "normal" human beings, are rendered remote. People and their duties vary.

Recognition of this plurality of human purposes and responsibilities continues in other Hindu texts, and particularly in the *Mahabharata*, a Sanskrit language epic that dates somewhere between the fourth century BCE and the fourth century CE. This text can be read as a reflection on the practical difficulties of recognizing and adhering to dharma (Doniger, *Hindus*, 277).

The Mahabharata

The *Mahabharata* chronicles the struggles of the five legendary Kshatriya sons of King Pandu with the one hundred sons of King Dhritarashtra,[5] a group of unscrupulous relatives known as the descendants of Kuru (the Kauravas). The text culminates in a battle in which the sons of Pandu (the Pandavas) defeat their rivals. After the battle and the later death of the Pandavas, the cosmos descends into our current epoch of ignorance and darkness (the Kali Yuga, an astrological era when tamas is preponderant).

The text contains numerous teachings about dharma, and many of these indicate how arduous it can be to recognize and abide by our duties. The human figure in the text who epitomizes fidelity to dharma is the eldest Pandava, Yudhishthira, and this hero appears not as a person who is assured of what is just but as one who struggles, and sometimes fails, to understand and do what is right. The narrative path to the final battle is laid out, for example, when Yudhishthira gambles and loses his wealth, kingdom, wife,[6] and freedom to the Kauravas in a rigged game of dice. Not only is inordinate gambling criticized in Vedic texts, but the *Mahabharata* also takes issue with Yudhishthira's treatment of the Pandavas' wife as property to be wagered. Yudhishthira embodies a life of commitment to dharma, not because he always knows what to do and does not make mistakes, but because, however imperfect the results of his actions, his motivations are steadfastly righteous.

Among the *Mahabharata*'s philosophical and folkloric explorations of dharma is the Bhagavad Gita, a division of the epic that elaborates a theory of practical morality. The Gita begins as the battle between the Pandavas and Kauravas is about to start. Arjuna, the third eldest of the Pandavas and a great warrior, looks across the battlefield and sees loved ones on both sides. He realizes that thousands of these loved ones will die, and he will kill many. Overcome with emotion, he attempts to apply the dharmashastras to his present crisis and convinces himself that slaughtering his family and friends would be immoral.

Rather than applaud Arjuna's refusal to participate in a battle that will have ruinous consequences, his dear friend and charioteer, Krishna, an avatar of the ultimate being,[7] tries to persuade him to fight and, in the process, purports to show Arjuna how to apply Vedic teachings to his life. He advocates a way of engaging the world that is also disengaged—a way of acting that is detached from concern for the fluctuating cosmos, the socially formalized fourfold varna system, and the explicit categories and rules of dharma stipulated in the shastras—yet, according to Krishna, is also maximally consonant with dharma. This yoga of detachment (from the Sanskrit verb root *yuj*, a cognate of the English verb "to yoke") ensures actions that are congruous with a dharma that is unique to oneself (*sva-dharma*).

Key to Krishna's teachings is a claim that people's true selves differ from their worldly manifestations. People do not stop existing after changing clothes or entering new phases of life. Aspects of existence that fluctuate, therefore, are not our selves. We are, instead, what persists through and exists apart from this changing manifest cosmos. We are, Krishna explains in chapter 2, identical to permanent, indestructible, unmanifest *purusha-uttama*—also known as Brahman—and do not cease to exist after death (Aurobindo 14–48).

According to Krishna, we fail to understand and adhere to dharma when we mistake the fluctuating threads of the cosmos for who we really are. Misidentifying ourselves causes us to become attached to impermanent phenomena, and this attachment makes us vulnerable to life's vicissitudes and, hence, confused about and prone to depart from our dharmas. As Krishna explains in II.62, "In him whose mind dwells on the objects of sense with absorbing interest, attachment to them is formed; from attachment arises desire; from desire anger comes forth" (Aurobindo 45). We might, for example, identify ourselves with our relationships, bodily or mental abilities, or reputations and, for their sake, not do what we would otherwise know needs to be done. Through misidentification, we make mistakes, just as Arjuna, overcome with emotion, is tempted to retreat from his duties on the battlefield.

According to Krishna, goals (arthas) and treasures (arthas) are, like clothes, bodies, and life stages, beyond our control and essentially different from our selves. They "roll like the wheels of a chariot, turning from one to another," as Rig Veda sūkta 10.117 says of riches; rather than clinging to them, we should "gaze upon the lengthening path." We should make all that we do a selfless, sacrificial offering to the fire of unmanifest, undifferentiated infinity. Otherwise, we will rise and fall in a karmic loop of sacrificial smoke. Consuming ephemeral arthas will consume us.

A second key theoretical element of the yoga that Krishna teaches Arjuna is his claim that moral rank in this life is primarily determined not by birthright but by the intentions that underlie our actions. In IX.32, Krishna says to Arjuna, "Those who take refuge with Me . . . though outcastes, born from a womb of sin, women, Vaishyas, even Shudras, they also attain to the highest goal" (Aurobindo 155). The arthas that motivate a person to act are, according to Krishna, colored primarily by sattva, rajas, or tamas. We become morally sweet smelling, we learn in chapter seventeen, not chiefly by being born male to twice-born parents but by acting on behalf of primarily sattvic ends. And we become morally pungent not chiefly by being conceived in the womb of a Chandala or dog but by acting with predominantly rajasic or tamasic ends-in-view (242–50). In this section of the *Mahabharata*, dharma is not only pluralized but is also disassociated from formal codifications of the sort found in the dharmashastras. The text articulates a novel theory of karma as well. Rather than rationalizing hierarchies of persons in ways that seem to deflect potential social critique, as the Chandogya Upanishad's path of smoke apparently does, the Bhagavad Gita's theory of karma justifies practices of moral discipline that are independent of social hierarchies and conventions.

Perhaps more than other religions, the polylithic Hindu tradition is defined by an abundance of efforts such as these to make novel, creative sense of ancient texts and concepts. Though the material presented here provides only a glimpse of the tradition's range and diversity, we should now be prepared to begin to address disability.

HINDUISM AND DISABILITY

Efforts to examine disability within Hindu contexts face an immediate challenge—the term "disability" has European roots and dates to the sixteenth century (*OED*). Its use to name a social identity is more recent, dating most clearly to post–World War II Europe and America. Therefore, studying disability in nonmodern and non-European traditions demands a sort of creative looking back and across. Initially, we must assume a modern, European understanding of the term and leaf through non-modern, non-European archives to find instances of the concept. An obvious risk of this initial approach is that we may ignore the parochial conditions in modern Western societies and cultures that first gave rise to the term. We may thus globalize conceptions that ought to be rooted in a provincial time and place, and, consequently, foreclose conceptions that could better suit other contexts, and perhaps better suit modern Western contexts. A second risk, associated with the first, is that uncritical application of this initial methodology may render studies of disability in non-modern and non-European contexts perfunctory. Once disability has been defined by modern Europeans, little is left for policymakers, activists, and scholars outside of the West except to catalogue responses and references to disability in non-Western traditions and societies, analyze the degrees to which they depart from an implicitly Western master image, and develop responses subaltern to this privileged standard. As international disability studies scholar M. Miles suggests, analyses such as these may lapse into the colonially inflected view "that 'local cultural beliefs' are barriers to be 'overcome' by a more vigorous application of modern (i.e., Western) scientific knowledge (or belief)" ("Community").

The first extensive study of disability in modern India, published in 1963, exhibits these faults. Usha Bhatt's *The Physically Handicapped in India* champions a rehabilitation model of disability that was developed in post–World War II Western societies. Rehabilitation models—the political, theoretical, and historical significance of which, in the West, would be hard to overstate—aim to maximize the autonomy and dignity of disabled persons. Bhatt's text offers useful empirical data on disability in twentieth-century India, but she also equates rehabilitation models with global progress and treats certain Hindu concepts, such as karma, as local cultural obstacles to be overcome. Writing of disability in ancient India, she contends, "The theory of *Karma* was instrumental in depriving the disabled of their inherent right to lead an independent life. It was believed that the disabled were reaping what they had sowed in lives bygone and any attempt to ameliorate their lot would, therefore, interfere with this divine justice" (96). Elsewhere, of disability in modern India, she argues:

> The proverbial fatalism that still pervades the masses in our country has also been responsible for this unhappy state of affairs. In other countries, the handicapped individuals themselves have raised their voices and fought for their rights to a successful end. Here, on the other hand, many of them have meekly resigned to the philosophy of *"Karma"* and thus sought a refuge in passivity, time and again blaming their stars. (26–27)

By "other countries," she means modern Western countries. In her work, these societies provide the master images through which disability-related conceptions and practices in India are measured.

Miles, a more recent pioneer of the study of disability in non-Western cultures, mostly avoids Bhatt's error of uncritically assuming Western master images of disability. Instead, he points to difficulties in recent efforts to formalize rehabilitation responses to disability in South Asia and argues that such efforts "could become more appropriate and effective by studying the previous 4000 years of cultural experience" ("Community"). Like Bhatt, Miles documents references to disabled persons in traditional Hindu texts but does so in ways that occasionally problematize the mechanical extension of modern Western models of rehabilitation to non-Western contexts ("Deaf-ness," "Glimpses"). Before returning to discussions of disability in South Asia by Miles and others, let us examine some of these ancient references.

Representations of disability within classical Hinduism are, as one would expect, varied. As Miles and Bhatt demonstrate, the literature often refer-ences disabled characters who live self-supported and dignified lives. A key figure in the *Mahabharata*, King Dhritarashtra, is blind. Though Dhritarash-tra's character is flawed, his faults are not linked in the text to his blind-ness but rather to a tendency to prioritize love for his sons over the good of the kingdom. This violation of kingly dharma is a vice that Dhritarashtra shares with non-disabled rulers in the *Mahabharata*. Overall, Dhritarashtra is represented as a powerful man who warrants admiration. Yudhishthira, for example, describes him as "wise," "venerable," "possessed of great learning," and "reverential to the old" (*Udyoga*, 52). Other self-supported disabled char-acters appear in the *Mahabharata*, and some are quite dashing. Miles ("Com-munity") and Bhatt point to Ashtavakra, whose name in Sanskrit means "he who is bent eight ways." A severely disabled Brahmin sage, Ashtavakra's wit and knowledge of the Vedas are unrivaled (*Vana*, 132–134). King Nala, living as a dwarf named Vahuka, also exhibits exceptional bravery and intelligence, as well as skill in horsemanship and the culinary arts (70–72). And Vishnu, before his incarnation as Krishna, is embodied as a dwarf (270). Textual ref-erences such as these prompt Bhatt to write:

> The eminence of *Ashtavakra* . . . who was first jeered at by the *Pandits* at the court of King Janaka, because of the crookedness of his body, but whose learning ultimately drew their plaudits; the status of *Manthara* as the favourite maid-servant of the royal queen, though hunchbacked, and the acclamation of *Vamana*, a dwarf, as an incarnation of God *Vishnu*, unmis-takably show that even in early times the Hindu society did not hesitate to recognize the individual merits of handicapped people. In India, the attitude toward [physically disabled people] never reached the height of cruelty that demanded their ruthless destruction. (93)

Classical Hindu texts also recognize that societies, communities, and families have duties to provide for the needs and comfort of their members, including their disabled members, as Miles and Bhatt observe. Citing several passages from the *Mahabharata*, Miles writes, "Part of the nobility of kings was represented by their sustenance of 'widows and orphans, the maimed and the poor'" ("Community"). He points to a greeting that Yudhishthira sends to Dhritarashtra's court:

Thou must ask, O sire, the women of the house as to their welfare. Thou must also represent unto the maid-servants and man-servants there . . . and also the many humpbacked and lame ones among them, that I am doing well, and thou must then ask them about their welfare. Thou must tell them—I hope Dhritarashtra's son still vouchsafes the same kindly treatment to you. I hope he gives you the comforts of life. Thou must also represent unto those that are defective in limb, those that are imbecile, the dwarfs to whom Dhritarashtra gives food . . . from motives of humanity, those that are blind, and all those that are aged, as also to the many that have the use only of their hands being destitute of legs, that I am doing well, and that I ask them regarding their welfare. (*Vana*, 30)

Miles further points out that "a catechism of kingly duties" listed in *Sabha Parva* 5 of the *Mahabharata* obliges rulers to cherish "like a father, the blind, dumb, the lame, the deformed, the friendless, and ascetics that have no homes" ("Deafness"). Attending to the needs and comfort of disabled persons is similarly recognized as dharma for family and community members. In *Sabha Parva* 51, a robber named Kayavya is said to achieve moksha partially because "he worshipped his old, blind, and deaf parents in the forest every day" and provided for their daily needs ("Community"). In the same *parva*, Miles notes, Draupadi, the Pandavas' wife, is praised for serving food to everyone, including "the deformed and the dwarfs," before herself ("Community"). Recognition of such duties is not confined to the *Mahabharata*. As Miles observes, the *Manusmriti* states that "the rule is for a sensible man to give . . . according to (his ability), both food and clothes without end" to all who are "born blind or deaf, those (who are) crazy, idiotic, or dumb, and all who are without manly strength" ("Deafness"). Hindu texts clearly recognize disabled persons as existent and worthwhile members of societies, communities, and families, although they also emphasize "top-down" charity models that contemporary rehabilitation advocates may wish to contest ("Community").

Traditional Hindu conceptions of disability can be considered troublesome for other reasons. Classical texts frequently subsume disability within the guna theory of cosmic purity/pollution that underlies the Chandogya Upanishad's doctrine of karma and exclude disabled persons from specific religious, political, and social institutions and practices on these grounds. For example, the *Manusmriti* includes mentally and physically disabled persons in an eclectic list of less than morally sweet-smelling folk whom a good Brahmin should exclude from certain Vedic sacrifices. The following is a partial excerpt from 3.122:

One should avoid at sacrifices to the gods and to the ancestors physicians, priests who attend on idols, people who sell meat, and those who make their living in shops . . . ; an epileptic, one who suffers from scrofulous swellings of the glands, a man who has white leprosy, a slanderer, a madman, a blind man, a man who criticizes the Vedas . . . ; a man who is criticized by good men, a man who keeps sheep or buffalos, a club-footed man, the husband of a woman who has been married before, a man who carries dead bodies—all these must be carefully avoided. (Doniger, *Textual Sources*, 129–30)

The text evicts physically and mentally disabled persons from other social and political contexts as well, presumably, again, to prevent inauspicious persons from cosmically polluting significant life events. For instance, the shastra lists mentally and physically disabled women in a different eclectic litany of supposedly inauspicious people, this time of women whom a twice-born man should avoid marrying (Doniger, *Textual Sources*, 101–3). Elsewhere, the text states, "At deliberation-time he [the king] should expel the foolish, dumb, blind, and deaf; the aged; women; the impure, diseased and deformed" (Miles, "Deafness"). Further, in the passage from the *Manusmriti* cited in the previous paragraph, the text stipulates that persons who are disabled should be denied inheritance rights. Finally, in 11.48–54, the dharmashastra explicitly appeals to karma to explain disability: "Thus, according to the difference in their acts, (men who are) blamed by the good are born dull, dumb, blind, and deformed in appearance" (Miles, "Deafness").

The *Mahabharata* likewise associates disability with notions of karmic punishment and moral pollution. In his greeting to Dhritarashtra's court (cited above), Yudhishthira does not merely send his regards and inquire about the welfare of persons in the court who are disabled. He also tells them, "Fear not, nor be dispirited on account of your unhappy lives so full of sufferings; no doubt, sins must have been committed by you in your former lives" (*Vana*, 30). Ashtavakra's disability is similarly explained as karmic punishment. He is said to have been born severely disabled after pointing out, from his mother's womb, mistakes in his father's recitation of the Vedas (Miles, "Community"). Further, as with the *Manusmriti*, certain characters in the *Mahabharata* assume that disabilities disqualify persons from holding certain political offices. King Dhritarashtra's reign is at first disputed, Miles notes, because he is born blind. And Dhritarashtra protests that his son "believes [him] to be a fool, and listens not to [his] words" because Dhritarashtra is blind, aged, and physically unable to exert himself (Miles, "Glimpses").

Hence, although her claim is too strongly stated, Bhatt's contention that Hindu ideas of karma can work against critical consideration of disability and advocacy for disabled persons' dignity is not without basis. Just as some threads within the Hindu tradition prescribe an inferior social and cosmic place to Shudras, Chandalas, and women, some threads within the tradition prescribe an inferior social and cosmic place to disabled persons. However, please recall, the tradition is polylithic and does not speak univocally on this or other issues. As we have observed, and as Miles notes, Hinduism offers "a repertoire of explanatory models" and karma is not necessarily the most central or prominent of these. Further, Miles remarks, karma is not a clearly formalized theory or "a tidy and logically coherent system of metaphysics," so much as it is a variously interpreted and contested cultural concept (Ursula Sharma qtd. in Miles, "Deafness"). The Bhagavad Gita's theories of karma and practical rationality, for example, offer plenty of resources to critique prevailing mores and assumptions. And, although consideration of them is beyond the scope of this chapter, so do theories elaborated in numerous text traditions of Indian philosophy, such as Advaita Vedanta, Mimamsa, Nyaya-Vaisheshika, Samkhya-Yoga, Buddhism, and Jainism.

Miles explains that he has focused his career on disability in non-Western contexts partially because, as an activist and scholar, he wishes to intervene against the ineffective extension of modern Western disability paradigms across the globe. He writes:

> For about 25 years I have been trying to generate wider interest in the 'disability world' of Asia, the Middle East and Africa, which runs with concepts and cultures significantly different from those of North America and Western Europe. I have suggested that those differences should be taken more seriously into account during the export of 'western' disability-related strategies, methods and technologies, and their import to the non-western world. These rather obvious suggestions have never been opposed; yet they continue to be largely ignored. ("Community")

Other scholars who have examined subjects related to disability in contemporary South Asia similarly stress the need to attend to this region's specific cultural practices and concepts when addressing disability. However, the most interesting contributions of these scholars do not merely show that disability-related strategies, methods, and technologies ought to take non-Western cultural differences seriously, as Miles' work does, but also call into question master images that underlie these strategies, methods, and technologies.

In a study of identity formation among members of the Delhi Foundation of Deaf Women (DFDW), for example, Michele Friedner not only highlights the specificity of disability in India but also problematizes cultural

models of disability, which, she says, advocate global disability-based identities which "can manifest disability pride in the same way that ethnic or
cultural groups can." According to her, these models "are seen by certain
activists, academics, and rehabilitation professionals to be universal and
unfettered by place and space" and have gained traction in India through "a
massive surge in Northern-created [Western-created] rehabilitation institutions and organisations, which bring their particular model of disability to
the South [non-West]" (366–67). She describes experiencing a peculiar sense
of déjà vu at the Sixth National Conference of Deaf Women/Second Deaf
Cultural Festival of India in 2005. After observing participants deploy the
cultural paradigm of disability, she writes:

> As a Deaf person who has spent a significant amount of time in Deaf schools,
> institutions and social gatherings largely in the United States, I had heard
> *all* of these things before—nothing that I heard was novel. The only thing
> that was different was the *place*. I was no longer in the global North where
> the disability-as-culture paradigm prevails. Instead, I was in India, a place
> where a certain kind of Indian culture, centered on family, caste, and reli-
> gion remains strong. So, what to make of this *doppelgänger* of Northern Deaf
> discourse? (370)

The cultural model of disability that Friedner critiques is one that advocates
and, she argues, globalizes "a highly specific concept of Deafness based upon
ideas of a universal Deaf culture and community" (367). However, her research
demonstrates that women in non-managerial positions at the DFDW did not
primarily define themselves through their Deafness, or share clear-cut, modern Western conceptions of political identity. Although they valued their roles
and duties as mentors, students, coworkers, and friends in the specific environment of the DFDW, they also valued roles and duties in other environments,
which, while overlapping, they considered distinct. Friedman writes:

> In fact, when I sat down with some of the younger women in the DFDW's
> workshop to discuss identity politics in the summer of 2006, identity as a
> concept did not resonate with them immediately, and initially they thought
> that I was asking them to tell me what was written on their government-
> issued identification cards certifying that they were disabled. While they
> eventually did get the drift of my query, they were quite clear that there
> were several identities that they *also* cared about, apart from and in addition
> to, being Deaf: their gender, religion, caste, family background and geo-
> graphic place of origin were equally important for them. (383)

Recall that Hinduism does not share the modern West's enthusiasm for uniform narratives of identity and duty. In Hindu contexts, people's responsibilities, aims, and embodied identities are plural and subject to change (e.g., across contexts). To the extent that cultural models of disability assume embodied identities that are overarching and static (i.e., modern and Western), they risk promulgating tactics and technologies that cannot take non-Western cultural differences seriously, perhaps despite their stated desires.

Much as Friedman problematizes cultural models of disability, Lawrence Cohen's *No Aging in India*, a study of Alzheimer's in Varanasi and elsewhere in India, problematizes master images that underpin modern medical models of disability. Cohen argues that cultural and conceptual peculiarities led to the emergence of geriatrics as a field of modern Western medicine and claims that culturally rooted paradoxes remain integral to medical notions of normal and abnormal bodies. Cohen states, for example, that he was surprised to discover that he rarely encountered elderly persons with Alzheimer's in India, and that, when he did, these persons tended to be modern and middle class (i.e., relatively more Westernized). He explains this dearth of dementia among non-middle-class elderly persons in India, thankfully not by suggesting that modern Western lifestyles cause Alzheimer's but instead by observing that aging in India tends to be conceptualized and pathologized differently than in the modern West. People in Varanasi sometimes talked with Cohen about older people "going sixtyish" and, in these discussions, deployed various traditional Hindu concepts, such as the three gunas and the dharmas appropriate to the four stages of life, as they worked to understand and express themselves, their relations with others, and their respective obligations. However, memory faculties did not feature prominently in these practical conceptual and moral negotiations (127). "Without dismissing the material nature of senility, we need to recognize," Cohen concludes, "that 'going sixtyish' in Varanasi or 'being a victim of Alzheimer's' in the United States are fundamentally dialogic processes, involving both an old person and some other" (32). We can extend Cohen's conclusion to models of disability more generally—disability is never simply a medically or culturally determined identity but is always a pliable negotiating of desires, anxieties, and needs in specific contexts. We will close with two brief narratives to illustrate the contingency of disability. Both are included in Veena Das and Renu Addlakha's article, "Disability and Domestic Citizenship: Voice, Gender, and the Making of the Subject," and each disrupts master images of disability.

Das tells the story of Mandira, a daughter of lower-middle-class Punjabi parents. Mandira had a birthmark covering nearly half of her face. "Subtle pressure was generated" on her and her parents to either forego marriage or accept Mandira's marriage to a man who was also in some way "defective" (Das and Addlakha 520, 514). Suitors who were deemed appropriate exhibited miscellaneous impairments. "The social circumstances in question," Das writes, "could include a variety of conditions ranging from extreme poverty to rumors of sexual violation or 'defects in character'" (516). Nonetheless, at considerable social cost, Mandira and her parents resisted these pressures, and in her early thirties, Mandira married a young man who "worked as a white collar employee in a reputable firm" and who seemed to have "a promising career ahead of him" (516). Rumors within the wider kinship group intensified and included allegations that Mandira and her parents had used tāntrik magical rites to get the young man to fall in love with her despite her birthmark. "As these rumors mounted, the family became more and more isolated from the kinship group" (516–17). Five years after Mandira's marriage, her husband died, and many within the wider kinship group felt vindicated. "For many of the relatives," Das writes, "there was almost a sense of satisfaction that she had received her just desserts. Her parents had played with the sacred in a clandestine manner—bought her happiness against what was written in her fate—and now she and her family were paying the price" (517–18). One cousin, however, suggested a different reading. "Perhaps," she said, "the *tāntrik* had not cast a veil over the husband's capacity to see and judge, as alleged by others—perhaps he had *lifted* a veil and allowed Mandira's husband to see her *as she truly was* . . ." (518). As Das notes, "Hindu mythology and iconography are replete with examples in which the capacity to behold beauty truly, to overcome feelings of repulsion and terror at the sight of that which to the uninitiated is ugly and terrifying, is the sign of a true devotee" (518). Mandira's disability was not culturally or biologically given; rather, as Cohen and Friedman suggest, it was shaped, refused, and reasserted, always contingently, within networks of desire, anxiety, and need. Persons contested the significance of Mandira's birthmark and interpreted concepts, including traditional concepts, in creative ways to support their normative claims.

The second story, narrated by Addlakha, similarly shows how disability labels are "fundamentally dialogic processes," to use Cohen's phrase, that work by circulating competing normative claims within local networks. Addlakha tells us of Pushpa, who was diagnosed at Lady Harding Medical College Psychiatry Ward with schizoaffective disorder. Her symptoms consisted of "not doing housework" and "not observing personal hygiene for the last six years" (521–22). Her alleged failures to observe personal hygiene included donning "a gray-colored men's *kurtā pājāmā*" in public, keeping the hair on her head in "an unevenly cropped crew cut," and allowing hair on her upper lip and chin to extend to a "thin but distinct growth" (522–24). Pushpa initially rejected this diagnosis and instead accused her husband of infidelity and abuse (523–24). She insisted, "There is nothing wrong with me. 'I am one-hundred percent medically fit'" (523). But in the eyes of her medical providers, her willingness to speak against her husband further confirmed the diagnosis. "Pushpa's brusque manner, the sharp tone of her voice, and her lack of deference to her husband were in sharp contrast to the demeanor of unobtrusiveness and self-effacement expected of a woman in public spaces" (523). In Pushpa's case, creative interpretations of available concepts support competing normative claims. Some concepts, such as ideas of womanly duties, are old, while others, such as the biomedical disability label "schizoaffective disorder," are modern. Available concepts are interpreted in ways that allow members of a familial and community group to displace anxieties about gender onto a body. The person is rendered disabled as a result of this displacement (524). As Das and Addlakha write, Pushpa's case not only provides "an uncanny illustration of a failure to live up to norms of femininity being glossed as defect" (521) but also illustrates "the problematic of disability's location off the body of the patient and within networks of connected kin" (527).

More than other religious traditions, Hinduism leaves space for competing efforts to make sense of diverse desires, anxieties, and needs, in part by allowing and encouraging various interpretations of concepts. The tradition's polylithic character neither implies an absence of critical engagement nor suggests disinterest in disability advocacy, as Bhatt's discussion of karma would imply. To the contrary, in Hinduism diverse and competing conceptions negotiate for voice and expression often in the same source material without subordination to overarching and unchanging narratives. The tradition's polylithic character therefore calls into question master images that underpin cultural and medical models of disability and perhaps problematizes their mechanical extension not only in South Asia but also elsewhere.

2

Buddhism and Disability

Stephen E. Harris

Although Buddhist texts do not theorize disability explicitly, the attention they pay to our vulnerability to suffering, the radical dependence and impermanence of everything that exists, and the fragility of health and life brings them into contact with several issues important to the study of disability. In Buddhist texts, explicit characterization of disabilities (e.g., blindness and deafness) as well as conditions partially overlapping with disability, such as long-term illness, are almost always negative.[1] Nevertheless, Buddhist texts value the recognition of suffering as conducive to a strong motivation to obtain liberation and develop compassion for others, and this recognition suggests Buddhists ought to value aspects of disabled experience. Further, the Buddhist commitment to the universal salvation of all beings implicitly commits them to making their teaching accessible to persons with mental or physical disabilities.

This chapter considers and develops these connections between disability and Indian Buddhism, drawing upon texts composed during the history of Buddhism in India, from the time of the Buddha in the fifth century BCE through the first millennium CE. The first section provides a brief introduction to the Buddhist religion and its main tenets. The next discusses how the Buddhist doctrines of impermanence and radical dependence undermine the depth of the binary opposition between able-bodied and disabled minds and bodies. This leads into a consideration of how these Buddhist insights relate to contemporary models of disability developed by scholars and activists to understand the relation between disability, physical and mental variation, and the environment. Although Buddhist ideas are compatible with multiple models of disability, they have a particularly strong resonance with the human-variation model that stresses continuity between disabled and able-bodied persons. The next section examines negative portrayals of disability in Buddhist texts, and shows how this is in partial tension with the Buddhist affirmation of the value of becoming aware of human suffering, a commitment which implies a positive evaluation of certain aspects of disabled experience. The final section discusses the Mahayana Buddhist doctrine of skillful means, in which teachings are adapted for the psychological propensities of various people, and suggests that this doctrine provides a partial analogue to the contemporary practice of reasonable accommodation which seeks to make work and services accessible to persons with disabilities.

BASIC BUDDHIST TENETS

The religion of Buddhism was probably founded in the fifth century BCE in northern India by the man who would come to be known as the Buddha.[2] Relatively little is known with any certainty about his life. We know that he was a member of the Śākya clan in northern India and that his given name was Gautama (Gethin 8). Tradition says that in his late twenties he went on a spiritual quest and after many years of meditation and spiritual practice attained deep insight into the true nature of reality. At this time he took on the title of Buddha, a Sanskrit word that literally means "one who has woken up."[3]

What the Buddha woke up to are certain facts about the universe that most of us only dimly acknowledge, such as that everything that exists is transient and depends on other things for its existence. Most importantly, the Buddha discovered that there is no enduring self (*ātman*) or soul that accounts for our identity and persists throughout a lifetime. Rather, humans are comprised of five groups of interrelated momentary events called aggregates (*skandhas*) of physical matter (*rūpa*), feelings (*vedanā*), concepts (*saṃjñā*), awareness (*vijñāna*), and miscellaneous mental factors like emotions and intentions (*saṃskāra*). The distinctive Buddhist claim is that there exists no enduring self or soul that possesses or stands in some kind of relation to these aggregates. All we are is an impermanent collection of these mental and physical aggregates in close causal relation.

One of the most powerful ways the Buddha's teachings have been conveyed is through a schema called "the four noble truths," which describes suffering (*duḥkha*); its cause (*samudaya*), which is craving; its cessation (*nirodha*), which is nirvana; and the path (*marga*) to achieving this cessation. The first noble truth refers to the fact that the lives of ordinary humans are pervaded by both gross and subtle sources of suffering. All of us have painful experiences such as physical suffering and emotional disappointment, but

Buddhists claim we also experience subtler forms of suffering. For instance, sensual pleasures cannot deeply satisfy us, and we find that our craving has increased after indulging in them. Further, because on some level we know things are impermanent, we experience a constant underlying anxiety that the good things we have will not last.[4] Because these kinds of suffering afflict us, Buddhist texts claim any kind of lasting happiness is impossible without undertaking the Buddhist path to liberation.

Like Hinduism and Jainism, two of the other major Indian religions, Buddhism professes that after death we take rebirth in another body. This rebirth can be in either a positive form—such as that of a human or even of a deity who will live for many millions of years—or a negative form of existence, including some in various kinds of hells.[5] All of these rebirths, including birth as a god or in a hell realm, are impermanent, and we will eventually take rebirth again. This cycle of continual rebirth and death is referred to as *samsara*, and escaping from it is the purpose of Buddhist teachings.[6]

Buddhists also believe that where we take rebirth in the future depends on our thoughts and actions in this life. A negative thought, such as anger or jealousy, or a harmful action, such as hurting another or stealing, creates a residue in the mind that can potentially cause rebirth in hell or as an animal. These imprints can also ripen to create the circumstances of one's present or future life. For instance, actions motivated by anger can lead to sickness or being the victim of violence. Likewise, positive thoughts and actions, such as compassion and generosity, will lead to good rebirths—as a human or deity—or to good conditions in present or future lives, like the possession of wealth or the ability to practice Buddhism. This is the Buddhist doctrine referred to by the Sanskrit word *karma* (action), which indicates these positive or negative thoughts or actions that ripen into future results.[7]

For Buddhists, countless rebirths mean the problem of suffering lasts longer than the present lifetime. If it were not for karma, we could escape all suffering simply by dying, but karma forces continual rebirth, making it necessary to practice Buddhist teachings to escape the continual cycle of death and rebirth.

The second noble truth is craving (*tṛṣṇā*), which is the cause of suffering. Craving in Buddhism is more than merely wanting something; it is an unrealistic mental state that is driven by false expectations about the thing desired. Craving is caused by ignorance (*avidyā*), which in Buddhism is a deeply rooted belief that things exist in a way that they do not. Ignorance refers primarily to our belief that we possess an enduring self (*ātman*) that subsists throughout a lifetime and travels to the next life. It also refers to the belief that experienced objects endure, exist independently of causes and conditions, and can bring lasting satisfaction. Because of ignorance, we view ourselves as enduring persons able to interact with a world of stable objects. In sharp contrast to expectations, everything exists as a radical flux of momentary dependent events. It is this mismatch between expectations and the world that causes suffering.

The third noble truth is that cessation of suffering and the cycle of death and rebirth is possible. This state of cessation is called *nirvana*, a Sanskrit word that means "blown out." It is suffering and rebirth, as well as their causes—ignorance and craving—that are extinguished. This is the state the Buddha achieved when he reached enlightenment. The final noble truth is the path to cessation, the Buddhist method by which one eliminates ignorance and craving and achieves enlightenment. Buddhist texts develop a series of practices, including ethical discipline (*śīla*), meditative concentration (*samādhi*), and insight into the nature of reality (*prajñā*), that enable the practitioner to progress toward nirvana.[8]

The Buddha was said to achieve enlightenment in his mid-thirties, and then he spent the rest of his life teaching others this path to salvation. After achieving his goal, one method he used to help others develop the same level of realization was by founding a monastic order in which monks and nuns lived communally, leaving their householder lives behind. One reason becoming a monastic is conducive to liberation is that monks and nuns can devote most of their time to various forms of spiritual practice like meditation and listening to teachings by the Buddha and his senior disciples. Furthermore, householder life stirs up powerful negative emotions like greed and hatred, which develop as one pursues a career, seeks a mate, and so on. By leaving such distractions behind, monastics are better able to escape samsara by focusing on the work of removing the mental afflictions of ignorance and craving from the mind.

THE STORY OF THE BUDDHA AND THE THREE MARKS

A traditional method Buddhists use to express central Buddhist themes is telling the story of the life of the Buddha, who was said to have been born to a powerful king in northern India. The Buddha's father was told by a sage that the boy would either become a great king or forsake worldly life and become a religious renunciant. Since the king wanted his son to inherit his kingdom, he devised a strategy to ensure the Buddha would not think of abandoning worldly pursuits. The king removed all signs of illness or aging from the palace in which the child grew up. All his attendants were youthful, and the older relatives of the prince, including the king and queen themselves, wore makeup and dyed their hair to hide their advancing age.[9]

The young prince spent thirty years in idle happiness in the palace, enjoying leisure activities like sports and theater. He married a beautiful woman and had a son. The king's plan was so completely successful that his son did not even know that aging, illness, and death existed. But one day he took a chariot ride outside the city walls and encountered a man stooped over with age. In response to the Buddha's shocked inquiry, his charioteer explained what age is and that it afflicts all beings. Subsequently, the Buddha, still distressed by what he had seen, took three additional trips outside the city during which he encountered a sick man, a dead man, and finally a religious seeker who had renounced householder life.[10] Horrified by his encounter with aging, sickness, and death, and inspired by seeing the renunciant, the Buddha abandoned his life in the palace. He engaged in various spiritual practices for five years until finally, during deep concentrated meditation, he attained perfect enlightenment. He then spent the next fifty years of his life teaching others the Buddhist path to salvation.

While the story is not historically accurate, its power lies in allowing us to imagine how horrifying it would be to suddenly discover that we are aging and will become sick and die. Although we all know on some level that this will happen, Buddhists claim that we hide the significance of these inevitabilities from ourselves. Contrast our relative indifference to the coming of death with the horror expressed by the Buddha in Aśvaghoṣa's telling of the story:

> Then, the king's son, as he learned about death,
> although steadfast, soon became despondent;
> leaning his shoulder against the railing,
> he said in a voice that was resonant:

> "This is the inevitable end of all men;
> yes the world rashly revels, casting fears aside;
> The hearts of men, I suspect, must indeed be hard,
> that they journey along this road so unperturbed.

> Let us turn back our carriage, therefore, charioteer;
> for this is not the time or place for pleasure groves.
> For, perceiving death, how can sensible man,
> keep on reveling here rashly at a time of pain." (Aśvaghoṣa 81)

The trauma to the prince is so great that he despairs. He is incredulous that ordinary people are willing to go about life as usual, all the while knowing that death is on the way. This behavior, he says in the final verse, is foolish. The story implies that all of us would have this violent a reaction to our mortality if we did not constantly hide these facts from ourselves. Massive delusion is a part of everyone's life.

Early Buddhist texts distinguish three errors in particular that ordinary humans make in relation to our experience. First, we experience impermanent (*anitya*) phenomena as if they were permanent. Although we appear to interact with a realm of relatively stable objects, Buddhists claim that everything we experience is actually composed of evanescent events arising and disintegrating in fragments of a second, an impermanence that exists at two levels. First, there is the ordinary level of change that all of us experience when objects break, people die, and so on. Second, this ordinary level of transience is itself made possible by a deeper radical disintegration of everything that exists at every second.[11]

The second error all people make is experiencing dependently arisen objects as if they are independent and self-subsistent.[12] Buddhist texts place particular emphasis on the nonexistence of any enduring unitary soul (*ātman*) that makes us who we are. Buddhist texts extend their analysis of selflessness to any object composed of parts.[13] The classic Buddhist example is the chariot.[14] There is no single unitary object called a "chariot" that exists over and above the collection of chariot parts; rather "chariot" is a convenient name (*prajñapti*) given to the wheel, axle, carriage, and so forth when they are put together in such a way that they can be used to travel quickly. However, even though no enduring unitary chariot exists in reality, the parts are experienced as if they formed one unified, independent entity able to function on its own.

The final error humans persistently make is believing that objects and events composed of impermanent, dependent phenomena are capable of bringing lasting satisfaction. It is this error that causes the deeper forms of suffering described in the opening section. These three features—the impermanent, the selfless/dependently arisen, and the unsatisfactory nature of everything that exists—are referred to in Buddhist texts as "the three marks of existence." The Buddhist claim is that our cognitive systems make numerous deeply ingrained errors in processing experience that result in this massive misperception of objects in the world.[15]

One of the consequences of accepting these Buddhist insights about the fragility, impermanence, and dependence of all existence is that our ordinary beliefs about the relative stability of health, physical fitness, and the other properties commonly associated with being able bodied are deeply mistaken. In this way, the Buddhist emphasis on the three marks undermines the depth of a set of binary distinctions upon which usual ways of perceiving disability are predicated. The disabled body and mind is ordinarily contrasted to a physically and mentally fit, able-bodied counterpart. Likewise, it is assumed that for able-bodied people, health and fitness are relatively stable and will continue. Finally, the able-bodied person is seen as independent, autonomous, and able to live successfully, in contrast to someone who is helpless, dependent, and disabled.

Buddhist insights affect how we view all these distinctions. Since Buddhists claim humans are massively deluded about ordinary features of our experience, the depth of the contrast between psychological disability and health is lessened. The Buddha as a young prince refers to ordinary people as insane for living their lives as if aging, sickness, and death did not exist. Psychological disabilities either arise from these underlying cognitive distortions or are insignificant in comparison. It is our ignorance of the impermanent and unsatisfactory nature of the world—not any particular medically recognized, psychological illness—that accounts for the deepest forms of suffering humans experience. Likewise, the Buddhist emphasis on radical impermanence undermines the distinction between physical and mental disability and a relatively stable, able-bodied norm. Human bodies and minds, like everything else that exists, are composed of radically impermanent events that originate and disintegrate continuously.

Finally, the mark of not-self, or selflessness, not only claims that things do not exist as unitary, independent objects but also implies how they do exist as dependently arisen phenomena based upon their parts, causes, and conditions. Emphasizing this highlights the fact that much of the stigma attached to many disabilities rests upon a series of relatively arbitrary distinctions between acceptable and unacceptable kinds of dependence. We claim that independence is not compromised when driving a car from home to downtown, but that independence is lessened if crutches or a wheelchair are used to get to the car. Having farmers, truck drivers, and grocery store clerks collaborate to make grocery shopping possible is somehow seen as consistent with independence, while using a personal care attendant to help reach items on a shelf is not. These examples can be multiplied without limit. The Buddhist doctrine of dependent origination lessens the contrast between able-bodied and disabled persons by emphasizing the radical dependence of everything that exists.

None of this means that Buddhists could not employ disability as a useful category to help distribute resources effectively and modify physical environments and social expectations to accommodate physical and psychological variety. Just as Buddhists hold that it is a useful fiction to group an assemblage of chariot parts together under the name "chariot," they can accept that labels like "blind," "deaf," or "developmentally delayed" may help facilitate successful interaction with the world. All such labels, however, are merely employed for convenience, marking out certain variation from amid a much deeper continuity of transience and dependence that characterizes everything that exists.

Moreover, as Lynne Bejoian has emphasized, the focus of Buddhist practice is on ending the suffering experienced by all beings. Specific pain associated with any particular disability is simply one aspect of the suffering experienced by all. The frustration of limitations to mobility from a physical disability is less painful than the constant dissatisfaction experienced by all non-liberated human beings. Therefore, no stigma need be attached to disabled experience.

BUDDHISM AND MODELS OF DISABILITY

One of the contributions disability studies scholars have made to our understanding of disability is developing contrasting models that define disability and explain how and to what extent negative effects arise from specific mental and physical impairments. Disability scholars generally call the dominant mode of theorizing disability the medical model, which identifies disability with a physical or mental impairment and claims that the various disadvantages associated with disability arise because of the impairment.[16] According to the medical model, disabilities are defects that interfere with ordinary human functioning and should be corrected whenever possible. The drawbacks to conceiving all disability under the medical model are that it views disabled persons, by definition, as defective, broken, and inferior to their able-bodied counterparts. Moreover, much of the frustration and pain experienced by disabled persons results not from impairment itself but from negative stereotypes and unfair treatment by able-bodied persons. The medical model errs in ignoring the effects of social barriers on persons with disability.

The minority model of disability seeks to remedy these defects.[17] It claims that the negative effects of disability—such as difficulty finding employment, social isolation, and an inaccessible environment—are caused by the discriminatory treatment of society itself, similar to the way some ethnic groups have been marginalized by racial discrimination. For instance, according to the minority model, mobility difficulties faced by a paraplegic are caused by able-bodied people's refusal to adapt the environment with wheelchair ramps and the like, rather than the impairment itself. Likewise, it is prejudice, as well as a lack of workplace accommodations like flexible scheduling, that prevent some people with psychological disabilities from securing employment. The minority model serves as a needed corrective to the medical model's overemphasis on the disabling role of impairment. It has acted as a powerful tool used by disability advocates in confronting abelist policies and attitudes and has contributed to the passage of disability rights legislation, such as the Americans with Disabilities Act. Nevertheless, although it correctly draws attention to the disabling effects of discrimination by society, the minority model's claim that *all* the negative effects associated with disability arise because of such discrimination is not realistic.[18] For instance, many impairments cause or contribute to a level of physical or mental pain that severely limits activity but is not in any obvious way attributable to social discrimination.

A third model of disability, the human-variation model, to some extent synthesizes the insights of the other two. The variation model claims that disability occurs when human variation exceeds our present ability to adapt the physical and social environment.[19] According to this model, all human minds and bodies exhibit certain variations, many of which are potentially disabling (Wasserman). Disability occurs when there is a lack of fit between certain kinds of variation and the existing physical and social environment. Therefore, what is considered a disability will change as technology improves, the physical environment is altered, attitudes change, and resources are distributed differently. Eyeglasses, for example, turn a formerly disabling impairment into a neutral variation. Wheelchair ramps and electronic doors likewise lessen the effects of mobility impairments, and given sufficient adaptation of the environment, many of these conditions would cease to be disabling at all.[20]

Although these models of disability are sometimes presented as being in competition with each other, the insights of both the medical and minority models can be incorporated into the human-variation model. According to the variation model, the medical model goes wrong in ignoring the negative impact of social discrimination, but the variation model agrees with the medical model in accepting that variations play a significant role in the disablement of some persons. This model claims that both the lack of curb cuts and the physical condition that requires the use of a wheelchair are disabling factors. Likewise, the variation model claims that the minority model neglects the role of physical impairment but agrees that social discrimination is an important element of the social environment that can make certain kinds of impairment disabling. Both the anxiety disorder and the lack of workplace accommodations play a role in preventing successful employment.

In comparing the language of Buddhist texts to these models of disability, the closest match would be the medical model. Buddhist texts pay relatively little attention to disability but do emphasize illness as one of the sufferings that should motivate us to escape from rebirth and samsara (Bodhi, *Connected*, 1844). Although scholars of disability have cautioned that it is misleading to associate disability too closely with physical or mental illness, there will be a great deal of overlap between some forms of long-term illness and disabling conditions.[21] Further, Buddhist texts take an almost universally negative view of sickness. In the Buddha's first sermon, he lists it as one of the eight major kinds of suffering afflicted on beings in *samsara* (Bodhi, *Connected*, 1844). Likewise, we have seen that an encounter with a sick person was so disturbing to the Buddha that he renounced householder life. Moreover, other Buddhist texts claim that certain disabilities, like blindness or mobility impairment, are karmic effects of past negative actions (Mrozik 30).

Note that the explicit way Buddhist texts treat illness and, on occasion, certain kinds of disability is, on the face of it, closest to the medical model. Illness and disability are seen as negatives, and there is seemingly no awareness that social discrimination accounts for at least part of the negative effects associated with disability. This is not surprising. Buddhists rarely, if ever, observe disability as an object of theoretical concern. It has taken the insights of several generations of disability activists and scholars, who themselves drew upon previous work in feminism and the academic study of race, to develop models of disability like the minority and human-variation models, which begin to recognize the disabling force of society itself. Keep in mind that the ancient Indian environment would be much less hospitable to physical disability than our contemporary one. Therefore, it is not surprising that Buddhist texts view disability as an intrinsically negative phenomenon.

Although the language they use resonates most closely with the medical model, relatively minor modifications could be made to Buddhist characterizations of illness and disability to adapt it to the variation model. Texts that stress the negative aspects of illness and disability could be amended to acknowledge that these ill effects depend on the environment as well as the impairment itself. The doctrine of karma could also be altered slightly to clarify that the bad effect of a negative action is not the disability itself but rather having to experience that disability in environments not suitably adapted to it. Buddhist texts do not present their doctrine this way, but this does not keep us from noting that there is no deep conceptual tension between Buddhist commitments and a human-variation understanding of disability.

Moreover, there is a sense in which Buddhist insights resonate more strongly with the variation model than the other two models. The medical and minority models sort the world into categories of disabled and able-bodied people. They do acknowledge that there will be boundary cases in which it is not clear if a person has a disability and that people acquire or lose disabilities as life progresses. Nevertheless, they tend to view disability as something that divides people into two groups that do or do not possess it. By contrast, the variation model emphasizes continuity between disabled and able-bodied persons, in that all humans already exhibit variation that could become disabling in a particular environment. The fact that our world possesses many different environments with different levels of accessibility further suggests there will be a lack of determinacy over who is disabled. Likewise, in a given environment, the same variation may present itself to disabling or innocuous extents by able-bodied persons in the same environment. Minor scoliosis, for instance, is unlikely to be disabling in most environments, whereas more severe cases may be. This suggests that the human-variation model views all humans in a spectrum of potentially disabling variation with no sharp boundaries drawn where categories of disability begin and end.

All of this resonates with Buddhist insights regarding universal dependence and impermanence. The Buddha, as a healthy young prince, and the old man he meets on his chariot ride are both already afflicted with aging, and they each possess a body with a fragile equilibrium that can be upset at any moment. Buddhist texts emphasize what on some level we already know: anyone can enter the category of disability at any time, and given the close relationship between illness, aging, and some kinds of disability, our fragile and decaying human bodies will all become disabled at some point if death does not intervene first. It is exactly this insight that led the young prince to renounce his kingdom in search of spiritual salvation.

Of the three major models of disability, the minority model seems most at odds with Buddhist insights. The minority model often stresses the potential positive aspects of disability, likening the experiences of people with disabilities to cultural experiences shared by ethnic minorities. Many authors writing from the minority model perspective seek to foster a sense of unity and pride in the disability community and explore aspects of disablement that can be viewed as positive. Moreover, the model is characterized by its claim that impairment is not, in itself, a negative but only becomes so because of societal oppression.

On the one hand, this conflicts with the Buddhist appraisal of disability as the result of negative karmic action. In addition, Buddhists extend their claim that no enduring self exists to all objects with parts and claim that partite objects only exist as useful ways of talking about groups of causally interacting parts. Ethnic, racial, and other social categories—such as Hispanic, homosexual, and disabled—will also be merely useful ways of talking, drawing attention to certain kinds of difference out of a vast spectrum of variation. In fact, the Buddhist monk Śāntideva makes exactly this point in relation to biological sex:

> What discerning person would be attached to form, which is
> just like a dream?
> Since the body does not exist
> then who is a woman and who is a man?[22] (126; 9.87)

Since even the physical body is only a useful fiction, properties of the body such as biological sex will only be real by convention as well.[23] Although Śāntideva does not extend this point to disability, the same analysis applies.

There is, then, at least the appearance of tension between the minority model, which stresses the importance of recognizing disability as a source of pride, and Buddhist thought, which emphasizes the ultimate nonexistence of any such category. Nevertheless, we should remember that even though Buddhists do not think the names we give to partite objects correspond to mind-independent reality, they also do not deny their pragmatic efficacy in helping us navigate through our lives. To return to the classic example, understanding the collection of chariot parts as a unified object called "chariot" helps us use it to get around quickly. Buddhists can also affirm the efficacy of social categories like disability; they can, for instance, recognize that providing additional parking privileges to persons with mobility impairments increases community access.

There is no obvious barrier to emphasizing the possibility of sharing experiences and building a community among persons with certain kinds of disabilities while keeping in mind that the various disabilities we recognize are all ways of talking about how pluralities of impermanent mental and physical moments causally interact. After all, Buddhist monks and nuns use various classificatory schemes in organizing their monastic communities, even though they recognize that all such classifications are merely useful ways of talking. Therefore, although we might recognize more friction between Buddhist insights and the minority model, there is no reason to hold that the Buddhist doctrine of not-self is incompatible with the minority model's emphasis on aspects of disabled experience as a source of identity and pride.

BUDDHISM AND THE NEGATIVE APPRAISAL OF DISABILITY

Although Buddhist texts pay relatively little attention to disability itself, they do talk about it as a negative effect of karmic action. As previously discussed, Buddhist karma theory claims that a harmful action—such as lying, stealing, or killing—or even a negative intention—such as a moment of malicious thought or covetousness—creates a karmic seed that ripens at some point in the future. Negative effects of karmic action include not only rebirth in a negative realm, a short life, or poverty but also a number of conditions that overlap with certain kinds of disability. "The Shorter Exposition of Action," for instance, links hurting others with sickness in future rebirths, and lack of attention to Buddhist teachings to low intellect (Ñāṇamoli and Bodhi 1053–57). Likewise, the *Lotus Sutra* claims that acting disrespectfully toward the sutra, or those who revere it, can result in rebirths without sight, or with various diseases (Watson 324).[24]

In addition, a number of Buddhist texts mention disability as one of several impediments to progressing on the path to liberation. The great Indian Buddhist master, Nāgārjuna, provides a list of eight impediments that make spiritual practice difficult or impossible:

> 63: To be reborn with false beliefs, or yet
> As animals, or pretas,[25] or in hell,
> Deprived of Buddha's words, barbarians
> In border lands, or reborn dull and dumb,
>
> 64: Or born among the long-lived gods—
> Of these eight defective states that give no opportunity
> You must be free, and, finding opportunity,
> Be diligent, to put a stop to birth. (Nāgārjuna 52–53)

The verses mention low intellect and muteness explicitly, but commentaries explain this also includes damaged sensory faculties and missing limbs (Tsong-kha-pa 118). What is jarring about these verses is that these disabilities are grouped together with rebirth in negative realms and living in an uncivilized land with no access to Buddhist teachings as conditions that interfere with an ability to progress toward enlightenment. Again, disability seems to be presented as an inherently negative impediment to living a valuable life. Part of the explanation for such remarks is that the physical and social environment in ancient India would have been particularly hostile to many types of disabilities; for instance, there would not have been trained interpreters to facilitate communication with the deaf.

Although Buddhist writers make remarks like these, which characterize disability as simply a defect, we also find a spirit of inclusiveness throughout the history of Buddhism that seeks to make its teachings accessible to many different kinds of people. In early Buddhist texts the Buddha provides a great variety of training tools to help people advance toward enlightenment. Study and sitting meditation are emphasized for the intellectually acute and physically able, but many alternative practices are also offered, including making offerings to monks and nuns—or simply visualizing offerings to the Buddha—chanting Buddhist scripture or mantras, and recollecting the good qualities of the Buddha. Great emphasis is also placed on the intention with which one acts, so physical disability provides much less of an obstacle to making spiritual progress than might at first be apparent (Bodhi, *Numerical*, 963).

Another feature of Buddhism that has implications for the value of disability is its emphasis on the great value of a human birth. Among all the possible forms of rebirth—be it as a human, an animal, a god, or in a lower realm like hell—human rebirth is seen as ideal for making progress toward liberation. Śāntideva expresses this attitude by emphasizing the rarity of human rebirth in verse 4.20 from *A Guide to the Bodhisattva Way of Life* (*Bodhicaryāvatāra*):

> Therefore, the Blessed One stated that human existence is
> extremely difficult to obtain, like a turtle's head emerging
> into the ring of a yoke on a vast ocean.[26] (41)

The reference is to a turtle that surfaces once every hundred years in a great ocean. The chance of attaining a human rebirth, according to Buddhism, is less than the possibility that the turtle will randomly put its head through a single ring floating on top of the water. This is because the number of animals is incredibly vast, including insects and beings in the various heavens and hells. Śāntideva goes on to praise the value of this rarely attained human birth in helping us progress toward liberation in 7.14:

> Upon finding the boat of human birth now, cross the great
> river of suffering. O fool, there is no time for sleep, for this
> boat is hard to catch again. (78)

Human birth is so precious because humans encounter just enough suffering to be aware of the need to practice Buddhism but not so much that it overwhelms us and makes practice impossible. Rebirth as a god results because of massive amounts of karmic merit created through good actions like generosity. Yet, in the verse quoted by Nāgārjuna, rebirth as both a god and a hell-being is an impediment to progressing toward enlightenment. The problem with rebirth in hell is that the torments experienced preclude spiritual practice. The gods face the opposite problem. Since they experience no explicit pain and dwell in pleasure for countless years, they have no motivation to practice Buddhism. However, Buddhist gods do eventually die, after which they face the possibility of being reborn in a realm with great amounts of suffering. Moreover, Buddhist gods still experience the subtler kinds of suffering like the inability to gain any kind of lasting satisfaction from enjoying sense pleasure. The gods, therefore, are much like the Buddha as a young prince enjoying himself in the palace with no awareness that illness and death are on the way.[27]

In addition to providing motivation to practice Buddhism, Śāntideva also points out that suffering has other aspects that help us progress toward liberation in 6.21:

> Suffering has another quality since
> arrogance diminishes because of despair,
> and one feels compassion for beings in the
> cycle of existence, fear of sin, and a
> yearning for the Jina.[28] (64)

Experiencing a limited amount of suffering reduces pride and deepens our compassion for others. These remarks show that a human rebirth containing some experience of fragility and pain can be, from a Buddhist perspective, a good thing since it can help us progress in our practice toward liberation; however, human rebirths in which very little suffering is experienced, like that of the young Buddha growing up in his palace, would be deficient in comparison.[29]

Following this logic to its conclusion suggests that Buddhist texts should value certain aspects of disabled experience as a potential aid to achieving liberation. Although they differ as to its underlying cause, all models of disability acknowledge that disabilities are often accompanied by a great deal of pain and frustration. For an advanced Buddhist practitioner, the additional frustrations that accompany disability could be an aid in motivating a strong commitment to Buddhist practice and in developing compassion for other suffering beings. From the perspective of Buddhist practice, disability might be seen as a negative only for those at relatively early stages of progress who have not yet developed the fortitude and mental flexibility to experience additional pain and frustration without becoming discouraged. Rather than being seen as intrinsically negative, disability could be considered an advanced training for those dedicated toward progressing quickly toward enlightenment.

One of the contributions contemporary disability activists and scholars have made is in drawing attention to the possibility that aspects of disabled experience can be positive (Smith 21–24). For example, Deaf people have developed their own culture, using their own language—American Sign Language—to communicate. Other authors emphasize the possibility that impairment of one sense organ may lead to increased development of other mental abilities. For instance, a recent study shows that blind persons perform better than seeing persons in recalling certain information (O'Neil; Silvers).

From the Buddhist perspective, some persons with disability are also in a privileged epistemic position in the sense that it is easier for them to understand the fragility and dependence of everything that exists. Since Buddhists claim that humans make an ongoing series of cognitive mistakes, whereby we experience, among other things, the impermanent as permanent and the dependent as independent, it is possible for some able-bodied people, especially when relatively affluent, to live the majority of their lives without deeply acknowledging the impermanence and vulnerability of the human condition. Buddhists see such ways of life as wasting the precious opportunity of being human. In this sense, the friction between disabled bodies and minds and the environment may be seen as an aid to making spiritual progress. Buddhists would still be committed to removing the pain and frustration that accompanies disabled experience; the purpose of all Buddhist teachings is to eliminate suffering. Nevertheless, this acknowledges that some persons with disability might be in a better position to initially recognize the fragility that underlies all human experience.

MAHAYANA BUDDHISM AND SKILLFUL MEANS

In very early Buddhist texts, there is no clear distinction drawn between the enlightenment of the Buddha and that of his disciples; the Buddha is distinguished, rather, in his achievement of being the first to attain awakening and in his consummate skill as a teacher of others (Bodhi, "Arahants"). As Buddhism continued to develop, however, it began to distinguish between two levels of spiritual accomplishment. The ordinary goal most people pursue is that of individual liberation, in which one eliminates craving and ignorance and escapes from suffering and rebirth. The higher goal is that of full Buddhahood, a process which takes an almost inestimable amount of time and requires a commitment to an arduous process of virtue development in which one completely removes all traces of ignorance and craving and develops the ability to teach and benefit others effectively.

Someone who undertakes the more difficult goal is called a *bodhisattva*, a being (*sattva*) who aims for the awakening (*bodhi*) of a fully enlightened Buddha.[30] The bodhisattva takes a vow to liberate all sentient beings from suffering and to take innumerable rebirths in order to develop the skill to effectively do this. Buddhists who stress the desirability of becoming bodhisattvas eventually begin to refer to themselves as the Mahayana (great vehicle), whose goal is the liberation of all; this contrasts with the early Buddhist teachings that aim for individual liberation. Śāntideva is renowned for his power in phrasing the Mahayana aspiration to benefit all beings.

> May I be a protector for those who are without protectors, a
> guide for travelers, and a boat, a bridge, and a ship for those
> who wish to cross over.

> May I be a lamp for those who seek light, a bed for those
> who seek rest, and may I be a servant for all beings who
> desire a servant.

> To all sentient beings may I be a wish-fulfilling gem, a vase
> of good fortune, an efficacious mantra, a great medication, a
> wish-fulfilling tree, and a wish-granting cow. (35; 3.17–19)

Many Buddhist texts affirm both the aspiration for individual liberation and the bodhisattva path of liberation for all beings as worthy aims. As Mahayana Buddhism developed, however, greater emphasis continued to be placed on the bodhisattva goal, until it became portrayed as a far superior option than individual liberation. Liberating all beings implies a commitment to making Buddhist teachings accessible to disabled persons, since they are among the beings to be liberated. But an even stronger implicit commitment to making teachings accessible can be found by examining the Mahayana doctrine of skillful means (*upāya*).

We have already seen at the end of the last section that early Buddhist texts offer diverse methods—including various forms of meditation, chanting, making offerings, and visualization—which help different kinds of persons to effectively practice Buddhism. In addition, early Buddhist texts portray the Buddha as teaching in many different kinds of ways to persons of various dispositions; he uses stories and parables for some and offers philosophical discussion for others. Skillful means, a Mahayana Buddhist teaching specifically developed to benefit persons with particular psychological dispositions, is a continuation of this commitment to flexible pedagogy found in the early texts (Pye 51–52).

The *Lotus Sutra*, a Mahayana text that is particularly influential in developing the concept of skillful means, provides a number of stories that illustrate the bodhisattva's skill in teaching sentient beings of various psychological dispositions. In perhaps its most famous story, a father is unable to convince his children who are fascinated by their toys to leave a burning house. He finally succeeds in doing so by telling them that there are various kinds of carriages waiting for them to play with outside. The *Lotus Sutra* explains that the bodhisattva must employ divergent strategies because the psychological makeup of humans differs greatly (Watson 56–62). In particular, given the presence of craving, anger, and delusion in our minds, people will often not understand what is in their best interests. The children will not leave the burning house because of their attachment to their toys, so the father diverts them toward other attachments to get them out. The toys represent samsaric pursuits, the father is the Buddha, while the carriages are different forms of Buddhism designed to appeal to different kinds of practitioners (59–60).

The justification for developing skillful means, therefore, is to minster to beings with various psychological tendencies. The doctrine does not explicitly address the issue of accessibility for disabled persons, although psychological disabilities themselves are instances of psychological variation, and so the explicit purpose of skillful means already partially addresses concerns about disability accessibility. Moreover, it is a small step from adapting Buddhist teachings to various psychological dispositions to adapting them to be disability accessible. A commitment to making teachings accessible to all beings is powerfully expressed in the following image from the *Lotus Sutra* that compares Buddhist teachings to clouds raining down on different kinds of plants:

> Kashyapa, it is like the plants and trees, thickets and groves, and the medicinal herbs, widely ranging in variety, each with its own name and hue, that grow in the hills and streams, the valleys and different soils of the thousand-millionfold world. Dense clouds spread over them, covering the entire thousand-millionfold world and in one moment saturating it all. The moisture penetrates to all the plants, trees, thickets and groves, and medicinal herbs equally, to their big roots, big stems, big limbs and big leaves. . . . The rain falling from one blanket of clouds accords with each particular species and nature, causing it to sprout and mature, to blossom and bear fruit. Though all these plants and trees grow in the same earth and moistened by the same rain, each has its differences and particulars. (Watson 98)

The image acknowledges the different propensities of sentient beings and claims Buddhist teachings are able to benefit them all. Although there is no explicit mention of disability, this guiding commitment to universalism implicitly commits Buddhist authors to develop their teachings to be accessible to disabled bodies and minds.

In contemporary society, the practice of businesses or workplaces changing their ordinary policies and ways of doing business to make them accessible to a person with a disability is called reasonable accommodation. For instance, a grocery store might have an employee help a person of short stature reach items high on a shelf or a supervisor might remove nonessential tasks, like climbing stairs to fetch mail, from the duties of a mobility-impaired administrative assistant. On occasion, we find something very close to reasonable accommodation in texts describing how the Buddha teaches others. One of the clearest examples of this is in an early Buddhist text that tells how the Buddha taught a monk of very low intelligence. The monk is unable to remember any of the teachings the senior monks give to him. To compensate for this, the Buddha gives him a clean cloth and tells him to say "removal of impurity" repeatedly while handling it. As the cloth becomes dirty, the monk suddenly realizes his mind is likewise defiled with negative mental states like anger and greed. After realizing this insight, he quickly progresses to liberation (Cowell 15–21).

Other Buddhist texts offer even more imaginative descriptions of how Buddhas can modify their teachings for beings of various psychological propensities. For instance, the Mahayana text, the *Vimalakīrti Sūtra*, portrays Buddhas in alternate universes using radically different means to minister to beings there. Some teach by light emanating from their body, others by special kinds of food, others attract beings through their physical beauty, and some even teach through silence (Thurman 86).

More down-to-earth examples of how a bodhisattva should accommodate disabled persons are given by the Mahayana monk Asaṅga, who offers lists of activities the bodhisattva should carry out to benefit others. In relation to disability, the bodhisattva should minister to the sick, guide the blind, carry persons without legs when necessary, and, significantly, communicate through hand gestures with the deaf (54). These examples show how the doctrine of skillful means begins to overlap with contemporary methods of reasonable accommodation. Since Mahayana Buddhism seeks to make itself accessible to all, when bodhisattvas encounter disability they adapt their teachings and behavior to benefit these beings.

CONCLUSION

When disabilities are mentioned in Buddhist texts, they are portrayed as the negative results of past karmic action and as obstacles to spiritual practice. This may be because disabilities are often accompanied by great amounts of physical or emotional pain, and Buddhists hold that pain results from past negative actions. Buddhist texts also emphasize the limited access people with intellectual disabilities and sensory impairments have to Buddhist teachings. This may explain why the language used in Buddhist texts is similar to the medical model which characterizes disabilities as intrinsic defects and impediments to human flourishing.

One benefit of comparative work between Buddhist and disability studies, therefore, is in highlighting the role societal attitudes and inaccessible environments play in creating these negative results that accompany disability. Limitations associated with particular disabilities, such as blindness and mobility impairment, can be lessened or even eliminated by appropriate accommodation and adaptation of the environment. A natural effect of accepting these insights would be an even greater commitment by contemporary Buddhists in making centers and practices accessible to disabled practitioners. There are also aspects of Buddhist theory itself that are conducive to rethinking usual characterizations of disabled persons. In particular, Buddhist texts pay extraordinarily careful attention to the impermanence and fragility of everything that exists. Disability is only a particularly visible manifestation of these ever-present underlying conditions. This insight undercuts any deep division between disabled and able-bodied persons and lessens stigma attached to disability.

Another area of intersection between disability studies and Buddhism is their shared concern with adapting practices to increase overall access to persons of various abilities. In Buddhism, this is expressed in the practice of skillful means, in which teachings are adapted for persons of varying psychological dispositions. Some of these adaptations resemble the contemporary practice of reasonable accommodation in which services or workplaces are made accessible to persons with disabilities. A natural development of Buddhist inclusive tendencies would be to integrate reasonable accommodations into Buddhist centers such as wheelchair ramps, no-step entrances, fragrance-free policies to help those with chemical sensitivity, and sign-language interpretation for teachings. Just as important will be the adaptation of particular Buddhist practices. Prostrations to a statue of the Buddha, for example, can be replaced by visualization of prostrations for those with mobility impairments, and sitting meditation periods might be shortened for those whose disability interferes with concentration. Many centers are already making adaptations like these to help disabled practitioners.

A final area in which Buddhists can benefit from the insights of disability scholars and advocates is the attention they have given to positive aspects of disabled experience. Buddhists claim that our propensity to deny the radical impermanence and fragility of existence prevents us from deeply practicing Buddhism and liberating ourselves from suffering. In relation to Buddhist practice, therefore, disability will be advantageous to the extent that it helps an individual accept these facts. Buddhist centers can also recognize that the participation of people with disabilities may enhance the spiritual health of a center. Since many disabled people have dealt extensively with physical or psychological pain, and the breakdown of the body, they have much to teach about the truths Buddhists emphasize like impermanence and suffering. Likewise, displaying the flexibility necessary to accommodate disabilities while maintaining the efficacy of Buddhist practices aids a center in avoiding rigid attachment to particular elements of practice.

Attention to the work of scholars and activists in the disability movement, therefore, can play an important role in the development of contemporary Buddhism. First, the traditional view that disabilities are negative results of past karmic action can be rethought. Second, contemporary practices of reasonable accommodation can be employed to facilitate the Buddhist commitment to expanding the availability of Buddhist teachings. Finally, positive aspects of disabled experience can be recognized, in relation to both the practice of disabled Buddhists and the overall spiritual development of Buddhist centers. Likewise, disability studies can benefit from the careful analysis of impermanence, fragility, and suffering developed in Buddhist texts, which suggests all humans lie somewhere in a spectrum of dependence and vulnerability that is often erroneously attributed to disabled persons alone.

3

Confucianism and Disability

Benjamin Lukey

INTRODUCTION TO CONFUCIANISM

The Challenges of Interpreting Confucianism

There are more than 2,500 years of text, commentaries, and cultural practices that can be identified under the Confucian umbrella, and, as is the case in many of the world's religious and philosophical traditions, a given understanding of Confucianism will be tinted by the particular lens through which it is viewed, especially when attempting to understand Confucianism and disability. Though the Confucian canon does not directly address the issue of disability, it offers a rich philosophical tradition focused on social relationships and what it means to be a human being and morally worthy person. This tradition can offer much to the field of disability studies, particularly in supporting philosophers of disability who strive to articulate a notion of personhood grounded in personal or familial relationships.

It is somewhat anachronous to classify Confucianism as a religion or philosophy. As Ronnie Littlejohn points out, the Classical Chinese had no character for religion. Instead they used the term *jiao* 教, which is often translated as "teachings" and is used to identify Buddhism (Fojiao 佛教), Daoism (Daojiao 道教), and Confucianism (Rujiao 儒教) (xx). As a set of teachings for self-transformation into an ideal person, Confucianism is rich in liturgy yet relatively sparse in theological dogma. This lack of dogma has allowed Confucianism to be very inclusive and maintain peace with other religions to the extent that, as Peimin Ni points out, "there is nothing oxymoronic about Confucian Christianity, or Confucian Islam" (94). It might seem more appropriate to call Confucianism a philosophy, but the concept of philosophy was not introduced to China until the late nineteenth century (99). Ni writes, "Confucius's thought, however, always focuses on how to live a better life and how to become a better person. His teachings are mostly instructions about *how* rather than descriptions of *what*" (100). While much of Western philosophy is characterized as propositional, Confucianism is more accurately characterized as instructional; using what Ni calls "intellectualist standards" to read Confucian texts (i.e., in the way that one might read Descartes, Kant, or Rawls) "is like eating the menu instead of the food" (100). While Confucianism may be considered, in the broad sense, as a set of ethical teachings for the benefit of humanity, it may also be considered a philosophy in the broad sense of pursuit of wisdom.

Herbert Fingarette recognizes that what made Confucian philosophy unique was its emphasis on human relationships and the ritual structures of those relationships. "To become civilized is to establish relationships that are not merely physical, biological, or instinctive; it is to establish *human* relationships, relationships of an essentially symbolic kind, defined by tradition and convention and rooted in respect and obligation" (76). This focus on relationships, rooted in respect and obligation, and the lack of theological dogma make Confucianism a welcome, but thus far underrepresented, addition to the discourse on disability.

The focus here will be on the texts and interpretations of classical Confucianism, meaning the *Analects* (*Lunyu*) of Confucius and the texts attributed to those within the orthodox transmission of Confucius' teaching, known as the Si-Meng lineage.[1] Because early Confucian philosophy is so far removed in time, language, and culture from many current readers, the choice of translations and translators assumes even more significance. Some of the earliest Western transmitters of the Confucian canon were Jesuit missionaries. Unsurprisingly, key Confucian terms were translated first with Latin and later English terms such as "heaven," "righteousness," and "benevolence" that would have been familiar to Western audiences. Wishing to avoid philological debate, I adhere to a strand of Confucian interpretation that is contemporary and somewhat unorthodox. Roger Ames, David Hall, and Henry Rosemont (and to a lesser extent Tu Wei-ming) have consistently attempted to present an interpretation of Confucianism that distinguishes the Confucian tradition from the predominant traditions in Western philosophy. While it may be argued that such translations take liberties with the text, they represent a sensitivity to importing Western philosophical biases into our reading of classic Confucian texts. If Confucianism is understood merely as another version of virtue ethics or a watered-down version of Christian theology, then its contributions to philosophical discourse, and in this case the discourse of disability studies, are marginalized; we must keep revisiting canonical Confucian texts to present the uniqueness of textually based Confucian insights. While it is ultimately impossible to say with certainty what Confucius intended, many modern translators are conscientiously attempting to present Confucian teachings in a way that is faithful to the philosophical insights of the classic texts.

Aspects of Confucianism

Many of the ideas to be examined with regard to disability introduce terms, such as "person" or "autonomy," that are meaningfully used in everyday conversation and which are also laden with philosophical significance. To assume that these terms carry the same philosophical baggage or are even everyday notions in early Confucian texts is to make a mistake that threatens to reduce the worth of examining such texts. As Rosemont and Ames write:

> A philosophical analysis of early Confucian ethical or moral thought must begin with the fact that there are no terms in the lexicon of early Chinese that correspond closely to our terms "ethics" or "morals." In itself this semantic fact might not initially give us pause, but there is more: Virtually *none* of the key terms employed in contemporary Western moral discourse—"freedom," "liberty," "rights," "autonomy," "dilemma," "individual," "choice," "rationality," "democracy," "supererogatory," "private," even "ought"—have close analogues in the early Chinese language in which the Confucian texts were written. Now, it seems, we must indeed pause; absent this concept cluster of basic terms, how can any issues of contemporary moral concern be discussed? (*Xiaojing*, 34–35)

This question can be addressed by (*a*) recognizing the unique methodological strengths of the Confucian emphasis on personal and social relationships and (*b*) limiting, somewhat artificially, the focus of the issue to be discussed. These methodological strengths can then be applied to a discussion of how to understand the issue of moral personhood with regard to those with disabilities.

A major shift in methodology is from the primacy of nouns to the primacy of gerunds, from things to processes. Rosemont and Ames characterize the language of the early Chinese canon as gerundive, meaning that nouns are expressed as verbs more frequently than in English or most other Indo-European languages (*Xiaojing*, 65). For example, instead of translating *xiao* 孝 as "family reverence," it would be more accurate (and more awkward in English) to translate it as "family revering." As Rosemont and Ames write:

> It is fairly well known that, apart from context, virtually every Chinese graph
> can sometimes be a noun, sometimes an adjective, verb, or adverb; less well
> known, or at least acknowledged by most translators, is the dynamic cosmos
> reflected in the language itself. "Things" are less in focus than events; nouns
> that would abstract and objectify elements of this world are derived from
> and revert back to a verbal sensibility. Indeed, a human being in this world
> is irreducibly a "human becoming." (*Xiaojing*, 65)

It is important to note that there is not a general rule for translating graphs into
verbs or nouns; ultimately it depends on context. However, it is certain that
almost every instance of a graph carries with it associations of multiple parts of
speech. This density of connotation should remind the reader that terms such
as "person," "respect," and even "family" are presented as nouns as a matter
of convenience but could be written as gerunds to express the shifted focus on
person-becoming.

In attempting to briefly describe Confucianism's vision of how to best
live one's life, we will introduce the distinctly Confucian importance of *ren*
仁, the attunement to others that makes one a moral person, and *li* 禮, the
domain of interactions within which that attunement or focus is cultivated.
Both of these concepts lead to the five socio-familial relationship models
(listed below) within Confucianism and the development of the dispositions
shu 恕 and *zhong* 忠 that enable mastery within those relationships. Finally,
we will briefly examine the exemplars, *junzi* 君子, that guide Confucians in
their cultivation of *ren*, *li*, *shu*, and *zhong*.

The gerundive nature of Classical Chinese has a profound impact on
the Confucian notion of person. The most common character for person in
both Classical and Modern Chinese is *ren* 人, which designates an individual
human being or the class of human beings and is used with varying connotations in a wide variety of contexts. Another closely related term for person,
one that more accurately captures the moral connotation of the term and is
central to Confucianism, is *ren* 仁, which Rosemont and Ames have translated as "consummate person/conduct." These two homophones indicate a
familiar distinction between human being and person. As Ni notes:

> In both Chinese and other languages, we find the need to give two meanings
> to the term "human," so that we can meaningfully say "a human should
> be like a human," or "a human should be treated like a human." We do
> not treat these statements as simple tautologies because, in these expressions,
> the first occurrence of "human" is used in a biological sense, whereas the
> second is used in a moral or cultural sense. . . . It is quite reasonable to say
> that for Confucius, *ren* (仁) must have meant a quality that makes a person

an authentic human being, for which every biological human should strive
toward. (101)

Though *ren* 仁 indicates a certain amount of growth or achievement, it
must be understood that this person-becoming is irreducibly relational. The
character itself, which is a combination of *ren* 人 and the indicator of two,
indicates the inseparability of persons and their relationships. As Ni emphasizes, "*Ren* is essentially relational, and the *ren* person defers to his or her
relationships and interactions with others for the completion of oneself. No
one can become fully human in isolation, nor can anyone say that what hap-
pens to others has nothing to do with one's self" (102). Wei-ming writes, "*Ren*
[仁] thus understood is one's 'field of selves,' the sum of significant relationships that constitute one as a social person" (75).[2]

Translated as a noun, *ren* 仁 has often been rendered as "benevolence,"
"humaneness," "goodness," or "humanity." While these translations capture
the moral importance of *ren* 仁, they are less successful in signifying the process of bettering one's "field of selves" through the innumerable relationships
one participates in.

It is in living these relationships to the utmost that *ren* 仁 is linked with
li 禮 (often translated as "ritual" or "rite," but translated by Ames and Rosemont as "observing ritual propriety"). If *ren* 仁 is the expression of human
beings becoming moral persons, then *li* 禮 is the set of guideposts that direct
this process. Fingarette argues that the central Confucian insight is that
human beings become persons through their familial and social relationships
and that these relationships are guided by *li*, context-sensitive ceremonies
that range from the shaking of hands to the burial of one's loved ones. Being
shaped by (and shaping) these ceremonies is what makes persons distinct
moral beings:

> These complex but familiar gestures are characteristic of human relation-
> ships at their most human: we are least like anything else in the world when
> we do not treat each other as physical objects, as animals or even as sub-
> human creatures to be driven, threatened, forced, maneuvered. Looking at
> these "ceremonies" through the image of *li*, we realize that explicitly sacred
> rite can be seen as an emphatic, intensified and sharply elaborated extension
> of everyday civilized intercourse. (11)

While many have interpreted the Confucian emphasis on ritual as an obses-
sion with tradition and justification for bureaucracy or oppression, it is actually, as Fingarette argues, calling attention to the social nature of our being in

the world and recognizing these workings of sociality as being of the utmost importance. *Li* is the notion by which we see the sacred in what is "already so familiar and universal to be unnoticed" (6). It is easy to overlook the everyday handshake or the sense of shared understanding that pervades a wedding, but these rituals are what elevate *ren* 人 to *ren* 仁, a unique status within the world.

The processes of *ren* 仁 and *li* 禮 are encompassed within the five socio-familial relationship models of Confucianism:

> According to the early Confucian tradition, we are most basically components of five relationships: (1) father-son; (2) husband-wife; (3) ruler-minister (subject); (4) elder brother-younger brother; (5) friend-friend. Role variations—mother-son, father-daughter, aunt-niece, elder cousin-younger cousin, village elder-village peer or youngster, and important, teacher-student—are all to be construed within this same spectrum of communal patterns. (Rosemont and Ames 49)

To be an individuated human-becoming, *ren* 人, one is a child, sibling, and so forth, but one *ren*s 仁 only insofar as one is consummate in these relationships, creating the sacred from the *li* 禮 within each relationship. As Fingarette notes, "social etiquette in general, the father-son relation, the brother-brother relation, the prince-subject relation, the friend-friend relation and the husband-wife relation—persons and their relationships are to be seen as ultimately sanctified by virtue of their place in *li*" (75). Contrary to a common criticism of Confucianism, the hierarchy characteristic of the five basic relationships does not entail that they are coercive or unfair. Since it is coercion rather than hierarchy that compromises creativity and growth within relationships, the five relationships, while unequivocally hierarchical, need to be understood as non-coercive relationships. Rosemont and Ames suggest that Confucian texts can be read as describing relationships between benefactors and beneficiaries (*Xiaojing*, 49). This shift in language alleviates the sense of coercion or mindless loyalty found in the common translation describing relationships between superiors and inferiors.

The coercive associations within the five relationships are also lessened by examining *shu* 恕 and *zhong* 忠, a pair of concepts that indicate the dispositions of compassion and responsibility that were so important for *ren* 仁 and *li* 禮 and for being better benefactors and beneficiaries. The importance of the concepts is illustrated in a familiar passage from the *Analects*:

> The Master said, "Zeng, my friend! My way (*dao* 道) is bound together with one continuous strand."
> Master Zeng replied, "Indeed."

> When the Master had left, the disciples asked, "What was he referring to?"
> Master Zeng said, "The way of the Master is doing one's utmost (*zhong*
> 忠) and putting oneself in the other's place (*shu* 恕) nothing more." (4.15)

These two terms function to guide all relationships between benefactor and beneficiary and, as can be seen in both the *Analects* and the *Zhongyong*, such relationships constitute the entirety of person-activity. The activity of *shu*, which has also been translated as "altruism" and "consideration," is pointed toward the achievement of *ren* 仁 and should be understood as a basic activity of person-becoming. As Ni notes:

> *Ren* is to "love people" (Analects 12.22), says the Master, and the method to
> be *ren* is *shu* (恕)—comparing one's own heart with other hearts with com-
> passion (6.30). The interrelatedness of a person is so important to Confucius
> that, as Rosemont puts it, for Confucius, one does not play the roles of a
> father, a friend, a teacher, etc.; one *is* these roles. (102)

Shu is a particularly necessary reminder to those in the benefactor roles of relationships; it guides those in a position of power to imaginatively place themselves in the role of beneficiary and thus serves as a check against unilateral coercion. Confucius acts upon his *shu* disposition when he provides seemingly inconsistent but contextually appropriate responses to his disciples when asked to clarify key concepts.

Zhong is *shu*'s sister concept both because the process of person-becoming entails mutual *zhong* 忠 and *shu* 恕 and because *zhong* expresses the motivation that is necessary to realize the insights from *shu*. *Zhong* needs to be understood not as simply doing one's best, which can be interpreted in an individualistic way, but also making the most of the guidance one receives from one's benefactors.[3] Yet *zhong* is also complementary to *shu* in that, as D. C. Lau expresses, "it is through *chung* [*zhong*] that one puts into effect what one has found out by the method of *shu*" (qtd. in *Xiaojing*, 91).

The two notions of *shu* and *zhong* are also linked to the Confucian golden rule, articulated in book 13 of the *Zhongyong*: "Putting oneself in the place of others (*shu* 恕) and doing one's best on their behalf (*zhong* 忠) does not stray from the proper way. 'Do not treat others as you yourself would not wish to be treated'" (Ames and Hall 94). Ames writes:

> This "negative" version of the Golden Rule is modest; it does not presup-
> pose some objective and universal standard that would serve as warrant for
> "doing unto others as you would have them do unto you." Just as the hewing
> of the axe-handle uses a model rather than a template, so the shaping of

one person in relation to another is directed at an accommodating harmony
rather than an imposed uniformity. (*Confucian*, 198)

As suggested by the notion of harmony, a metaphor for understanding one
who is adept at *shu* is that of a musical virtuoso who can play multiple instruments and multiple musical styles.[4] Like *shu*, *zhong* should also culminate in
a virtuosity that is antithetical to complacency. For those who might take to
heart an overly passive interpretation of the Golden Rule expressed by *shu*,
zhong is a reminder that doing nothing is an evasion of responsibilities.

Since Confucianism is prescriptive and not propositional, *ren* 仁, *li* 禮,
shu 恕, and *zhong* 忠 are understood through exemplars, not principles or
definitions. In Confucianism these exemplars are *junzi* 君子, translated as
"exemplary persons." The notion of *junzi*, like *ren* 仁, is both immediate—
when one behaves as a *junzi*, one is *junzi*—and in some sense unattainable, a
strived-for ideal. *Junzi* and *ren* are immediate because the instructive examples are taken from ordinary life, from family life. As Tu Wei-ming writes:

> The profound person [*junzi* 君子] in *Chung-yung* [*Zhongyong*] seeks to man-
> ifest the ultimate meaning of *ordinary human existence*. . . . And *Chung-yung*
> makes it explicit that the profound person's knowledge of the Way is shared
> and practiced by men and women of simple intelligence as well (XII:1-2).
> After all, the way of the profound person is also the way of the commoner.
> (23; emphasis added)

It may be as easy as pointing to one's own family or community for certain
exemplary relationships or situations, though such pointing may exemplify or
highlight only a narrow efficacy in relationships. To be an effective model,
junzi, like *ren*, must be near at hand.

Though *junzi* are immediate and familiar, the idea of *junzi* is also a call
for ever more progress, an ideal asymptote that can be infinitely approached
but never reached. Confucius did not consider himself a *junzi*: "As far as
personally succeeding in living the life of the exemplary person (*junzi*), I have
accomplished little" (*Analects* 7.33). It was less important to reach the ideal
than it was to continually strive toward it. Therefore, Confucius recognized
that his strength was his constant learning and study (*xue* 學) (7.34). This
commitment to learning with others, and learning from what is near at hand,
is one of the distinguishing characteristics of Confucianism. The Confucian
emphasis on process and growth is more appropriate for cases of disability, particularly cases of mental disability, than are traditions or schools of
thought that focus on innate capacities or ontological status. Before we apply

Confucianism to disability studies, it is necessary to understand a bit more about the disability issues that Confucianism can contribute to.

PERSONHOOD AND MENTAL DISABILITY

In the documentary *Murderball*, a paraplegic rugby player who plays for the US National team in the 2004 Athens Paralympics recounts a story where he was introduced as a participant in the Special Olympics. He proclaims his anger at the mistake and vehemently disassociates himself from those with mental disability, "I went from being a hero to being a f—— retard." In the film's commentary, the player clarifies that he has great respect for what Special Olympians do. But he is disturbed by the conflation of the two Olympics. His vehemence is directed at society, which often does not recognize the difference.

This scene from *Murderball* highlights a prominent tension within disability studies, one that Confucianism may help to lessen. The tension is deeper than the apparent one between the status of those with physical disabilities and those with mental disabilities; it touches the depths of how and why we treat individuals as moral persons.[5] The claim of personhood is not trivial and highlights both the differences and similarities between how those with physical disabilities and those with mental disabilities are received within the moral domain ("moral recipiency").

Narrowing the Focus of Disability

The importance of names and labeling in disability studies and disability literature cannot be understated. The first distinction to make is between terms that imply devaluation and terms that simply identify function. "Disability" and "impairment" are terms used by Anita Silvers, a prominent philosopher of disability, because they neutrally describe a loss or difference in conventional function.[6] However, "inferior" or "disadvantage" imparts a normative tone to the neutral description. Though common in use, "handicap" is a term that is felt by many to contain a negative normative tone, and it will not be used. Instead, value-neutral language accepted by many of those involved in disability studies will be adhered to. This *intention* should be remembered since language has a tendency to accumulate normative tone in unintended ways, often furthering practices of devaluation that the language was originally meant to overcome.

"Mental disability" itself is a vague and problematic term. It identifies impairment in performing certain mental tasks or a deviation from cognitive processes that are deemed normal within a particular culture, community, or society. "Mental" rather than "cognitive" is used because it is broader in scope and more clearly includes impairments in affect, which can be just as challenging as impairments in reasoning. Although impairment may be a biological fact, disability references conventions of functioning. Dyslexia, for example, is a disability only in cultures that rely on written language. It is in this way that disability is socially defined and constructed. Furthermore, while the range of diseases, illnesses, conditions, disorders, and syndromes that can create mental disability is staggering, there is still a range of *ability* within any particular diagnosis.

Stress, physical or emotional abuse, diet, drugs, and aging cause cognitive impairments that are often responsive to treatment. Everyone is susceptible to these cases of mental disability. Yet these kinds of impairments, even if they last for decades, are still viewed as temporary, as an unfortunate deviation from the person's normal state. Though troubling and perhaps philosophically interesting, these cases of mental disability present a different challenge. Instead, the focus should be on the types of mental disability that do not clearly represent a temporary deviation from the norm.

The Seeming Tension between Physical and Mental Disability

As seen in the *Murderball* scene, for some of those with physical disabilities the conflation of physical and mental disability is perceived as threatening their place at the table. Many of those with physical disabilities would rather be grouped together with the non-disabled than with those with mental disabilities; the difference of mental disability places those individuals in an undesirable category. In cases of physical disability, whether individuals were historically excluded from the moral domain or included through pity or charity, advocacy for change used the strategy of revealing underlying equality. Ron Amundson argues that we must focus more on the level of function than on the mode of function. Individuals with physical disabilities are able to function at the same level as normal people, but not in the same mode ("Biological Normality," 106–7). Grounded in the assumption of equal moral agency, philosophers and activists have successfully argued that with accommodations to the constructed environment, which has historically been constructed in such a way that it discriminated against those with disabilities, individuals with physical disabilities can achieve levels of function equivalent to those of normal individuals. The Americans with Disabilities Act (ADA) is legislation that removes the bias against modes of functioning and ensures that all those of equal levels of function should be treated equally. As long as the case can be made that those with physical disabilities are equal in the relevant aspects to those in the majority, they have already been assured a place at the table as equals.

In cases of mental disability, the distinction that philosophers of disability make between impairment and handicap is no longer as clear since no amount of change within the social environment (e.g., access ramps and "talking signs") will enable those with certain mental disabilities to become functionally normal members of society. In these cases, where differences may be less easy to ignore and more easily perceived as a biological fact instead of a product of discrimination in the environment, justification of equal moral status cannot immediately appeal to sameness.

It is therefore unclear whether many individuals with mental disabilities can be called persons in the same way that those with physical disabilities sometimes take for granted. The arguments and activism of scholars such as Silvers and Amundson rely upon revealing the moral agency of those with disabilities; moral recipiency will necessarily follow from recognition of such agency. In other words, many of the arguments that have been advanced for inclusion of those with physical disabilities into the moral domain assume autonomy as an essential characteristic of moral personhood. Thus, a deeper tension emerges between the personhood of those with mental disabilities and the notion of autonomy.

Personhood and Autonomy

The grounding of respect for persons in autonomy, while it might seem intuitive, is in fact a development of the past forty years. Understanding this development indicates some of the philosophical richness that has been lost in the concept of person, richness that Confucianism can help restore. M. Therese Lysaught provides an "intellectual archaeology" of how the term "respect" has shifted in bioethics. Her findings can be used to helpfully frame the challenge of including those with mental disabilities in the moral domain (665).

In its 1979 *Belmont Report*, the National Commission for the Protection of Human Subjects of Biomedical and Behavioral Research defined principles and guidelines for the treatment of human subjects. Lysaught writes:

> Two components of Belmont's argument are worth noting. First, in their discussion of "respect for persons," the authors of the report distinguished between those with autonomy and those without, but they presumed that the notion of "persons" applies to both. They did not define who is a person and who is not; they did not distinguish between "persons" and "nonpersons." Autonomy is certainly not co-equal with personhood. Respect does not apply to some but not to others. Second, the meaning of "respect" clearly cashes out differently for persons with different levels of autonomy. But importantly, Belmont presupposed an inverse relationship between

autonomy and protection. For Belmont the need for protection increased as the individual's proximity to autonomy decreases: "Respect for the immature and incapacitated may require protecting them as they mature or while they are incapacitated." (668–69)

The fact that personhood did not depend on autonomy or agency, and that respect was flexible enough to encompass those with profound impairments who were wholly dependent on others, indicates a notion of person that has positive implications for acknowledging the moral considerability of those with mental disabilities.

Also in 1979, Tom L. Beauchamp and James F. Childress published their *Principles of Biomedical Ethics*. They too professed a principle of "respect for persons" but defined the principle in a more restricted way:

> In *Principles of Biomedical Ethics* the principle of "respect for persons" became the principle of autonomy or *respect* for *autonomy*.
>
> . . . In making this move, the principle of respect for persons has deftly been redefined as a sub-category of the principle of autonomy. It is no longer the principle of *The Belmont Report*. (Lysaught 675)

This new conception of respect meant "noninterference and correlatively an obligation not to constrain autonomous actions—nothing more but also nothing less" (Beauchamp and Childress 62). Whereas in *The Belmont Report* respect entailed obligation and active protection, Beauchamp and Childress made the principle of respect into one of leaving people alone. This difference also entailed a different order of moral consideration for those who were not autonomous. "Respect no longer pertains to the non-autonomous. Instead, their fortunes are determined by the principles of nonmaleficence and beneficence" (Lysaught 676). The non-autonomous are therefore subject to the kind of pity that Silvers criticizes as signifying inferiority.

The third and final notion of respect that Lysaught unearths comes from another 1979 report, this time by the Ethics Advisory Board (EAB) of the Department of Health, Education, and Welfare:

> Whereas Beauchamp and Childress decoupled autonomous and nonautonomous persons *vis a vis* respect, the EAB decoupled "respect" from "persons." . . .
>
> The EAB began the conversation about which beings that share human genetic heritage, in the words of the National Commission, ought to be included in the category of "persons" and thereby protected from the canons of respect. (677)

And yet, Lysaught concludes, the notion of respect that the EAB put forth was empty. "In the third configuration (EAB), respect is decoupled from persons and becomes a free-floating, essentially meaningless term, trading on cultural associations to mask that the sole ethical consideration has become that of utility" (678). This decoupling is evident in the conclusions of the EAB that "the human embryo is entitled to *profound respect*; but this respect does not necessarily encompass the full legal and moral rights attributed to *persons*" (qtd. in Lysaught 677; emphasis added). Lysaught accuses the EAB of trading upon a Kantian notion of respect—as was done in *The Belmont Report* and the *Principles of Biomedical Ethics*—in order to disguise their true policy principle: utility. Thus, according to developments in bioethics since *The Belmont Report*, what individuals with mental disabilities confront then is either inclusion in the moral domain via principles of non-maleficence and beneficence, à la Beauchamp and Childress, or being objects of an empty respect, à la the EAB.

The fact that respect for persons has been transformed into respect for autonomy poses few problems for those with physical disabilities; by establishing their autonomy, they establish themselves as persons. Yet this transformation of respect creates more significant limitations for many with mental disabilities.

Personhood and Capacities

As Lysaught's research indicates, the shift in focus to capacities has compromised the moral status of those who may not be seen as possessing such capacities. Though much discussion surrounds the definition of "morally relevant capacities," moral is often a mask for utilitarian considerations: which capacities offer the greatest potential for pleasure and the least risk of pain? Comparisons on the basis of such morally relevant capacities often call into question the personhood of those with mental disabilities. Jeff McMahan has asserted that the radically cognitively limited do not warrant full human rights. He writes:

> I have argued that the cognitively impaired are not badly off in the sense relevant to justice and indeed do not come within the scope of comparative (and, by extension, noncomparative) principles of justice. Not only do they not have special priority as a matter of justice, but *their claims on us seem even weaker than those of most other human beings. And my arguments have explicitly compared them to nonhuman animals with comparable psychological capacities.* (31; emphasis added)

Conclusions such as those of McMahan may be valid on the basis of such comparisons, but it is by no means established whether such comparisons are a sound means of determining moral worth, particularly personhood.[7]

Eva Kittay, a prominent philosopher of disability, takes issues with comparisons such as McMahan's. She tries to see the issue through the lens of comparing capacities but recoils because she recognizes that such comparisons not only fail to capture what makes a child a person but also may have morally abhorrent practical consequences.

> And if *I* sensed the comparison cutting me off from my own daughter, then imagine the wedge the process of juxtaposing the cognitively disabled and the nonhuman animal would place between a person with severe cognitive disabilities and those who lack any familiarity with such individuals. In the case of the theorist the wedge may be merely conceptual, but it has the potential to translate into one with horrific consequences on a practical level. ("Personal," 613; emphasis original)

Furthermore, as Kittay points out, such comparisons are based on the assumption that we can know the capacities of another, an assumption that is often proven false. She, like other parents, is often surprised at what her daughter Sesha, who has severe cognitive and physical impairments, is capable of.

> Now what cognitive capacities Sesha possesses *I* do not know, nor do others. And it is hubris to presume to know. I am often surprised to find out that Sesha has understood something or is capable of something I did not expect. These surprises can only keep coming when she and her friends are treated in a manner based not on the limitations we know they have but on *our* understanding that our knowledge is limited. ("Personal," 619; emphasis original)

If a comparison of capacities is grounded in questionable assumptions and potentially leads to unjust policy, then another means of claiming personhood is required, one that resuscitates the claims of *The Belmont Report*. Admittedly the notion of person in *The Belmont Report* is vague; there is no attempt to distinguish person from non-person, so we need to draw upon some philosophical resources that offer more clarity.

Personhood and Relationships

Kittay suggests that claims of personhood are grounded in familial relationships, particularly focusing on parent-child relationships, and it is this approach that recommends the resources of the Confucian tradition. Before turning directly to Confucianism, it is helpful to briefly acknowledge that there is an acceptance of grounding personhood in relationships within some spheres of American sociology.

Robert Bogdan and Steven Taylor analyzed more than fifteen years of research beginning in the mid-1970s (when the notion of respect for persons was prominent), primarily examining the relationships between those with disabilities and those without. Their primary finding is that, in such relationships, disabilities do not hinder recognition of personhood:

> In our case, those involved are people with severe and obvious disabilities and ostensibly nondisabled others. In such relationships, the deviant attribute, the disability, does not bring stigma or discredit. The humanness of the person with a disability is maintained. The difference is not denied, but neither does it bring disgrace. (137)

For them, humanness defines the domain of moral considerability, much like respect does for Lysaught. Even though theirs is a sociological study, they recognize that they are studying a moral property:

> The nondisabled view the disabled people as full-fledged human beings. This stands in contrast to the dehumanizing perspectives often held by institutional staff and others, in which people with severe disabilities are viewed as non-persons or sub-human (Bogdan et al. 1974; Taylor 1977, 1987). . . . The term "humanness" captures the underlying perspective on severely disabled people held by the nondisabled people described in this study. Whether or not people with severe disabilities "really are" human is not a matter of social definition. This is a moral and philosophical question and not a sociological one. (138n2)

Most importantly, they give equal philosophical weight to the perspectives of those interviewed. Their conclusions capture the open-minded attitude that characterizes the philosophical examination of personhood informed by the accounts of those most intimate with mental disabilities:

> It is easy to dismiss the perspectives described in this paper. One might argue that the nondisabled people are deceiving or deluding themselves when they attribute these qualities and characteristics [e.g., humanness and "someone like me"] to people with severe and profound mental retardation and other disabilities. . . . Yet it is just as likely that those who dehumanize people with severe disabilities, dispute their human agency, and define them as non-persons are deceiving themselves. After all, no one can ever prove that

anyone else is "someone like me" or that the assumption of common experience is anything but an illusion. What and who others, as well as we, are depends on our relationships with them and what we choose to make of us. (146)

This final observation, made in 1989, anticipates Kittay's response to philosophers such as McMahan and captures one of the central insights that Confucianism offers disability studies.

Kittay recounts an exchange with philosopher Naomi Scheman at a 2008 conference when Kittay challenged McMahan's questioning of the claims that Sesha has on others:

> "It is not that you cannot now do certain things to her that you couldn't do before because it would hurt me, it's because you can't do certain kinds of things to her because *now she is a different kind of being*." The difference between Naomi Scheman's cat and Sesha or any other human with cognitive disabilities, however, is that human beings do not survive long as feral beings. We human beings are the sorts of beings we are because we are cared for by other human beings, and the human being's ontological status and corresponding moral status need to be acknowledged by the larger society that makes possible the work of those who do the caring required to sustain us. ("Personal," 625; emphasis original)

Kittay is pointing toward a different kind of approach, not only rejecting the focus on capacities but also urging us to see persons as a unique kind of being, one grounded in socio-familial relationships. As indicated, there are challenges associated with this approach, but these are challenges that Confucianism can uniquely help to address.

CONFUCIANISM, PERSONHOOD, AND MENTAL DISABILITY

A turn to Confucianism can help address a bias in Western philosophy of seeing persons as collections of capacities. Kittay critiques this bias when she writes,

> This is why I just reject the idea that you should base moral standing on a list of cognitive capacities, or psychological capacities, or any kind of capacities. Because what it is to be human is not a bundle of capacities. It's a way that you are, a way you are in the world, a way you are with another. (Kittay, "Personal," 621)

Kittay's appeal to a different kind of being should remind us of the Confucian notion of *ren* 仁 and the uniqueness of the human being understood as a social being. Confucianism offers a deep understanding of what kind of being the human person is and the corresponding moral status that it has within the larger society. Moreover, as the title of Kittay's article suggests, she is attempting to use the case of those with cognitive disabilities to connect what are often three distinct domains:

> For moral personhood is . . . importantly connected with the ability to make claims of justice and receive the resources and protections that justice is meant to guarantee. . . . I have been attempting to affirm in this essay that the personal is philosophical and the philosophical is political. ("Personal," 624)

While this affirmation is a relatively new tack within philosophy of disability, it is, as seen in the introduction, almost a defining feature of Confucianism; many Western philosophers have struggled to appreciate Confucianism precisely because it is nearly impossible to separate the personal from the philosophical from the political. In turning to examine how the personal and philosophical are closely interwoven in Confucianism, we can see how Confucianism strengthens Kittay's approach by helping her respond to challenges from philosophers such as McMahan.

Confucianism and Capacities

The gerundive nature of Confucianism should immediately be recognized as a challenge to the capacities-focused approach to personhood. Individuals are constituted by the relationships within which they grow. *Ren* and *shu* need not be understood as nouns (i.e., capacities) but are more appropriately understood as activities (i.e., verbs) that one participates in, hopefully more adeptly over time. Thus, *ren* might be more accurately phrased as "person-becoming" and *shu* as "what-if-I-were-you-ing."[8] Undoubtedly, some perform these activities better than others, sometimes depending on context and other times depending on skill, but there is no attempt within Confucianism to use these notions to include or exclude persons from the moral domain.[9]

The Confucian emphasis on *li* 禮 also helps us move away from the focus on capacities. For Kittay, the personal project of preparing Sesha to be a part of society is intimately connected with the philosophical and political project of shaping the society that accepts Sesha.

> When Sara Ruddick describes the practice of mothering, a central feature is socializing the child for acceptance into society. The mother with a disabled child hears this requirement somewhat differently from most (Ruddick 1989). For her, socialization for acceptance means that you have both to help the child make her way in the world given her disabilities *and* to help shape a world that will accept her. ("Personal," 611)

Li 禮, because they are inherently relational and connected to a wide web of relationships, are personal, philosophical, *and* political; they are the mechanism by which we improve ourselves and the world. Sam Crane describes the ritual of bathing his son who has severe physical and mental impairments before taking him to school (167–69). Rituals such as these not only help develop distinctively *ren* relationships, socializing the child for society, but also socialize the society for that child. Crane writes of one such ritual, "My purpose was not just to display my fatherly pride, but also to remind all of Aidan's caregivers that he was more than a recovering *status epilepticus*: he was a brother, a family member, a person embedded in a complex web of loving relationships" (108). The Confucian insight is that to parent is not to separate one's child from other relationships but to facilitate the development of those relationships so that the child is also a sibling, classmate, friend, student, colleague, and perhaps eventually a parent, teacher, or leader. Since the extension of *ren* (i.e., person-becoming) is interwoven with the extension of *li* (i.e., recognizing more socio-personal signposts for guiding one's conduct in the world), parents such as Kittay and Crane want their children to be part of the world, to participate in human *li*. Moreover, their particular rituals with their children are, and should be, instructive for those of us who do not, or cannot, participate in such particular forms of *li*. Thus, if one seeks maximum efficacy of *ren*, then one is willing and able to learn from each and every person (*Analects* 7.22 and 19.22) and does not look to exclude or include others based upon assumptions of what they are capable of.

One of the most significant consequences of examining person-becoming, guided by exemplars rather than looking for necessary attributes, is an inherent inclusivity. We are not looking to sort individuals into persons and non-persons; rather we are asking how each individual is progressing in relation to their ideals. The notion of *junzi* that guides this process of person-becoming is efficacious for everyone. Drawing from book 10 of the *Zhongyong*, Wei-ming writes:

> *Inequality among human beings in intelligence and ability notwithstanding, a person can always improve himself through self-effort no matter how adverse his existential situation.* What really matters is not the quality of his native

endowments or the nature of his immediate surroundings, but how he can make the best use of them. (74–75; emphasis added)

"Self-effort" is an ambiguous term here because it does not specify whether the self is inclusive or exclusive. It does not necessarily mean a solitary practice of meditation and discipline. Rather, self-effort implies an awareness of the relationship between one's inner states and the environments and relationships of which one is constituted. Everyone has obstacles to this awareness—that is, obstacles on the path of the *junzi*—and some obstacles are greater than others, but the *junzi* ideal is not regulative for only the intelligent, noble born, or artistic. Furthermore, self-effort is misleading in its implication that the individual pulls himself up by his own bootstraps. While self-conscious, solitary effort may characterize certain stages in the process of person-becoming, growth inevitably begins and continues as one does childing, younger-siblinging, friending, and so forth.

Relationships and Vulnerability

McMahan articulates one challenge faced by philosophers of disability like Kittay who, knowingly or not, advocate a Confucian turn to personal relationships. He argues that if the personhood of an individual is grounded in the fact that that child matters to its parent, then such a variable type of *mattering* cannot be the basis for a moral concept like person. The variability of mattering leaves others vulnerable to abuse (e.g., children halfway across the world). Kittay acknowledges this vulnerability; indeed, her central concept of "some mother's child" indicates the responsibility that arises from vulnerability. "It is a moral claim upon me, only if the other is vulnerable to *my* actions." (*Love's Labor*, 55). However, because vulnerability is often perceived negatively, even by some disability advocates, it is an unpopular basis for moral obligation.

The existence of vulnerability does not weaken a Confucian response. In fact, vulnerability exposes a moral concept already at play. Children, for example, are vulnerable to the parents to whom they are supposed to matter most, to neighbors to whom they matter somewhat less, and to governments to whom they probably matter even less (as individuals). Each of these increasing vulnerabilities identifies a potential breakdown in a particular relationship: parents are not treating their child as they should *as parents*; neighbors are not treating their neighbors' children as they should *as neighbors*; and governments are not treating their children-citizens as they should *as governments*. There is an underlying, normative sense of person-in-relationship that is necessary for vulnerability to even be an issue in the first place. For Confucianism, vulnerability is a fact of relationships, and relationships are the basis for our moral development.

The outward, other-seeking aspect of Confucianism, manifest in the concepts of *shu* and *zhong*, can make Kittay's notion of "some mother's child" explicitly prescriptive. The reciprocity indicated by *shu* and *zhong* does not exist only between the partners in a particular relationship; it calls for an expansion of *shu* and *zhong* to those with whom one might not be familiar. Kittay wants to bring others into her relationship with her daughter and to bring her daughter into relationships with others. Again, this is characteristic of parenting in general and not something unique to parents of children with disabilities.

> Now what sort of things are important to the parent qua parent? Foremost is the need that the wider society recognize the worth and worthiness of the child. It is incoherent to grant the special relationship I have with my daughter and then to turn around and say, "But that daughter has no moral hold on anyone but her parent." Her parent cannot fulfill her role as parent, unless others also have an acknowledged moral responsibility to the child—a moral responsibility on par with the one it has to anyone's child. ("Personal," 623)

What *is* different is the ease with which those other relationships are formed.[10] Another person, such as a neighbor or teacher, might have never met someone as singular as that particular child with a disability. Thus the parent must facilitate the creation of a novel relationship that is distinct from both the parent-child relationship and most likely the other's previous experiences of such relationships (e.g., neighbor-neighbor, teacher-student). This requires *shu* on the part of the parent (putting himself in the place of the other) and on the part of the other (putting himself in the place of a person that is undeniably different). For Kittay, the fact that some seem indifferent or resistant to *shu*, by both rebuffing her *shu*(ing) and by denying that such *shu*(ing) is possible with Sesha, is either an epistemic limitation (i.e., the result of an incapacity) or a moral offense (i.e., the result of an ill will).[11] Thus, it is possible to characterize Kittay's notion of "some mother's child" as a moral reminder, a reminder of the importance of *shu* and *zhong*. The recognition of another as "some mother's child" is that a relationship of reciprocity exists (or existed) and that that relationship ought to be extended into other relationships.

Kittay has a unique relationship with her daughter. Confucianism would not assert that all must have such a special relationship with Sesha (which would be impossible). Rather, the contribution of Confucianism is to recognize that those not in such particular relationships can still enrich and be enriched through relationships with parents, caregivers, and advocates like Kittay. The importance of these particular relationships, however, raises another challenge to dominant trends in moral philosophy.

Particularity and Moral Status

Kittay's moral grounding in the notion of "some mother's child" appeals to *particular* relationships of care. This is problematic because the particular obligation felt by a mother is not universal and seemingly cannot be used as a basis for ascription of personhood that expresses a universal moral value. It is this universality that many within disability advocacy strive for because they see discrimination against those with disabilities as unfairly denying them their status as equals.

The concern for equality is often mistakenly translated into a demand for symmetry, where the participants in a relationship are envisioned as giving and receiving in equal measure. David Wong describes how Confucianism challenges this common avoidance of asymmetrical equality:

> The Confucian acceptance of hierarchy in life is often an awkward subject for those Western liberals otherwise sympathetic to the philosophy. While we need to condemn Confucianism's tendency to accept the subordination of women to men, we should also recognize that it rightly accepts the necessity of certain other unequal relationships for viable life among human beings. Some feminist philosophers have noticed the tendency of much Western moral philosophy to focus on equal relationships such as contractual ones between "normal" adults, to the neglect of relationships between parents and young children, or adult children to their elderly parents, and it might be added, to the neglect of teacher-student relationships. *The result is a neglect of the very processes that make relationships between equals possible, since equals are made and nurtured by those who stand in an unequal relationship to them*. (347; emphasis added)

Part of the challenge of incorporating the kind of personal relationships mentioned by Wong (and highly valued by Kittay) into a modern moral framework that highly values equality is trying to explain how one's child can be special insofar as they are one's child and not special insofar as they are an equal member of society and not to be excluded from moral laws. This challenge is of particular importance to those with disabilities and prompts the question: how does one reconcile what makes one special (i.e., what distinguishes oneself from those without such impairments) with one's equal moral status (i.e., what makes one just like everyone else)?

Confucianism does not attempt to de-emphasize the fact that each of us *is* particular and special. If I ask you to help me, then I expect that you will, like Confucius, tailor your response to my particular needs so as to best help *me*. If I think that you are giving me boilerplate advice or run-of-the-mill assistance, then, while I may not consider you unfair, I may think that you are lacking in moral development (i.e., you are not very *ren*). Responding to the richness of particular persons, we are not only allowed to make exceptions as the situation or context demands, we are also encouraged to do so.

We can recognize that we are not special, insofar as special means "preferential" (positive) or "delegitimized" (negative); we ought not to consider ourselves above or beneath moral laws that apply to all. We can also recognize that we are special, insofar as special means "unique"; our particular interests, capabilities, and goals entail consideration when deciding exactly what we ought to do. These two senses of special are both at play in a popular chapter from the *Analects*:

> The Governor of She in conversation with Confucius said, "In our village there is someone called 'True Person.' When his father took a sheep on the sly, he reported him to the authorities."
> Confucius replied, "Those who are true in my village conduct themselves differently. A father covers for his son, and a son covers for his father. And being true lies in this." (13.18)

While this story is certainly about partiality (and the specialness of fathers to sons and sons to fathers), it does not promote unfairness. Instead, it may be seen as a discussion of specialness and the compatibility of fairness (i.e., not being unfairly preferential) and uniqueness.[12] While Confucius certainly recognizes the crime that the father has committed, he differs from the Governor of She in thinking of how to address the crime. The Governor is proud of True Person for not being preferential in his application of the law. But Confucius does not necessarily ignore the law. He may recognize that the law has been broken, but, given his commitment to remonstrance, he has a different understanding of the proper response to such a violation. By saying that a son should cover for his father, he seems to be suggesting that the father should be held accountable to the son, whose duty it is to help his father resolve the breach of conduct that occurred (perhaps by paying for the sheep or offering labor in exchange).[13]

The fact that the father took the sheep was unfair because the father treated himself preferentially. However, the initial unfairness may be more effectively resolved by considering the unique relationship between father and son and the role that the son can play in correcting the wrong. Fairness can play just as significant a role in addressing some ethical breach as it does in creating the law that defines the breach in the first place.

The notions of impartiality or universality (non-specialness) are helpful in revealing what we ought *not* to do (e.g., "Do not lie" and "Do not steal sheep"). However, they are less effective at telling us what we *ought* to do. To help us determine what we ought to do, an awareness of particularity and specialness can be quite helpful. Moreover, an awareness of specialness may actually be necessary to prevent unfair maxims from becoming laws. For example, to make the guideline "use the stairs" into law would be unfair to those requiring wheelchairs, using walkers, or even carrying heavy boxes. However, we are aware of this failing only to the extent that we are aware that there are particular persons and contingencies that prevent such a guideline from being universal law.

Unlike much of modern and contemporary moral theory, Confucianism does not presume to offer clear principles to determine who is equal or what is right or fair when tackling issues prevalent in disability studies. Instead, it is instructional rather than propositional. It suggests that we look and add to our own exemplars (the *junzi* in our midst) to help guide our judgments of what we ought to do.

One advantage of narratives is that, although they do not provide clear guidance for what we ought to do in all situations, they can be very effective at revealing when unfairness (i.e., the veil of impartiality) actually conceals morally relevant exceptions. Likewise, it is stories (our own and others') that illustrate how we are both special and not special. For example, after reading Michael Bérubé's *Life as We Know It*, a narrative about his son Jamie, born with Down syndrome, a reader may have a much clearer sense of how Jamie deserves to be treated just like everyone else (e.g., being allowed to attend school, not being manipulated for someone else's personal gain, and being allowed to participate in discussions regarding his well-being) and how some cases of being treated like everyone else may be unfair (e.g., being required to take Algebra III in order to graduate and being expected to live independently). Similarly, the *Analects* and, by extension, the predominant narrative style of much of Confucian philosophy continually offer examples and exemplars that help guide our judgment in applying our moral laws.

CONCLUSION

In closing, it is worthwhile to revisit the seeming tension between those with mental disabilities and a notion of moral personhood grounded in autonomy. Insofar as autonomy is understood as a capacity, Confucianism stands with philosophers such as Kittay in asserting that moral status should not be contingent upon such capacities. There may be other understandings of autonomy that would fit better into a Confucian worldview.[14] While an extended examination of Confucian autonomy is beyond the present scope, Confucianism reminds us that the moral capacities we value, including autonomy, depend on and emerge from relationships. These relationships are often asymmetrical (or even hierarchical) and cannot be broken down into reductive parts. Thus, if we face moral issues regarding those with disabilities, it serves us poorly to limit ourselves to symmetrical relationships among equals or to deny that the relationships those with disabilities participate in are extraneous to the issue. Doing so denies the person-becoming truths that underlie everyone's moral development.

4

Daoism and Disability

Andrew Lambert

INTRODUCTION

What can the early Daoist texts teach us about disability? Studying Daoism with the hope of gaining insight into contemporary discussions of disability might appear to be misguided. The two canonical texts of classical Daoism, the *Daodejing* and the *Zhuangzi*, do not explicitly discuss disability as an object of theory or offer a model of it; however, these texts do provide resources and concepts that can enrich contemporary discussions of disability. Two particular ideas are discussed here. First, attribution of the label "disabled" often relies upon certain normative assumptions about the body, but Daoist thinking about the body reveals the contingent nature of those assumptions; second, Daoism warns against the premature inferential leap from an initial judgment of incapacity to a more general judgment of uselessness. In general, Daoism's skepticism and particularistic approach to experience suggest caution about the value of appealing to models of disability. To appreciate this contribution, it is helpful to articulate something of the worldview and sensibility conveyed by the Daoist tradition.

The Daoist tradition is diverse and defies simple definition. When understood as a religious tradition, it encompasses multiple deities, studies in alchemy, quests for elixirs of eternal life, and various health manuals. Daoism is perhaps most simply understood, however, as the ideas expressed in two foundational texts, the *Daodejing* and the *Zhuangzi*. These were the basis for later, more diverse schools of Daoist thought, and will be the focus here. The most widely known text in the Daoist canon, the *Daodejing*, is traditionally attributed to the shadowy figure of Laozi (sometimes written Laotsu or Laotze) and thought to be a settled text by the fourth century BCE, though authorship of the received text's eighty-one concise and poetic passages is uncertain. The second canonical text of classical Daoism is the *Zhuangzi*. Consisting of thirty-three chapters, it is named after its supposed author, Zhuangzi or Zhuang Zhou (ca. 370–290 BCE). Scholarly consensus has the historical Zhuangzi writing the first seven chapters of the text, known as the "inner chapters." Later disciples or like-minded scholars wrote additional chapters embellishing the themes of the original chapters.

DAOIST METAPHYSICS: HOLISM AND TRANSFORMATION

What unites these texts and makes possible the label of a Daoist school of thought is a shared worldview and corresponding sensibility. At its simplest, this worldview emphasizes holism and unity (*yi* 一), also translated as "oneness," "one," or "singular"). As a metaphysical account of what the world most fundamentally is, holism is the view that objects or entities cannot be individuated—separated from the background that gives rise to them—even if they might be nominally differentiated. The characteristics of any object, including persons, remain ineluctably linked with the network of background conditions that give rise to and are implicated in them.[1] The *dao* 道, from which Daoism takes its name, consists of an ineffable mass of interacting forces and particles that form a single, great unity and give rise to the phenomena and events of the world.

In contrast to a world of discrete objects, the early Daoist texts see the world as made up of constantly shifting forces that interact and congeal to give rise to objects (including people) and then dissipate at some future point. These imperceptible and unarticulated forces that influence life and human affairs is one meaning of *dao*. This world is always in flux, even if some objects persist for a relatively long time while a stable and balanced configuration of forces arise. The importance of change to the Daoist worldview is clear in the number of words for change found in the classical texts, and in the fine-grain distinctions in different aspects of change that each term denotes. Transience and transformation are primary. Within this stream of ongoing transformations, attempts to individuate objects within such a fluid web are provisional, yielding at best contingent and temporary results. Given this, the essence or defining characteristics of an object or event are not sought, and no attempt is made to locate them within broader categories and identify the laws governing their behavior.

However, the world is not so full of change and transformation that it is chaotic and unknowable. There can be regularity or consistency (*chang* or *tong*) within this broader framework of transformations. For example, while still being part of process and transformation, day and night reliably follow each other, as do the cyclical seasons, and human forms persist for some time. There is, however, much change within these broader contexts of continuity.

One simple image that captures this worldview is mentioned several times in the *Zhuangzi*: mushrooms.[2] Consider a grassy field initially devoid of mushrooms. Given the presence of certain elements and forces—such as nutrients in the soil and the relevant temperature and humidity as conditions shift imperceptibly during the night—dawn breaks to reveal a collection of freshly-sprouted mushrooms. They emerge only because conditions in the environment came together in a timely way. But within a few hours or days the mushrooms wither and disappear, reabsorbed into the environment that gave rise to them.

The *Zhuangzi* tells us that a human life is somewhat like the mushroom. Unseen and unknown "cosmic" forces of various kinds cohere and give rise to a human form, which persists for a while (the duration of that particular life) and then dissolves as those forces move apart: "The human form is merely a circumstance that has been met with, just something stumbled into, but those who have become human take delight in it nonetheless. Now the human form in its time undergoes ten thousand transformations, never stopping for an instant" (*Zhuangzi*, 43; 6.26).

This, the *Zhuangzi* tells us, is why excessive human grief at the death of a loved one is often misplaced.[3] It is to misunderstand the source and nature of human life and to demand a human form from constitutive forces that bring no intrinsic guarantee or disposition toward such form. This account also makes clear that the Daoist worldview does not place explanatory weight on a powerful creator being who oversees worldly events.[4] Even more removed is the idea of a creator with a special interest in the welfare of humanity. Humans are, the *Daodejing* tells us, like straw dogs used in a ritual sacrifice (ch. 5), used when needed and then discarded, tossed on the fire or trampled underfoot when their allotted role has been fulfilled. The world (*tiandi*) is indifferent to human concerns. In contrast to the spirit of scientific inquiry, what lies behind the ceaseless transformations of the natural world and human life is left open. What matters is whether one can come to terms with the events that transpire within them.

Within this worldview, the human predicament is the challenge to find a *way* or a *course* through these changes and transformations, so as to fulfill our natural span and avoid an early demise (*quanming* 全命). This is a second meaning of *dao* and includes the social goal of finding a way to preserve the larger social order.[5] This requires accommodating or yielding to the forces implicit in each situation while also making the most of them, nudging them in our favor or taking advantage of opportunity as it arises.

DAOIST METAPHYSICS: QI (VAPOR, ENERGY, PSYCHO-PHYSICAL FORCE)

The Daoist view of the world as endless process and transformation derives from a metaphysics founded on *qi* 氣. The character *qi* is sometimes glossed as the character for vapor above the character for rice, suggesting the image of steam billowing above boiling rice. Other accounts explain it as mist forming in clouds. Qi is typically understood as a kind of psychophysical force or energy, which straddles the divide between matter and energy, including different forms of energy. The forces or manifestations of qi are further divided into *yin* and *yang* qi (or phases of qi), suggesting mutually opposing bilateral forces that interact dialectically and give rise to change. For example, anything hot contains within it a movement toward cold since it loses heat to cooler surroundings; similarly, the depth of night is the point at which there is a turn toward daylight.

Qi refers to the environment and to atmospheric forces, such as wind and rain,[6] and to the various fluid systems that, according to the Daoist, constitute the human body. These include the "flow" of the nervous system, the circulatory system or blood, the breath, and reproductive fluids. The concept of qi also describes both physical and mental aspects of the person. As the *Daodejing* notes, "In carrying about your more spiritual and physical aspects and embracing their oneness, are you able to keep them from separating?" (ch. 10). Healthy qi refers to both a strong pulse (physical) and feelings of vigor and motivation (mental). Recognizing the role of fluid qi systems in bodily health yields an initial comment on the meaning of disability. On this view, disability is the impediment of the flow of qi, where blockage leads to detrimental effects on the body. Traditional Chinese medicines, such as acupuncture, aim to remove these blockages and restore a healthy circulation of forces.

Within the body, qi energy is to be conserved.[7] To overexert and thereby use up qi is dangerous (*Daodejing*, chs. 52, 55). Put simply, people can wear themselves out by living in ignorance of the way forces unfold around them and wasting energy by acting against these forces. In the *Daodejing*, one ideal manifestation or configuration of qi in human life is that found in an infant (*Daodejing*, 10). The ideal qi here is described as pliant or soft (*rou*). The image of the baby tells us much about how the Daoist thinks people should approach the world. It suggests flexibility of the body and a mind not filled with knowledge, potency, or power (screaming all day without becoming hoarse) and fear (*Daodejing*, ch. 55). Further, the baby lacks the apparatus or inclination to impose and be guided by conceptual or linguistic distinctions of the world. The absence of familiarity with conventions and the freedom from habitual mental associations and ways of seeing the world are valuable because they allow greater responsiveness to transformations in qi forces and the surrounding environment.

Qi also provides a reliable basis for action. The world is constituted by shifting qi vapors and forces, which coalesce to form discernible objects before dissolving and reforming. Subsequently, the capacity of human language to track such change is limited. Discrete objects can be identified and labeled, but out of expediency rather than as a reflection of a basic reality. Words and names applied to an ever-changing world of transformation could be misunderstood as picking out enduring objects or natural kinds, leading to error. Given suitable preparation, it is better for people to "listen with their qi" and act accordingly.

Given this worldview and qi metaphysics, what kind of ideal behavior is implied? Human conduct for the Daoist should be informed by both forgetting and knowing. The Daoist texts call for a forgetting of the social doctrines, especially those of the classical Confucians (*Daodejing*, ch. 38; *Zhuangzi*, ch. 4). Conventional social rules, rituals, and methods of social control are insufficiently sensitive to the nuances and subtle changes in the forces shaping most situations. Similarly, too much reliance on logic and argumentative debate leads to overly abstract distinctions that lack relevance in everyday interactions.[8] The world is too complex to model.

Ideal Daoist conduct might also be described as a know-how or confidence that, by removing doctrines and allowing cultivated, internal qi forces and intuitive skills to express themselves, results in actions appropriate to context. "You will come to hear with the vital energies (*qi*) rather than with the mind" (*Zhuangzi*, ch. 4.9). The Daoist ideas of spontaneity (*ziran*) and effortless action (*wuwei*) express this idea,[9] as do the many skill or "knack" stories in the *Zhuangzi*.[10] The important form of knowledge is thus a knowing how to act or what to do, even if the reasons for and origins of the action remain unknown.

DAOISM AND DISABILITY

Having sketched the worldview and the way of being human presented in the two Daoist classics, how this outlook contributes to the understanding of disability can begin. The texts contain several ideas that are relevant. First, the emphasis on holism, a unity of all constitutive elements that make up the world and where each has a place, means that the distinction between able and disabled is greatly muted. Several *Daodejing* passages exhort the reader to treat the inept (*bushan*) or weak (*ruo*) as being on a par with the able or strong (chs. 27, 62).

Similarly, wariness about conceptual categories that divide the world and invite dispute (*Daodejing,* ch. 2) compels restraint in dividing people into the "able" (*shan*) and its correlate the "un-able" (*bushan*). Singling out the worthy and promoting them to public office, for example, invites people to label those not deemed worthy as inept. The Daoists seem to believe that thinking in dichotomous categories has such intuitive appeal that, once an initial distinction is made, people cannot resist identifying its opposite and thinking in terms of mutually opposed and divisive categories.[11]

Relying on such categories also creates problems for the worthy. Mimicking the *Zhuangzi*'s playful style, an excess of ability can be seen as "disabling," since those of outstanding merit who become public figures also become targets of envy, abuse, or violence and are less likely to live out their natural term. It is much better, suggest the Daoists, to recognize the dependency of the esteemed on what gives rise to them but is not so valued—that is, the indeterminate background conditions (*wu*) (*Daodejing*, chs. 11, 40, 64). Better still is to avoid all social discourse that relies on mutually opposed terms and whose fit with a fluid reality is tenuous.

Rejecting elaborate structures of knowledge and dichotomous categories, the Daoist sage dwells at the hinge point: "Where neither 'this' nor 'that' has an opposite is called the hinge of the course (*dao*)" (Ames and Hall, *Dao*, 119). Finding the hinge point means remaining in the eye of the whirlwind or the stable center of the potter's wheel (Ziporyn 14) while still aware of the transformations going on around and able to respond without distortion or doctrine. The Daoist way or path through life is one that is constantly unfolding and lacks clear articulation or definition; but this, as Schumm and Stoltzfus point out, also describes the disabled person's experience in an environment constructed according to the categories of "normal" human beings and the able bodied (143).

Several of these themes might be developed further, but two Daoist ideas in particular hint at novel ways of approaching disability. These are Daoist thinking about the body, and the Daoist defense of the usefulness of the useless. There is a conception of the body in the texts that identifies a more expansive and collective entity than the single physical body. Understanding this higher level collectivity or identity has consequences for how disability is understood, especially when it is premised on the idea of a normal human body. The usefulness of the useless suggests that people who appear to lack capacity or function are not only useful but can even exert an influence on those around. This idea suggests that disability itself can be a form of usefulness and relieves the need for the disabled to meet standards for usefulness imposed by the non-disabled.

The Body in Daoism

Daoist texts, especially the *Zhuangzi*, react against what they perceive as an exaggerated belief in the separateness of the individual body from the circumstances in which it is embedded. According to this view, the body is a self-contained unit with its own particular form or structure. This mistaken belief leads to normative connotations being attached to the normal and intact human body, and this in turn generates an opposite and inferior category—the incomplete or disabled body. The Daoists reject the ideal of a normal body and the normative judgments derived from it. Discussions and presentations of the body are only one aspect of disability, but are important nonetheless. People can and do react to others on the basis of how their bodies differ from what is perceived to be the standard type.

This rejection of the normal human body takes several forms. Perhaps the simplest is the rejection of the attachment of social prestige to a wholly intact physical body. The Confucians in particular valued the maintenance and preservation of the body bequeathed by parents, exemplified by being a good son.[12] But failure to keep the physical body intact was not merely an insult to family or ancestors; it was often a sign of criminality. Amputation was a common punishment in the classical period. An incomplete body was thus not only a physical disablement; it was also a shameful failure to uphold the honor of parents and an explicit sign of transgression of communal norms and reduced social status.[13]

The *Zhuangzi* rejects the prevailing social attitudes toward the body. In a critical riposte to conservative elements of Confucian thought, several stories feature amputees and cripples who are also popular and influential sages and teachers. The story of Wang Tai begins chapter 5:

> In the state of Lu [Confucius' home state], there was a man called Wang Tai, whose foot had been chopped off as a punishment. Yet somehow he has as many followers as Confucius himself. *Chang* Ji questioned Confucius about it. "Wang Tai is a one-footed ex-con, and yet his followers divide the state of Lu with you, Master. When he stands he offers no instructions, and

when sitting he gives no opinions. And yet they go to him empty and return filled. . . . What kind of man is he?" Confucius said, "That man, my master, is a sage. Only procrastination has kept me from going to follow him myself. If he is master even to me, how much more should he be so to you. I shall bring not only the state of Lu but all the world to follow him!" (32)

Wang Tai is a "one-footed ex-con," yet his influence is equal to or greater than Confucius' influence. The author has us believe that Confucius himself becomes a follower. Wang Tai's body is incomplete but his clarity (*ming*) of mind (*xin*) about the world (its processual and transforming way) constitutes a form of influence or power. Others are drawn to him. In the Daoist sage, the physical body is rendered tangential to social influence and prestige.[14]

But the Daoist rejection of the normal body is not limited to the rejection of conventional social judgments of its importance. It prizes a particular kind of attitude or personal response toward a body that deviates from physical norms. Daoist stories of sickness and deformity reveal sufferers whose attitude is not one of suffering and who do not call for a pitying response. Rather, their attitude blends curiosity, awe, and acceptance. One *Zhuangzi* story features four friends—Ziji, Ziyu, Zili, and Zilai—one of whom, Ziyu, falls ill.[15] When Ziji goes to visit him, Ziyu's attitude is striking:

> Ziyu said, "How great is the Creator of Things, making me all tangled up like this!" For his chin was tucked into his navel, his shoulders towered over the crown of his head . . . his five internal organs at the top of him, his thigh bones taking the place of his ribs, and his yin and yang energies in chaos. But his mind was relaxed and unbothered. He hobbled over to the well to get a look at his reflection. "Wow!" he said. "The Creator of things has really gone and tangled me up!"
> Ziji said, "Do you dislike it?"
> Ziyu said, "Not at all. What is there to dislike?" (44; 6.39)

Ziyu is unconcerned with the loss of his normal or healthy form. His case is distinguished by a sense of awe and fascination at the transformations his body is undergoing, and even curiosity at what will come next. Ziyu's next words highlight this wonder:

> Perhaps he [the creator of things] will transform my left arm into a rooster, thereby I'll be announcing the dawn. Perhaps he'll transform my right arm into a crossbow pellet, thereby I'll be seeking out an owl to roast. Perhaps he will transform my ass into wheels and my spirit into a horse; thereby I'll be riding along—will I need any other vehicle? (45; 6.39)

His attitude to the changes is movingly pragmatic. He is determined to understand these bodily changes in a way that renders them as enabling, as bringing new opportunities rather than regret at the loss of familiar human form and its usual function.[16] Through invention and resilience, disability should be integrated into everyday life. Of equal importance, however, is the story's didactic force and implicit normative demand; this attitude of pragmatic coping toward disability should be the norm, adopted by the able-bodied as well as the disabled.

The story of Ziyu also offers a deeper comment on the place of the physical body in Daoism. This is the rejection of the ideal of the human body as a natural kind; ideally all human bodies are to be understood by reference to a natural template and knowledge of this generic human form informs understanding of any human. The ideal of an intact and normal human body does not feature in the thoughts and actions of Ziyu. He has no attachment to any conception of what his body should be like and therefore no anxiety or revulsion as his body transforms into novel configurations. More important to an accurate understanding of the body are the transformative forces that shape it and its integration into a larger whole.

Why is this significant for disability studies? Arguably, the basic categories through which the world is parsed provide the basis, and thus influence, for value judgments. They are central to questions of whether something is an X (e.g., a human), including the positive or negative associations attached to that identification (e.g., respect directed at a human), and whether something is a good example of an X (e.g., a good human being). Part of the discriminatory force associated with disability is the underlying belief that a human body, in some ideal sense, has a certain structure or composition, which is responsible for familiar human capacities and characteristics. Although subtle, such implicit assumptions can lead to a mild degree of shock when encountering a body lacking these familiar specifications. This is sometimes described as a kind of revulsion due to the incongruence between the normal body ingrained in thought and the presented incomplete body, which resists ready categorization.[17] Such an abnormal body is thus deprived of the faint feelings of approbation and the useful conceptual associations that recognition of the familiar engenders. However, as the *Zhuangzi* story suggests, when there is no attachment to a natural kind, there cannot be a failure to identify an object in terms of its natural kind, nor a negative and discriminatory reaction when such failure arises.

The question then arises: why doesn't the *Zhuangzi* place value on the ideal of a normal physical body? The answer is because it recognizes another conception of body more important than the intact human physical form.

Recognizing this alternative body is integral to understanding the basic processes constituting the world and human experience. To understand this alternative conception of body, we should first understand the diversity of ways in which the human body is conceptualized in the early Chinese texts. These extend far beyond the ideal of the human body as a generic physical form.

As Deborah Sommer points out, there are several different terms for body in the classical texts, each associated with a distinct cluster of ideas. While the conceptual distinctions between them are not always clear, the terms give rise to a range of informative heuristics for thinking about the body. The classical texts also contain a term for the body as a structure (*xing* 形). *Xing* can refer both to the structure of the body ("skeleton" 形骸) and to its superficial appearance or surface form ("a person's appearance" 外形), but it is *wuxing* 無形 (literally "no body" or formlessness) that appears more often in the Daoist texts. There, *xing* is often a temporary form, assumed against the background of formlessness or inchoateness. The elemental forces flow into or congeal as a body but disperse in time. The human form is temporary and contingent, and its value should not be overstated. Returning to Ziyu, he offers a poignant analogy to illustrate this view:

> Now suppose a great master smith were casting metal. If the metal jumped up and said, "I insist on being nothing but an Excalibur!" the smith would surely consider it to be an inauspicious chunk of metal. Now, if I, having happened to *stumble into human form*, should insist, "Only a human! Only a human!" Creation-Transformation would certainly consider me an inauspicious chunk of person. So now I look upon all heaven and earth as a great furnace, and Creation-Transformation as a great blacksmith—where could I go that would not be right? (46; emphasis added)

The prioritization of *wuxing* over *xing* can be understood as a commitment to uncover the metaphysical assumptions that create the very idea of bodily disability.

Another term for the body is *shen* 身. While this has several meanings, shen often refers to the social status of the body—a person's standing in the eyes of others. For the Confucians in particular, shen is the public manifestation of the degree of self-cultivation and can, as it were, be read off the "surface" of the body by others. Amputation diminishes the *shen* body's social standing whereas graceful movement and comportment enhance it, conveying cultivation and refinement.[18] The shen body thus marks the point at which the inner world of self-cultivation meets the public realm of family and state, and its status is a comment on the successfulness of this integration into social life. Here, the physical form of the body is less important than how well the cultivated body integrates.

This conception of the body also suggests a novel conception of disability. For the shen body, disability is the uncultivated body, which proceeds vulgarly or clumsily through public space and social interactions. In fact, there is another dedicated word for such a body: *qu* 軀. The disabled qu body lacks refinement and learning. Those who are typically regarded as able bodied can still be disabled in body since they lurch from social interaction to social interaction without shame, acting inappropriately, inciting resentment, and so forth. Failing to integrate socially, they are a disruptive influence.

The Daoists deny the importance of the body as it is defined through social practices and accrued status. But shen has a meaning relevant to the Daoist account—the identification of the body by reference to an extended framework, which extends beyond the boundaries of the individual body. In Confucian thought, that from which the body derives its identity is an extended web of social roles and relationships, as illustrated by the Confucian five cardinal relationships: father-son, husband-wife, ruler-minister, elder brother-younger brother, and friend-friend. For the Daoists, the larger corpus into which the individual person is integrated is the *ti* 體 body.

What is the ti body? Sommer describes it as "a corpus of indefinite boundaries, which might encompass multiple persons" (324). As this vague definition suggests, the ti body is not a clearly defined or bounded entity like the biological human body. It is broader and more capacious, extending spatially or temporally beyond the individual body. It indicates a fuzzy composite, the unity formed by the person's physical body and a larger whole.

The ti body is recognized in several schools, and the Daoist account of the ti body follows the Daoist worldview, and qi metaphysics in particular. This body is conceptualized as the unity formed between the individual biological body and the surrounding environment. The body is constantly transforming, but these transformations are in harmony and integrated with the larger entity. This is vividly illustrated in the story of one-armed ex-con Wang Tai. When asked to explain Wang Tai's influence, Confucius compares Wang Tai to:

> A man who takes heaven and earth as his own bodily organs, and the ten thousand things [all phenomena and events] as his own guts, a man who is merely lodging for the moment in his particular limbs and trunk and head, a man who regards even his own eyes and ears as mere semblances. He takes all that his consciousness knows and unifies it into a singularity, so his mind always gets through unslaughtered. (34)

The claim that the sage forms one body with an extended field of beings or forces is repeated several times in the *Zhuangzi*.[19] The figures are sages because they understand the unity of their physical bodies with the broader forces and energies that give rise to them. We are told that "he could see the singularity" (6.37), "I am the same as the transforming openness" (6.54), and "the sage gets through to the intertwining of things, so that everything forms a single body around him" (108). The *Daodejing* also takes awareness of unity as crucial to conduct: "The sage grasps the oneness" (ch. 22); "*Dao* is the flowing together of all things" (ch. 62).[20]

Anthropologist Brian Knaft's study of the body in Melanesian culture, though lacking any direct connection with Daoist thought, is helpful in developing a fuller account of the ti body. In agrarian Melanesian culture, the collectively constituted body begins at birth and is expressed through the medium of food or the food chain. The unborn baby is nourished by food provided by family members, and the growing child is formed by this food. The food is the product of their physical labor, and their labor is also exchanged for food with other members of the community. This generates a series of connections which are symbolic yet can be traced through various related processes. The energy of physical labor, including economic transactions with others in the community, and the nutrients in the ground transform into foodstuffs; in turn, the food transforms into the body of the growing child. In this way there is a sense of body that unites a group of people through tangible connections. As Knaft notes, "Those whose food you consume are those whose labor, land and essence constitute your own being. Most Melanesians concretely appreciate the physical energy used in subsistence cultivation, and the way this is converted into bodily substance to maintain health and well-being" (qtd. in Sommer 318). Here we see a heightened consciousness of the powerful link between labor, food, and life, and of a corpus or body that emerges from this way of seeing the world.

An analogous case exists in the Daoist worldview, albeit one that extends beyond the food cycle and recognizes a wider range of constitutive forces. This shifting between mediums or modalities while maintaining identity and continuity aptly expresses the qi metaphysics and cosmology described earlier. The ti body can be identified with qi. Here qi refers to forces or energy that are not restricted to a single medium but can pass between superficially different substances or modalities—from the kinetic energy of labor to the chemical energy of foodstuffs, and even to the feeling of vigor or motivation experienced by a person. Qi is not confined within a single physical body but circulates among, and in some sense demarcates, a ti body.

To explain the ti body in this way is not to offer a clear and concise definition of it.[21] This vagueness, however, is consistent with the Daoist wariness about attempts to impose a rigid conceptual structure on reality.[22] Even without conceptual clarity, the recognition of a larger collective body has normative, action-guiding significance in the Daoist texts. In the *Zhuangzi* in particular, the sense of body most relevant to action is not the individual physical unit or body. Those who truly understand the forces at play in the world are guided by awareness of this larger corporate entity. Returning to the Wang Tai passage, Confucius describes the benefits of recognizing the ti body.

> Looked at from the point of view of their differences, even your own liver and gallbladder are as distant as Chu in the south and Yue in the north. But looked at from the point of view of sameness, *all things are one*. If you take the latter view, you become free of all preconceptions about which particular objects might suit the eyes and ears. . . . Seeing what is one and the same to all things, nothing is ever felt to be lost. (33; emphasis added)

People habitually think of themselves as individual entities with determinate form, but this is a mistake. Grasping the processual and transformational nature of reality means recognizing the unity of one's body with a larger whole, the relative unimportance of a normal body within that whole, and the porosity of the boundaries of the human form.

If one identifies with the larger unity, then nothing can be lost;[23] lacking a limb or any other diminution of the individual body is not regarded as a deficiency. Since the Daoist does not regard the individual physical body as normative, the basis for ascriptions of disability predicated on the normal body is lost. Viewing the world as a unity or a whole invites an attitude of seeing things in terms of sameness and dispels such exclusionary judgments of difference.[24] The Daoist view of the body presented here might be summarized as the belief that diverse forms of human embodiment can be integrated into a mutually complementary whole. This is one of the ideals of modern disability studies (Tremain, "Impairment," 1–24).

The *Zhuangzi* gives us one final image to express this guiding ideal: the tally. Chapter 5 of the *Zhuangzi* is entitled "De cheng fu" 德成符, translated as "Markers of Full Virtuosity" by Ziporyn or "The Signs of Fullness of Power" by A. C. Graham. *Fu* 符, here translated as "marker" or "sign," originally meant "tally." In ancient China, a tally was an official seal or disc that was broken into matching but irregular halves and carried by the envoy to guarantee his authenticity or that of an official command. Each half of the tally formed an irregular shape not easily categorized or replicated. Yet it also formed a perfect whole when matched with its complementary half.

In the *Zhuangzi* chapter, the broken tally symbolizes the irregular or "broken" bodies of cripples or amputees. But the tally image suggests that although these bodies do not fit into the conventional mold of the normal body, they nevertheless integrate into and form a unity, one body, with some larger whole—in this case, the surrounding environment.

A discriminatory sense of disability comes from taking only a partial view of things. Focusing on a broken piece of jade (a jagged half of the tally) and failing to appreciate the whole renders it useless. Further, its irregularity also suggests its uselessness, especially to those ignorant of tallies.[25] The beauty of the tally metaphor is that not only does the half tally find its counterpart, but it is precisely this irregularity that is the source of its usefulness and bestows upon it a form of power. This is the power possessed by the cripple Wang Tai and other figures. They fit themselves into the world and somehow make it fit around them. This usefulness of the superficially useless is the second contribution of Daoism to disability debates.

The Use of the Useless

A reoccurring theme of the *Zhuangzi* is the usefulness of the useless (*wu yong zhi yong* 無用之用). A story featuring Zhuangzi's friend and opponent, the dialectician Huizi (or Hui Shi), illustrates the idea:

> Huizi said to Zhuangzi, "The King of Wei gave me the seed of a great gourd. I planted it and when it matured it weighed over a hundred pounds. I filled it with liquid, but it was not firm enough to lift. I cut it in half to make a dipper, but it was too large to scoop into anything. It was big and all, but because it was so useless, I finally just smashed it to pieces."
>
> Zhuangzi said, "You certainly are stupid when it comes to using big things. . . . How is it that you never thought of making it into an enormous vessel for yourself and floating [*you* 友] through the lakes and rivers in it? Instead, you worried that it was too big to scoop into anything, which I guess means our greatly esteemed master here still has a lot of tangled weeds clogging up his mind!" (1.14)

Gourds were often used as water containers or ladles, and Huizi acquires an unusually large one. Unable to think otherwise, he acts on that conventional view of gourds and finds his giant container useless. Zhuangzi points out how a little more imagination would have presented Huizi with a great opportunity: to roam freely (*you* 友) around the realm. Huizi simply needed to reconceptualize the relationship between the gourd and water, and he would discover that his conclusion of uselessness was premature.

There are several similar stories in the *Zhuangzi*, many featuring a tree initially condemned as useless but later revealed to be useful in some sense.[26] In these, a tree does not meet the standards applied to trees by society—useful for building materials, producing fruit, coffins, and so forth—and is deemed useless. But in its alterity, the tree finds a use and exerts an influence—that is, people are drawn to it because it provides shade. Since being perceived as less useful or, *in extremis*, useless is a concern in disability discourse, the *Zhuangzi* stories offer various responses to this unsympathetic perception. In the gourd story, this is a warning against thoughtlessly applying familiar categories, failing to see the potential of what is in front of us, and arriving at hasty judgments. The tree stories highlight how people habitually take their own interests as adequate standards to evaluate objects but without adequate understanding of the object. The carpenter judges the tree useless, but his limited and highly selective understanding of trees is no basis for a fair judgment of the tree.

Several other useful ideas can be derived from these stories. One is the practical advantage of being deemed useless. In the *Zhuangzi*, the classic statement of this is the greatly deformed Shu the Discombobulated. When the authorities called for troops, he simply presented himself along with the able bodied, flailed his arms, and was immediately exempted from the draft. Then when the time came to "take on any great labors" (public works), Shu's condition again exempted him. He was thus "able to live out his natural span." In the right context, incapacity becomes an advantage. Shu is disabled if warfare is valued as the norm, but not if a long life (31).

This advantage accrues in several ways. One is the liberation from social rules. In Shu's exemption from the draft, rules that would have brought an unwanted burden are not applied. There is also a sense in which disability can be skillfully used by the disabled to create advantage. Shu makes the most of what he has; his dramatic performance before the authorities spares him the draft, and when the authorities "handed out rations to the disabled," he got "three large measures of grain" (31). From a contemporary perspective, however, such use of disability is a double-edged sword. It appears to be a case of relying on a disability to secure charity or help, but this threatens to undermine the sense of empowerment that recent developments such as the Americans with Disabilities Act sought to provide.

But disability can create advantage without recourse to pity or charity. Shu, for example, by washing, sewing, and "pounding the divination sticks and exuding an aura of mystic power" could "make enough to feed ten men"

(31). Advantage can also result directly from the disability itself. In ancient China, for example, the blind were considered to have a particularly refined sense of hearing, and many famous music masters were blind.[27]

There is another distinctively Daoist sense in which disability can be a useful advantage. This is when it creates a particular kind of freedom from both the expectations of others and the self-given pressures of desire and ambition. The *Daodejing* and the *Zhuangzi* promote being oblivious to social standards and conventional norms, are unbothered by peer pressures, and are impervious to categories such as beautiful and rich and the negative correlates they generate. In the *Daodejing*, the uncarved block (*pu*) is a metaphor for Daoist living. Unrefined wood is regarded more highly than carved and sculpted wood. Lacking refined tastes or far-reaching ambitions, someone who is like an uncarved block is immune to the frustrations that accompany them. Lacking sophisticated tastes and thoughts, there is little about daily life that can disappoint. This constitutes a kind of freedom; at the very least it is a liberation from familiar and substantial worries about what others think of one, what one thinks about oneself, and how one measures up to others. This state of indifference can be the (beneficial) result of disability.

Sam Crane's account of life with his severely disabled son, Aidan, in his book *Aidan's Way* illustrates this. Aidan was born with severe physical and cognitive impairments and is liable to frequent brain seizures. He requires constant assistance and, in a sense, lives suspended in infancy. Yet the infant is one of the models of Daoist living—free from preconceptions and indoctrination.[28] Crane writes of his son:

> Is my life better than his? Is his somehow less than mine?
> . . . I am also caught up in the frenetic workaday world. Although I can point to an array of achievements—a PhD, a good job, publications—I often wonder if I really am getting anywhere. At times I feel enslaved to the demands of the economy and society. . . . And there lies Aidan, completely disconnected from such worries. There is so much he cannot do, but also so much he does not have to do. He does nothing but nothing is left undone. (Crane 189–90)[29]

The absence of pressures, both from outside and those placed upon oneself by ambition, shame, and doubt, is a feature of Aidan's life that might be regarded as "useful." However, to claim too much for impairment might appear to romanticize disability, suggesting that it is really not so bad while overlooking the realities of disability. While there may be excellent blind musicians, few people would prefer their children to be blind instead of sighted. In his account of coming to terms with Aidan's disabilities, Crane also acknowledges this worry (190).

Perhaps the best response is to avoid sweeping judgments of the comparative worth of different lives and instead develop two lines of response. The first is an account of the nuanced freedom that accompanies disability despite the apparent loss of freedom; the second concerns how disability can still exert a form of power or influence at the local level despite its superficial uselessness. Developing these responses by focusing on cases of cognitive impairment will complement earlier discussions of the body and demonstrate a further dimension of disability studies to which Daoism might contribute.

One kind of freedom, the loss of which is associated with disability, is that of organizing a life according to a personal conception of how it should be. A person forms a life plan or develops projects and then instrumentally reasons toward them, directing the objects of the external world accordingly.[30] Intellectual impairment means the loss of this freedom. This form of freedom in which autonomy and individual choice are crucial is highly valued in liberal consumer societies.

The Daoist worldview, however, presents a different picture; outcomes are subject to forces that the individual cannot control but can only react to and enjoy, accepting and also opportunistically making use of circumstance. Insisting that a life take a particular form is somewhat like the metal leaping up at the blacksmith and insisting, "Only an Excalibur!" But since this kind of freedom is not prized in Daoist thought, its loss cannot be a significant impairment. Instead, a second kind of freedom can result from the loss of this freedom to organize a life plan. To see this, consider the following self-narrated story of Jan, a woman with early dementia, taken from Stephen Post's study of Alzheimer's:

> Things began to happen that I just couldn't understand. There were times I addressed friends by the wrong name. Comprehending conversations seemed almost impossible. My attention span became quite short. . . .
>
> One day, while out for a walk on my usual path in a city in which I had resided for eleven years, nothing looked familiar. It was as if I was lost in a foreign land, yet I had the sense to ask for directions home. . . .
>
> She was a strong and independent woman. She always tried so hard to be a loving wife, a good mother, a caring friend, and a dedicated employee. She had self-confidence and enjoyed life. She had never imagined that by the age of 41 she would be forced into retirement. . . .
>
> Then one day as I fumbled around the kitchen to prepare a pot of coffee, something caught my eye through the window. It had snowed and I had truly forgotten what a beautiful sight a soft, gentle snowfall could be. . . . As

I bent down to gather a mass of those radiantly white flakes on my shovel, it seemed as though I could do nothing but marvel at their beauty. Needless to say [my son] did not share in my enthusiasm; to him [shoveling] was a job, but to me it was an experience. . . .

I am still here, I thought, and there will be wonders to be held in each new day; they are just different now.

Quality of life is different to me now from the way it was before. I am very loved, in the early stages, and now my husband and sons give back in love what I gave them. I am blessed because I am loved. . . . Now my quality of life is feeding the dogs, looking at flowers. My husband says I am more content now than ever before! (18–20)

This account shows the movement from one kind of freedom to another that accommodates the cognitive impairment. It is one that consists of the ability to enjoy the moving present and experience delight and wonder at the ordinary objects encountered there. This does not require locating those objects within practical projects or life goals. This freedom is similar to Ziyu's attitude to the transformations of his physical body. A worthwhile life is reconceived and now consists of a series of rolling encounters with everyday scenes and objects, each delightful on its own terms. Collectively these serial experiences amount to a worthwhile life, especially because they are shared with others who can also participate in them.

The second use of disability is to appreciate how a cognitive impairment can influence events and exert a certain power in unexpected ways. Let us return to Aidan. Aidan is blind, unable to speak, and wheelchair bound. But he is still able to exert power (*de* 德) over those who come into contact with him. The first lesson that Aidan administers is one in the psychology of desire. As his father notes, interacting with Aidan has taught him much about how he structures expectations and the kinds of desires he allows himself to be influenced by:

Aidan's life was all about us letting go of expectations and desires. We had to let go, continually, of whatever image of him we held in our minds. As the typical became the impossible, we had to redefine his normal, our normal. (Crane 136)

Aidan's father learns to let go of existing desires and instead allows his desires to track the situations, to respond to and be limited by the possibilities present therein. Such sentiments are exactly those of the *Daodejing*. In chapter 41 we are told that the greatest image has no shape (*wuxing*). In other words, that the most important representations by which we live are constantly shifting. The Daoist ideal of *wuyu* is a response to such fluidity. One of the variants on the more familiar Daoist ideal of *wuwei* (effortless action or doing without action), wuyu literally means "desireless action." But rather than the removal of desire, it actually recommends cultivating desires appropriate to context and the flow of events, which are less vulnerable to being thwarted. Contrast this stance on desires bound up with the realization of more complex projects and life goals, which are more liable to frustration and friction with circumstances.

The benefit of allowing desires to be reordered or restructured is the creation of delight in everyday interaction with Aidan. Enhanced attentiveness made possible by greater openness to outcomes and imagination enables his father to find meaning and delight in the subtlest of actions. One such example involved a baby jumper:

> It was an odd-looking contraption that hung in a doorway: a long slender spring attached to a little seat, allowing a toddler, one not quite ready to walk to happily bounce up and down and swing to and fro. . . . Aidan never progressed to standing and striding, but he was able to use his ability to hop and twist in the jumper. . . . When properly positioned, he would push down with his legs and throw himself about with great abandon. This was one of our developmental milestones and we cherished the times he cheerfully bobbed about in the living room portal. (Crane 113)

From one perspective, Aidan's actions represent failure. He cannot walk or even stand when in the device intended to help him learn to walk. But the perception of uselessness only arises when the situation and objects are understood conventionally, as with Huizi and his gourd. There is clearly another experience of this event, one invisible to those with only a partial perspective of the situation and an understanding conditioned by conventional expectation, and it is a success story. His father knows that Aidan's happy bobbing is an achievement for Aidan, but he can only see this as such because he has discarded expectations of Aidan and early infanthood that would otherwise have produced disappointment. Aidan's uselessness becomes a tiny ability.

A second way in which Aidan's incapacity constitutes a power is his ability to get those around him to do things without any obvious effort or striving on his part. Aidan provides an example of the wuwei ideal of conduct—effortless action or doing without action. As he grows older, Aidan begins attending school. He is integrated into a typical class with the aid of a personal assistant. One child in the class, Ricky, has a speech impediment and is told as part of his therapy that he must speak more to practice the relevant movements of the jaw and tongue. However, because of his impairment, Ricky is wary about speaking with other children, scared that they will make fun of his irregular pronunciation. Things are different with Aidan. He presents no such judgmental front, and Ricky is willing to speak freely with him without fear of rejection. As Crane notes:

> In Aidan, however, he had a friend, one who did not strain to understand his words or laugh when they came out garbled. Aidan did not judge or correct. He just sat silently, varying little in his countenance whatever Ricky might say. On more than one occasion when I was in the classroom, I noticed Ricky close to Aidan, happily chatting away, gaining the practice he needed to clarify his speech, sustained by the presence of an uncritical buddy. Aidan was yin to his yang, and able to help. (149–50)

It is the things that Aidan cannot do that enable another to achieve something useful and beneficial. Without Aidan's impairment the above interaction would presumably have been very different. When the impact of disability in highly particular and private contexts is recognized, then its use becomes apparent. This is also seen in how Aidan effortlessly influenced his father's career path, directing him into local politics. Aidan's father joined the local school board and became heavily involved in education policy; but, as Crane admits, it is unlikely he would ever have considered such a path without Aidan's narrative to guide him.

We might summarize the usefulness of Aidan in general terms. Through close contact those regarded as disabled can teach others about assumptions toward disability, facilitate the actions and development of others, and even exert influence on others' actions, though not necessarily in obvious ways. In contrast to brief and superficial encounters, prolonged interaction enables a richer picture of the person to emerge, along with the contribution of the "useless" to the world around them.

CONCLUSION

In one sense, it is unclear to what extent the Daoist texts can engage directly with contemporary disability studies. Daoist thinking on disability was unable to definitively shape attitudes to disability in the larger population exposed to that tradition. Miles suggests the Daoist appreciation of the useless was confined to the educated classes (96).

Daoist thought does not yield a developed alternative model of disability. In its reluctance to theorize it prompts critical reflection on the use of such models. At the same time, the texts offer imaginative ways of seeing the world that might inspire novel approaches to familiar themes in contemporary debates concerning the body, freedom, and agency. The two texts invite us to question any claims about the normal human body or the independence of that body from the surrounding environment. Similarly, appreciating the subtle ways that the impaired person can still influence events elevates the status of those regarded as deficient by conventional standards. In this way, Daoism contributes to a reimaging of what normal is and highlights assumptions behind its ascription.

There are limitations to approaching disability from a Daoist point of view. For example, Daoist insights might have only indirect relevance to the contemporary production of public policy. A feature of bureaucratically managed mass society is the use of general rules and policies that apply to large numbers of people, including the question of how to distribute limited resources among a diverse population. Disability advocates must contend with this framework, fighting to secure their own interests alongside other interest groups and factions. It is not clear what contribution Daoist thought can make in such a context, however. Daoist texts typically focus on particularity and change, suspicion of public office, and the rejection of social conventions.[31] Further, there are advantages to addressing disability through such contested public discourse, and viewing people in terms of generalities and conventions. A term such as disability can be useful in securing recognition for various subsets of a larger population, and as a step toward reform and more informed debate. A common theme in Daoism, however, is to avoid fractious public debates. These are seen as necessary only when communal life and implicit trust break down and people must consciously take up opinions and positions (*Daodejing*, chs. 18, 19, and 38).

Daoism can make a contribution. Public policy can be insufficiently sensitive to the experiences of people at a local level such as those with a disabled family member. It is perhaps in this realm, as resources applied in everyday personal experience, that the Daoist texts make their contribution. Through their images and metaphors the Daoist texts serve to create a site of resistance to, or critique of, public policy. In imaginatively presenting alternative realities, they help to make disability clearer when more abstract and general rules and conventions are failing to track the personal experiences of those who directly confront disability.

This personal viewpoint may be captured by one final metaphor from early China. Disability can be thought of as being like the patterning or striations in jade. Every community has its distinctive collection of human idiosyncrasies and particularities that collectively constitute a distinctively patterned whole. What is thought of as disabled is simply a further set of features or characteristics within this community, characteristics that are perhaps statistically more unusual, including the magnitude of the impairment, but not of a different kind or type. They merely provide some of the patterning that, as in jade, can increase the value of the whole. Daoist literature helps us see this.

5

Judaism and Disability

Julia Watts Belser

Disability offers an important and often overlooked lens for considering critical issues in Jewish thought and practice. From the biblical prophet Moses to the Babylonian rabbis Rav Sheshet and Rav Yosef, Jewish tradition remembers and honors a number of religious leaders and teachers with disabilities. Yet Jewish sacred texts also grapple with disability as a religious problem. Over the centuries, Jewish authorities have debated whether people with disabilities may participate in certain religious practices or fulfill legal and ritual obligations. Because Jewish law holds such a significant place in structuring Jewish religious practice, examining disability in Jewish tradition requires considering how biblical and rabbinic texts have conceptualized the place of people with disabilities in Jewish life as well as how these texts have been interpreted and implemented through the centuries. But while disability offers a vantage point for assessing how the religious tradition conceptualizes and responds to human difference, it also offers an opportunity to consider how people with disabilities contribute to the development of Jewish culture and religious life. In modern Jewish life, Deaf and disabled Jews have created cultural institutions, articulated theological insights, and developed alternate expressions of Jewish ritual and prayer that illuminate the dynamic potential of disability to reshape religious practice and contribute to the ongoing development of the tradition.

Judaism centers on reverence for a single, all-encompassing God and the observance of God's commandments as expressed in the Torah and interpreted through the ages. The Torah is God's revelation to the Jewish people, the sacred text that lies at the heart of Jewish religiosity. Torah means "teaching." While Torah can encompass a variety of traditional texts in the Jewish canon, it is also used to refer to the first five books of the Hebrew Bible: Genesis, Exodus, Leviticus, Numbers, and Deuteronomy. According to Jewish tradition, these texts were revealed by God to the prophet Moses on Mount Sinai. The Torah recounts the creation of the world and tells the sacred history of the biblical Israelites—the ancestors of the Jewish people. It lays out the central ethical obligations of the Jewish people and serves as the cornerstone of Jewish ritual practice.

The gift of the Torah is often described as God's greatest gift to the Jews, and study of the Torah lies at the heart of Jewish life. Though the text of the Torah is frequently reprinted in books, its most revered physical form is the Torah scroll. Written by hand on parchment by a specially trained scribe, a Torah scroll is a masterful work of art that holds a central place in Jewish worship. During most worship services in the synagogue, the Jewish house of prayer, a reader chants from the Torah scroll—a ritual practice designed to remind Jews of the continuing obligation to serve God, seek holiness, observe the commandments, and work for the betterment of the community and the wider world. Over the course of a Jewish year, traditional synagogues will chant aloud the entire text of the Torah. In other communities, a smaller portion of the traditional weekly portion is chanted and expounded. Regardless of practice, the established cycle of weekly readings serves as an important, unifying force in Jewish culture. In diverse communities around the world, Jews read and study the same texts week by week, year after year.

While Judaism is a tradition rooted in the Hebrew Bible, Jewish practice throughout history has evolved and developed significantly from its biblical origins. In addition to the "written Torah," or Hebrew Bible, Judaism is based upon postbiblical texts known as the "oral Torah." In traditional Jewish thought, the oral Torah was given at Sinai together with the written Torah and contains essential interpretive insights for understanding the biblical text (Fraade 31). From a historical perspective, these texts can be dated to the rabbinic period, an era in Jewish history that began after the destruction of the Jerusalem Temple in 70 CE. This period is marked by the rise of the rabbis, a group of Jewish scholars and teachers who developed a flexible system of Jewish law that aimed to sanctify and hallow every aspect of Jewish life (Strassfeld 139–75; S. Cohen 205–23). During this period, many hallmarks of biblical Israelite religion such as the practice of animal sacrifice and the ritual significance of the priesthood ceased to be a significant part of Jewish practice. The rabbis also developed many practices and traditions that are not discussed in the Hebrew Bible or that evolved significantly from their biblical origins (Satlow 69).

Rabbinic sacred texts have become the cornerstone of the traditional Jewish bookshelf. The Mishnah, one of the earliest texts of rabbinic Jewish law and practice, was canonized in 200 CE. Even more influential is the Babylonian Talmud, a massive work of Jewish law and lore completed several centuries later. The Babylonian Talmud is structured as a commentary on the Mishnah and records wide-ranging debates between different rabbis about Jewish law and practice. Rather than simply recording the settled law, the Babylonian Talmud emphasizes the process of inquiry and argumentation, initiating its students into a complex world of study and intellectual development. While the Talmud does aim to articulate Jewish legal norms and clarify points of practice, it also emphasizes the importance of honoring multiplicity in the law, concluding at many points that seemingly contradictory rabbinic opinions about Jewish practice are both "the words of the living God" (bEruvin 13b).

The rabbinic emphasis on study and interpretation remains a central characteristic of Jewish life to this day. The rabbis practiced a mode of biblical interpretation they called *midrash*, a way of reading and interpreting that expands and explores the biblical text. This practice fills in gaps in the biblical text and embellishes the histories and life experiences of biblical characters. It is also used to draw out correspondences across the biblical text and reconcile apparent contradictions between individual biblical verses (Holtz 177–80). Midrash became an important tool for expressing Jewish theology and recounting Jewish stories. Though rabbinic authorities differentiated between the binding nature of the law and the expressive, imaginative character of the midrash, both law and lore remain a central part of Jewish tradition. In the contemporary period, the practice of midrash has been reclaimed by feminist Jews who use it to express more expansive readings of biblical women, reassert women's experience within the tradition, and articulate a new vision of feminist Judaism (Plaskow 53–56; see also Myers, "Midrashic Enterprise"). Lesbian, gay, bisexual, and transgender Jews also make use of contemporary midrash to express queer Jewish culture in conversation with the tradition (Ramer xviii–xix). Judaism is a living, dynamic religious system that has developed over the centuries and continues to change today.

Religious practice is a central category in Jewish life, and it is generally regarded as more important for constituting Jewish identity than are formal assertions of belief or faith. Judaism teaches that God formed a covenant with the Jewish people. When the people accepted the covenant, they accepted the obligation to keep God's commandments (*mitzvot*) and live according to God's law. While most of the mitzvot are associated with a verse in the Hebrew Bible, later Jewish thinkers expanded the legal thinking surrounding these commandments and developed an expansive tradition of Jewish law known as *halakha*. Medieval Jewish thinkers canonized 613 mitzvot, which together comprise the key obligations and prohibitions of Jewish law. Many of the mitzvot are ethical in orientation and regulate conduct between people, such as the prohibitions on gossip or hurtful speech, the laws of appropriate conduct in business, or the obligation to give generously to those in poverty. Jewish tradition strongly emphasizes social justice and communal responsibility, articulating an obligation to work for *tikkun olam*, "the repair of the world" (Jacobs 24–25). Other mitzvot are ritual in orientation and structure the obligations that a Jew has to God—such as prayer, the observance of Shabbat (the Jewish sabbath) and other Jewish holidays, and keeping kosher according to the Jewish dietary laws. The system of mitzvot aims to sanctify everyday life, turning every moment and every action into an opportunity to serve God and pursue holiness.

While virtually all Jewish communities today recognize the significance of the mitzvot in some way, contemporary Jews differ significantly in how they relate to Jewish law. Surveying the four major Jewish movements, a central difference between them lies in their approach to Jewish law and their degree of observance of the mitzvot. Orthodox thinkers tend to emphasize a strict view of Jewish law and a more punctilious observance of the mitzvot. The Conservative movement also emphasizes the importance of law, but its leaders are more willing to adapt the law and introduce changes that will bring the law into closer harmony with contemporary non-Jewish culture. The Reform movement tends to focus almost entirely on the ethical mitzvot and the larger prophetic voice of Jewish tradition, while de-emphasizing the significance of the ritual mitzvot and Jewish law. The Reconstructionist movement highlights the evolving nature of Jewish tradition. While it aims to take into account the teachings of Jewish tradition and its legal thought, the classic stance of Reconstructionist Judaism holds that tradition "has a vote, not a veto" (Kaplan 263). Though the stances of the different Jewish movements can be a helpful way to conceptualize different approaches to Jewish practice and chart variation in the Jewish community today, individual Jews need not identify with any particular movement. Even when people identify with one of the Jewish groups named above, individual practice may diverge significantly from the official stance of the movement (Sarna 368–70).

Judaism is both a religious tradition and a cultural system. While Jewish identity often has religious dimensions, Jewishness is commonly expressed and mediated through cultural affiliation with Jewish community and Jewish family. In contemporary American contexts, it is not uncommon for Jews to identify religiously as atheists or as practitioners of other religious traditions, such as Buddhism, while still maintaining a strong Jewish identity. In the modern period, secular Judaism is an important cultural reality (Biale, *Heavens*). A large percentage of Jews both in America and in Israel identify as secular Jews. While secular Jews are generally uninterested in synagogue life or in the religious practice of Judaism, they often remain deeply invested in Jewish culture. Many continue to observe certain Jewish holidays, to practice "culinary Jewishness" through cooking or eating distinctively Jewish foods, and to share in Jewish humor, literature, art, and pop culture.

Jewishness also serves as a marker of ethnic identity. Over the centuries of Jewish history, Jews have lived within and adapted to diverse cultures around the world. Jewish social life is often characterized by a complex blend of integration and distinctiveness (Biale, *Cultures*, xx–xxii). While Jews often adopt and adapt aspects of local culture into Jewish practice, Jews have also resisted assimilation into the dominant culture and have consistently been marked as other within their host cultures. Consequently, Jews often have a strong sense of ethnic connection to other Jews, even those living in distant lands and regions. Jewish ethnic identities are traditionally divided into three main groups that reflect significant cultural differences within the Jewish community: the Ashkenazim of eastern European descent, Sephardim of Spanish heritage, and Mizrahim of Middle Eastern descent. In the modern period, racial and ethnic diversity within the Jewish community has continued to grow. There are significant communities of Jews of African descent in Israel as well as increasing numbers of African American, Latin American, Asian American, and multiracial Jews within the United States. Increased attention to racial and cultural difference within Jewish communities may also set the stage for a renewed appreciation of disability as a manifestation of Jewish diversity, as an expression of valued human difference.

CONCEPTUALIZING DISABILITY: THINKING DISABILITY STUDIES THROUGH THE JEWISH TRADITION

One of the signal contributions of disability studies has been to challenge the idea of the "naturalness" of disability as a stable and easily recognizable category. While popular notions commonly assume that disability is rooted in the "obvious" deficiency of certain human bodies, disability studies insists on a social and political understanding of disability. Many theorists have emphasized a distinction between the biological dimension of impairment and the sociocultural component of disability, the process by which a particular culture turns certain bodily or mental differences into stigmatized disabilities (Shakespeare, "Social Model"). By advancing a social and cultural conception of disability, scholars emphasize that disability is produced through social processes: the tendency of observers to stare at and single out particular bodies that deviate from society's expectations, architectural and design choices that privilege certain kinds of moving and being in the world, and conceptions of rationality and behavior that expect all people to fit within narrow expressions of cognition and emotion (Davis; Garland-Thomson, *Staring*). Disability studies has also politicized the idea of the "normal" body, which exists only in relation to bodies marked as disabled. Rosemarie Garland-Thomson has coined the term "normate" to designate "the figure outlined by the array of deviant others whose marked bodies shore up the normate's boundaries" (Garland-Thomson, *Extraordinary*, 8).

This social and political approach to disability has important implications for how we conceptualize disability in Jewish tradition. Disability studies theorists emphasize that notions of disability vary profoundly in different cultures and in different historical periods. To offer an example, consider that there is no single term in the Hebrew Bible that aligns precisely with the modern English term "disability." Perhaps the closest equivalent is the Hebrew word *mum*, usually translated as "blemish." The term *mum* appears in a variety of biblical passages, including an extensive list of blemishes that disqualify a priest from offering a sacrifice at the altar (Lev 21:17). The list of exclusions includes a number of conditions that contemporary readers readily recognize as disabilities, including blindness, lameness, or a hunchback. But it also prohibits the service of priests with a broken leg or broken arm. Where a modern reader is likely to consider a broken arm a temporary condition that will heal without lasting injury, the Hebrew Bible reflects a world in which a once-broken limb remains an enduring blemish. The list is also striking for its absences. While most contemporary readers would include intellectual disability and deafness as prominent, representative forms of disability, neither of these conditions are mentioned in Leviticus 21. Other passages in the Hebrew Bible do present deafness and intellectual disability as undesirable conditions but do not describe them as *mumim*. Some have suggested that the exclusion of these conditions stems from the fact that, in contrast to the *mumim* enumerated in Leviticus 21:17, they are not visible to the eye. Saul Olyan argues that this explanation does not hold. Genital damage would not ordinarily be visible to the casual observer, yet it is classified as a *mum*. By contrast, the frequently discussed biblical skin condition *tsara at* is visible to the eye but is not described as a *mum*. Olyan maintains that "the criteria that determine whether biblical sources classify physical conditions or qualities as 'defects' remain obscure" (*Disability*, 29). Rather than treating disability as a fixed, stable category, I examine the native categories that Jewish texts use to conceptualize certain stigmatized body-mind conditions as different from the norm. I also draw on contemporary Western conceptions of disability to examine how Jewish tradition responds to people that "we" consider disabled. By shifting back and forth between native and essentialized categories, I aim to make plain the way in which ideas of disability are complex, changeable, and fluid.

Disability is an experience of difference that commonly carries social stigma, the process of marking out certain physical, mental, and emotional characteristics as undesirable. Emphasizing the way that stigma can result in social rejection, Erving Goffman charts the way stigma shapes social relations between the stigmatized and those whose bodies remain normalized (see Goffman, *Stigma*). Stigma is profoundly tied to social context. Stigma, Lerita Coleman argues, becomes particularly palpable when "we move out of one social context where a difference is desired into another context where the difference is undesired" (148). Deafness provides a striking example of how social context determines whether a particular difference is considered disabling. Within Deaf communities, the birth of a Deaf child is often cause for celebration as parents welcome their child into a close-knit linguistic minority and shared culture.[1] Within majority culture, by contrast, a child who is unable to hear is generally viewed as disabled.

Within ancient Jewish culture, infertility provides a striking example of how stigma and social context shape the experience of disability. Most modern readers recognize that infertility can cause profound emotional distress and lead to considerable medical intervention. Yet in the contemporary American context, people who experience infertility are generally not considered disabled. In the Hebrew Bible, however, infertility appears as a significant disability. Jeremy Schipper shows that biblical writers commonly mention infertility in conjunction with other physical, sensory, and speech impairments ("Disabling," 105). The biblical portrayal of infertility has a strong gender component. While Hebrew Bible texts occasionally reflect on men's inability to sire children, the biblical representation of infertility as disability centers on women's experience of barrenness.[2] Rebecca Raphael highlights the profound cultural and religious significance of infertility within the biblical narratives, arguing that a number of biblical texts use female infertility "as a narrative prosthesis" to convey the nature of God's power and to drive the sacred story forward (*Corpora*, 57–62).

By emphasizing the cultural production of stigma, disability studies shifts the focus away from the idea of disability as an individual experience and toward the analysis of how and why certain human variations come to be regarded as undesirable. Disability studies theorists critique the tendency to individualize disability, to view certain stigmatized conditions as regrettable circumstances of a particular body-mind. By contrast, it adopts a politicized, critical view of disability, challenging the "givenness" of a particular norm (Kafer 1–19). Disability studies also highlights how the lived experience of disability challenges prevailing social patterns and cultural assumptions about the nature of humanity and the experience of embodiment. It chronicles the way disablement shapes the lives of those whose bodies or minds are marked as failing to measure up according to the norm (see Linton, *Claiming Disability*). While disability studies pays attention to the social cost of stigma and marginalization, it also considers how disability serves as a cultural resource. Feminist disability studies has often emphasized how disabled people can shape disability into a dissident stance that forces majority culture to reevaluate its disdain for difference and its tendency to treat the disabled as Other (Garland-Thomson, "Staring").

B'TZELEM ELOHIM: HONORING ALL HUMAN BEINGS AS A REFLECTION OF THE DIVINE

Jewish tradition affirms the full humanity of people with disabilities. Jewish recognition of the dignity and inherent worth of people with disabilities is often linked to a principle known as *b'tzelem elohim*, a phrase which evokes the Hebrew Bible's affirmation in Genesis 1:27 that God created all humanity "in the divine image." In contemporary Jewish thought, the conviction that all humans were fashioned in the divine image is one of the most consistently cited ethical principles on behalf of the rights and full inclusion of people with disabilities. Rabbi Lynne Landsberg, senior advisor on disability issues to the Religious Action Center of Reform Judaism, references the principle of *b'tzelem elohim* to bolster her call for Jews to support the United Nations Convention on the Rights of People with Disabilities (see Landsberg, "Tell the Senate"). Similarly, Rabbi David Saperstein links the Reform movement's steadfast support of the Americans with Disabilities Act in 1990 "with the knowledge that each individual is created *b'tzelem elohim* in the image of God, and worthy of dignity and respect" (Banks). Rabbi Elliott Dorff, affiliated with the Conservative movement, uses *b'tzelem elohim* to ground his affirmation of the inherent worth of all people, regardless of disability (108). Human rights lawyer Melinda Jones, writing from an Orthodox perspective, likewise argues that "the belief that all human beings were created in the image of

God presupposes an acceptance that each life is of inherent value to the creator despite apparent imperfections" (101–2).

Despite the contemporary appeals to *b'tzelem elohim* as a principle that asserts the equality of all human beings before God, its intellectual history reveals a troubling tendency in traditional Jewish thought to conceptualize "the human" in ways that are problematic for people with disabilities. Though *b'tzelem elohim* can be understood as a great equalizer between human beings, it has also been used to articulate a difference between humans and other creatures or to claim that humans more profoundly reflect the divine image than do any other created beings (Marx 21–25). The influential medieval philosopher Moses Maimonides emphasizes that human cognition and intellect sets human beings apart from the rest of creation and grants them the capacity to reflect godliness (*Hilchot Yesodei HaTorah* 4:8). Nachmanides, his contemporary, locates human distinctiveness in the capacity for speech, following a long chain of commentators who have described humanity as "the speaking being" (Ramban on Gen 4:11). This link between humanity and the capacity for intellect and speech has had negative consequences for people with intellectual disabilities and those who are unable to speak. Traditional Jewish emphasis on intellectual cognition and sacred study as a means of drawing near to the divine has long marginalized both people with intellectual disabilities and deaf people, who were excluded from traditional oral modes of study (Abrams 124).

Despite these historical intellectual tensions, the contemporary use of *b'tzelem elohim* emphasizes the ethical imperative to value people regardless of disability and to include people with disabilities in all aspects of Jewish life. The principle of *b'tzelem elohim* undergirds many Jewish initiatives that support the inclusion of Jews with disabilities in synagogues, Jewish education initiatives, and Jewish cultural programs. Shelly Christensen, program manager of the Minneapolis Jewish Community Inclusion Program for People with Disabilities, emphasizes the importance of creating robust communities that welcome and support both individuals and families whose children have disabilities. Drawing on the example of Genesis 18:1, Christensen calls Jewish communities to expand their welcome to people with disabilities in ways that mirror the hospitality and generosity exemplified by Abraham and Sarah, the biblical patriarch and matriarch who welcomed strangers into their tent for shelter from the desert sun (1–2). She likewise evokes the biblical example of the community's response in Numbers 12:10-15 when Miriam, a prophet and sister of Moses, experienced a skin disease that kept her out of the camp for seven days. The Israelites waited until Miriam returned to camp before the entire community moved on together. Drawing on that biblical narrative, Christensen argues that "inclusion is meant to remind us that, like our ancestors, we cannot move on unless everyone is present. . . . We must learn to accept that when one member of our community is left behind, we are not whole" (1–2).

REPRESENTING DISABILITY: DISABILITY AS EXEMPLAR
AND METAPHOR IN JEWISH TRADITION

Biblical narratives feature many people with disabilities, including a striking number of leaders and heroes who experience disability. Elliot Dorff argues that the Torah's example contrasts sharply with the prevailing Greek and Roman idealization of the hero as physically perfect. By valorizing heroes and heroines with disabilities, Dorff maintains that the Torah teaches that disability is no obstacle to leadership and responsibility within the community (107). Perhaps the most frequently discussed example of a biblical hero with a disability is the prophet Moses, whom classical and contemporary interpreters commonly regard as having a speech disability (Marx 51–52). When Moses is singled out by God to serve as a prophet and leader to the community, he initially attempts to refuse God's call, saying, "Please, O Lord, I have never been a man of words. . . . I am slow of speech and slow of tongue" (Exod 4:10). In response, the Hebrew Bible asserts that Moses' disability is irrelevant to the question of his leadership, that God has given humans the power of speech and endowed them with diverse abilities. When Moses continues to protest his role, God instructs him to convey God's word to his brother Aaron, who will voice Moses' words before the people. Considering the brothers' partnership from the perspective of disability studies, Devva Kasnitz and Naomi Steinberg describe Aaron as Moses' "revoicer," highlighting parallels with a common practice in disability circles whereby a designated interpreter repeats and amplifies the words of a person with a speech disability (Steinberg and Kasnitz 2011). Despite the deployment of Aaron, however, it is Moses himself who delivers the most celebrated address in Jewish history. The entire book of Deuteronomy consists of Moses' speech before the gathered Israelites. The man who first protested his inability to speak eventually utters the most influential and enduring words of Jewish scripture.

While Moses is often lifted up by contemporary disability advocates as an example of a positive link between disability and communal leadership in the Jewish tradition, Jewish sources elsewhere use disability imagery as a negative metaphor. The Hebrew prophets commonly use blindness or deafness as a rhetorical characterization to portray the Israelite community's stubbornness, ignorance, or refusal to act in accordance with God's will. Raphael examines how negative images of the gendered and disabled body are used in Jeremiah to condemn what the speaker regards as Israel's wrong relationship with God ("Whoring," 103–16). Olyan shows how disability imagery appears in biblical polemics against idolatry to castigate other deities as powerless and ineffectual in contrast to the fully able God of Israel ("Ascription," 89–102). Prophetic texts deploy the miraculous healing of disability as an expression of deliverance and redemption. Isaiah 35:5-6 uses disability to portray the joyous return of the liberated Israelites as a time when "the eyes of the blind will be opened and the ears of the deaf unstopped. Then will the male leap like a deer and the mute tongues shout for joy." The rhetoric figures redemption as the erasure of the disabled body and portrays embodied disability as a sign of all that is not yet redeemed in human experience. Disability studies has sharply criticized the negative associations these texts make with disability as well as the way that a metaphorical treatment of disability makes instrumental use of disability for theological ends. Jeremy Schipper critiques the tendency of biblical texts and their interpreters to focus on disability as a theological trope rather than as a lived human reality. "The divorce of disability imagery from lived experience," he writes, "can create the dangerous impression of a biblical world full of imagery of disability but free of people with disabilities" (*Suffering*, 8). By using the disabled body in service of a literary trope or theological message, metaphor overwrites the actual body, scripting itself onto and over the lived experience of disability and further eclipsing the complex realities and religious experiences of people with disabilities.

LIFNEI IVER: DO NOT PUT A STUMBLING BLOCK BEFORE THE BLIND

Jewish tradition articulates a strong ethical imperative to treat people with disabilities fairly and to avoid taking advantage of them. An oft-repeated refrain within the Hebrew Bible exhorts the people to care for the orphan, widow, and stranger, emphasizing the moral necessity of concern and aid to those who are often neglected within society. The Torah explicitly forbids the mistreatment of people with disabilities: "Do not insult the deaf, and do not put a stumbling block before the blind; you shall fear your God. I am your Lord" (Lev 19:14). While traditional sources and commentators emphasize that this commandment forbids these acts against *any* person (Babylonian Talmud, Sanhedrin 66a), the biblical verse particularly singles out behavior that targets a person's disability. Leviticus 19:14 offers a strong example of the Jewish tradition's compassion for people with disabilities, with its particular concern of protecting disabled people from exploitation. Yet disability

studies scholarship has called critical attention to the way that efforts to "protect" people with disabilities may inadvertently intensify disparities of social
power. Raphael suggests that the very premise of compassion for people with
disabilities reinforces a mode of relationship that is marked by paternalism,
charity, and pity. Though she acknowledges the kindly intent of this legislation, Raphael argues that it underscores the marginalization of people with
disabilities. The passage assumes that the people addressed by the commandments are able bodied; it does not speak directly to the deaf or the blind
themselves. By positioning people who are blind or deaf as particularly vulnerable and in need of explicit aid, the commandment diminishes the agency
of people with disabilities (*Corpora*, 22).

In traditional Jewish interpretation, Leviticus 19:14 is read in a way that
moves significantly beyond its literal meaning. Rashi, an eleventh-century
rabbi who authored one of the most influential commentaries on the Torah
and the Talmud, interpreted the verse as a prohibition against deceiving
those who are vulnerable. He argued that the Torah already forbids causing
harm to another person, especially when the harm results from a malicious
act. Because he read according a classic Jewish hermeneutical principle
that assumes the Torah will never be redundant, Rashi sought an additional
meaning of this commandment. Since setting a physical obstacle before a
blind person is already prohibited by other commandments that govern
human behavior, Rashi read Leviticus 19:14 metaphorically, arguing that
the commandment forbids purposefully giving bad advice to a person who
is ignorant in that particular situation, thereby putting "a stumbling block
before the blind."[3] His interpretation hinges upon a symbolic reading of
blindness that has been roundly critiqued by disability studies for the link it
forges between blindness and ignorance (Koosed and Schumm).

RITUAL AND PRACTICE FOR JEWS WHO ARE BLIND

Jewish tradition includes ample examples of blind people who held positions of
significance within their communities, and Talmudic sources testify to a broad
inclusion of people with vision disabilities in many aspects of Jewish ritual.[4]
The Talmud attributes a number of halakhic teachings and debates to blind
rabbis, including some that reflect on the significance of blindness for Jewish
ritual practice. Consider the following text, attributed to the blind Babylonian
rabbi, Rav Yosef:

> Rav Yosef said: At first, I would have said—someone who taught the law
> according to Rabbi Yehudah, who said, "the blind are exempt from the *mitz-
> vot*," I would make a feast for the rabbis. What is the reason? Because I am

not commanded, and yet I perform the *mitzvot*. But now I have heard that which Rabbi Hanina said, "Greater is the one who is commanded and who does it, than one who is not commanded and who does it." The one who says to me that the *halakhah* is *not* like Rabbi Yehudah, I will make a feast for the rabbis. What is the reason? If I am commanded, then I will have a greater reward. (Babylonian Talmud, Baba Kamma 87a)

The account of Rav Yosef testifies to a significant change in rabbinic thought about the nature of obligation and exemption from the commandments. At first, Rav Yosef assumed that it would be to his advantage to be exempt from the commandments. He would be able to express his devotion through *voluntary* observance of Jewish ritual and law, which he assumed would be even more meritorious than obligatory actions. Yet Rav Yosef later learned that certain rabbis were teaching that it is superior to perform mitzvot in response to an explicit obligation, that the fact of being commanded conveys higher religious status and brings greater merit. Rabbinic Judaism eventually came to link exemption with exclusion, arguing that only a person who was commanded to perform a ritual act could fulfill that duty on behalf of the community. In addition to its implications for men with disabilities, this principle had significant ramifications for undercutting women's ritual performance because rabbinic law also considered women exempt from many ritual commandments (Alexander).

Most halakhic authorities maintain that people who are blind are generally obligated to the mitzvot, with only select exemptions for acts that specifically require vision (Nevins 29–32). The Mishnah permits a Jew who is blind to lead the congregation in prayer, allowing him to recite the central unit of blessings and scriptural passages known as the Sh'ma, a declaration that calls the congregation to affirm God's unity (Mishnah Megillah 4:6). One of the first blessings that surrounds the Sh'ma praises God as the creator of the heavenly lights. Rabbi Yehudah, however, dissents from the majority opinion that a blind person may lead the congregation in prayer, arguing that someone who has never seen the sun with his own eyes should not praise God for its creation. In keeping with the opinion cited above by Rav Yosef, Rabbi Yehudah rules conservatively with regard to a blind man's ritual obligations, but medieval commentators expressed discomfort with his position. They point out a logical contradiction, arguing that if he exempted the blind from *all* the mitzvot elsewhere, he surely need not specify that people who are blind are exempt from reciting these blessings on behalf of the congregation. They reason that Rabbi Yehudah must have meant that people who are blind are actually obligated to fulfill the commandments on the basis of rabbinic authority and only specifically excluded them from this particular obligation because of its association with vision.[5]

Vision serves as a key issue in certain other ritual and legal obligations. The Mishnah explicitly allows a Jew who is blind to serve as the translator of the Torah reading, an official position in the early synagogue (Mishnah Megillah 4:6). Yet most authorities rule that a blind person cannot recite the Torah during the synagogue service because the liturgical ritual requires the reader to chant the words directly from the scroll itself. Rabbinic sources specifically forbid a reader to chant from memory during this part of the synagogue service as they see the practice of reading from the scroll as central to the ritual of the public recitation (Fraade 36–38). This exclusion has been particularly challenging in the contemporary era because of the significance of Torah reading during the bar or bat mitzvah ceremony, a signal ritual of Jewish belonging. In historical practice, a young man was considered bar mitzvah when he was old enough to be considered personally obligated to the mitzvot; he was now responsible for his own actions according to Jewish law and thereby eligible to perform ritual responsibilities on behalf of the congregation. (Bat mitzvah is also used today for young women.) In contemporary Jewish life, new bar or bat mitzvah customarily lead a celebratory service in which they perform key roles in the synagogue service for the first time, leading certain prayers and chanting from the Torah. In a 2003 *responsum* written for the Conservative movement, Rabbi Daniel Nevins affirmed that a person who is blind may lead services and fulfill many other ritual responsibilities, including chanting the *maftir* (repeated) portion of the Torah after it had previously been chanted by a sighted reader and chanting the prophetic reading from a Braille text. Nevins could not find a way to permit a blind reader to chant the regular Torah portion, but he concluded his *responsum* with the hope that new technology might one day make it possible for people who are blind to read directly from the Torah scroll (44–47).

Jewish legal authorities also debated whether a blind person could serve as witness before a Jewish court. Traditional Jewish law concerns all aspects of life. Because Jewish communities have been subject to the rule of other governments throughout most of Jewish history, Jewish courts have rarely had jurisdiction over criminal cases, but they have exercised authority in certain realms of civil and family law. Blindness was rarely judged to affect a person's legal status before the court except in the case of serving as a witness. Maimonides argues the Torah requires witnesses to testify on the basis of what they have *seen* and therefore disqualifies a person who is blind from serving as a witness before a Jewish court (*Mishneh Torah*, Eduyot 9). An alternative reading of the halakhic tradition, however, argues that a blind person is disqualified only in certain situations that specifically require sight. According to Jewish law, some situations do require eyewitness testimony. But in all other cases, people who are blind are qualified to serve as witnesses based on the knowledge gained from their other senses (Central Conference of American Rabbis). In modern Jewish contexts, serving as a witness often has a ritual and ceremonial function as well. A recent *responsum* from the Reform movement rules that a person who is blind may serve as a formal witness to a Jewish wedding, both on halakhic grounds and because of a strong desire to fully include people who are blind in all aspects of Jewish ritual life (Central Conference of American Rabbis).

PHYSICAL DISABILITY

As with blindness, physical disability has surfaced in Jewish thought primarily when rabbinic interpreters found it relevant to a specific biblical law or felt it would impede the performance of a particular mitzvah. Within the Hebrew Bible, physical disability appears most prominently in the discussions of priestly blemishes in Leviticus 21:16-23. Though this passage is often read as a broad reflection of negative biblical views about disability, recent scholarship emphasizes the importance of reading this passage in light of the specific ideologies of the Israelite priesthood. Judith Abrams argues that priests represent physical exemplars of holiness within the context of divine service and any detraction from the priests' physical form represents a danger for both priest and community (23–27). As Olyan emphasizes, the religious structure of Leviticus still privileges a disabled Israelite priest above a lay Israelite who has no disabilities. While he is excluded from sacred service at the altar, the disabled priest is still eligible to eat the consecrated food and perform other priestly duties that the able-bodied, lay Israelite is forbidden to do (*Rites*, 112). Priestly identity is constructed as the preserve of an exemplary, elite male lineage. A priest with a disability is, in religious terms, still significantly privileged over an ordinary, able-bodied Israelite.

Within the context of rabbinic Judaism, priestly duties no longer include sacrifice, yet rabbinic Jewish tradition still draws on this biblical paradigm to consider how disability affects a priest's ability to offer the priestly blessing in the synagogue. In contrast to the broader prohibitions on the service of biblical priests with a variety of blemishes, the rabbinic tradition prohibited priests from performing the blessing only in cases where they had a visible blemish on their face, feet, or hands. In addition to narrowing the relevant forms of disablement, the rabbinic texts suggest that the primary "problem" with a disabled priest lies not in the physical fact of his body but in the potential that his bodily difference will cause observers to stare and thereby become distracted at a critical religious moment. Echoing a principle of contemporary disability studies theory, these texts suggest that disability is produced in part through the stare. Disability lies not in the body of the priest but in the eye of the beholder. The Talmud closes its discussion of priestly disability by recognizing several examples in which a priest with a visible blemish blessed the community. It resolves the contradiction by concluding that a priest who is well known in his town is allowed to bless, thus positioning *familiarity* as a cultural solution to the problem of stigma (Belser). Jewish jurists continue to use the principle of familiarity in modern rulings about whether disabled priests may bless. Yosef Karo, author of the *Shulkhan Arukh*, a frequently referenced sixteenth-century law code that remains highly influential today, follows this principle and rules that a person becomes familiar after a mere thirty days in a new place (Marx 81–85).

In contemporary Jewish life, improving the accessibility of synagogues and other Jewish venues remains an important priority for many people with physical disabilities. While progress continues to be made in this respect, disability advocates note that it remains common to provide limited access to Jews with disabilities, allowing them access to a part of the sanctuary, for example, but not to the *bimah* (raised platform) from which the prayers are led and the Torah is read. Such institutional and architectural barriers limit the access of clergy with disabilities and often keep other Jews with physical disabilities from accepting the honor of reciting the blessings before recitation of the Torah or opening the ark during the synagogue service. Architectural barriers can also limit people's ability to perform other Jewish rituals. Chava Willig Levy, an Orthodox woman with a physical disability, notes the inaccessibility of her local *mikvah*, the ritual bath in which observant women immerse themselves after their menstrual cycle. But Levy also speaks to the way in which the mikvah experience intersects powerfully with her experience of disability and the way immersion in the waters infuses her with an experience of physical and spiritual renewal. "Time after time," Levy writes, "I feel the exhilaration of that plunge. The *mikvah* waters transform me from a woman with four atrophied limbs into—honest to God—a ballerina! For a few glorious moments, my arms extend effortlessly. And as I ascend unassisted the three bottom-most steps, I marvel at the miracle of human grace and motion" (141).

CATEGORIZING STIGMA: THE LEGAL EXEMPTION
OF PEOPLE WITH HEARING, SPEAKING, AND
INTELLECTUAL DISABILITIES

While Jewish tradition has tended to treat blindness and physical disability as experiences that limit a person's performance of only specific mitzvot, classic Jewish texts treat disabilities of hearing, speech, and cognition as a "master status" that often served to categorically exempt the person with a disability from the performance of mitzvot (Abrams 129). Jewish legal texts often address triads of frequently excluded individuals—for example, treating "women, enslaved persons, and minors" as a group who are excused from the performance of certain mitzvot and thereby excluded from significant portions of Jewish ritual. Another triad singles out two categories of disability—the *heresh* and the *shoteh*—who are grouped with minor children as stigmatized in virtually all legal situations. The heresh is usually understood to refer to a person who is both deaf and mute, while the shoteh is variably treated as a person with intellectual disability or with mental illness. Judith Abrams argues that the heresh and the shoteh are both profoundly stigmatized in Jewish culture because their disabilities are believed to render them unable to participate in the central activity of rabbinic culture: the study of the Torah and its oral transmission through the centuries. In her view, the critical question surrounding these disabilities is whether a person possesses *da'at*—the ability to understand, discern, and take deliberate actions that has legal significance in rabbinic culture (*Judaism*, 168).

The shoteh has been understood to encompass a variety of human experiences, ranging from developmental or other disabilities that affect a person's intellectual cognition to mental illness, psychosis, or other psychiatric disabilities. While some contemporary legal authorities continue to include people with mental retardation in the general category of shoteh, Rael Strous argues that the rabbinic category of shoteh indicates a person who displays disordered and destructive behavior, a definition that most closely approximates the modern diagnostic category of psychosis (Strous 159). Strous argues that rabbinic legal thought distinguishes between a person who should always be classified as a shoteh and those whose conditions are cyclical or transitory in nature. Jewish legal thought is particularly concerned with the potentially erratic behavior of the shoteh. During a period of mental disturbance, Jewish law limits a person's ability to contract a marriage, initiate a divorce, provide evidence in court, perform ritual obligations on behalf of others, or transact business dealings (160–61). A number of halakhic provisions aim to protect the shoteh from financial exploitation. Because a shoteh is regarded as one who does not act with discernment or deliberate knowledge, such a person is commonly treated more leniently in matters of civil and criminal law. Yet even though the shoteh is excused from many of the obligations of Jewish life, the community remains obligated to assist the shoteh in religious matters and to support their integration in family and communal life. The Hatam Sofer, a nineteenth-century rabbi whose legal authority remains profoundly influential today, emphasizes that the well-being of people with mental illness or intellectual disability cannot simply fall on individual families but must be undertaken by the Jewish community as a whole (Strous 174).

While Jewish legal authorities continue to refine the category of shoteh to better align with contemporary medical insights and social principles of appropriate treatment for people with mental illness, the rabbinic category of heresh has undergone an even more significant transformation. Rabbinic sources describe the heresh as a person who can neither hear nor speak, a condition that was tantamount in the rabbinic mind to being entirely unable to communicate. This perceived inability to communicate profoundly stigmatized the heresh in rabbinic thought, causing the rabbis to exempt the heresh from the performance of all mitzvot. In the intervening centuries, however, the revolution in Deaf education and the strengthening of the Deaf community has resulted in major changes in the categorization of deaf people within Jewish thought. In his reappraisal of deafness in halakha, Moshe Taub argues that the classic rabbinic heresh now exists only rarely, if at all. Instead, contemporary rabbinic authorities recognize the cognitive and communicative capacity of deaf people and regard them as fully bound by the mitzvot, except for specific mitzvot that require hearing (Taub 7–9). In making this shift, Jewish thinkers have revisited rabbinic texts that address deafness and shown how the sources offer significantly more lenient rulings regarding the ritual performance of deaf people who can speak or who are otherwise able to communicate and indicate their legal understanding (see Gracer 2003; Mishnah Terumot 1:2). Rabbinic texts affirm that communication need not rely on speech. The Mishnah, for example, rules that a heresh could transact business by means of manual communication via signs or by lipreading (Mishnah Gittin 5:7, Mishnah Yevamot 14:1). Rabbinic texts also recount the successful education of deaf children such as the sons of Rabbi Yohanan ben Gudgada who participated in rabbinic education and eventually became experts in a particular aspect of Jewish law (Babylonian Talmud, Hagiga 3a).

In contrast with the profound exclusion of deaf people in classical rabbinic texts, contemporary Jewish legal thought generally considers deafness relevant only in specific situations where it might implicate a person's ability to perform a certain mitzvah, thereby paralleling the approach that halakha has long taken to visual and physical disabilities. Hearing is religiously significant in certain Jewish rituals, especially the commandment to hear the sound of the *shofar*—the ram's horn which is sounded during Rosh Hashanah (Jewish New Year) and Yom Kippur (Day of Atonement). The sounding of the shofar has potent ritual significance in Jewish culture. It is commonly understood as a call to awaken from symbolic slumber, engage in the process of repentance, and return to God as well as a particularly powerful call to God that gives voice to the crying of the heart (Strassfeld 262). Because the mitzvah is understood to refer specifically to *hearing* the shofar, virtually all halakhic authorities rule that when the shofar is blown publicly for others, it must be sounded by someone who can hear the sounds (Taub 19–20). Centuries of audist interpretation that privilege the hearing world have marginalized the qualities of Deaf Jewish perception. Rabbi Elyse Goldstein, who served as student rabbi at Temple Beth Or of the Deaf, argues that "for deaf Jews, to hear the *shofar* is also to feel its vibrations" and notes that the congregation incorporates a phrase to that effect into the traditional blessing during their celebration of the holidays (Goldstein 57).

DEAF JEWISH CULTURE AND PRACTICE

The rise of communities and cultural networks led by and for Deaf Jews has been critical for their social and religious advancement, fostering the development of Deaf Jewish culture as a distinctive form of Jewish religious practice. The early twentieth century saw a sharp increase in Jewish Deaf organizations in America, including a number of Deaf Jewish congregations, schools, and social welfare societies (Burch 49–50). Deaf Jewish activism resulted in the creation of Deaf-led support for Deaf Jewish immigrants, vocational training, labor advocacy, and cultural developments. In the early decades of the twentieth century, New York City was home to a substantial Deaf Jewish community, making it a crucible for the development of Deaf Jewish cultural institutions, such as the Hebrew Congregation of the Deaf, the Society for the Welfare of the Jewish Deaf, the Institution for the Instruction of Deaf Mutes, and the Horeb Home and School for Jewish Deaf-Mutes, which had a congregation that developed its own prayer book and a choir that sang hymns "in the deaf style" (Stein 288). Sarah Abrevaya Stein argues that these schools were critical inculcators for Deaf Jewish leadership and allowed students to forge vital cultural networks with other Deaf Jews. Samuel Cohen, a Gallaudet University Student from New York who became the first Deaf rabbi ordained by the Jewish Theological Seminary of America, received his initial training at the Horeb

Home (289). The emergence of a vibrant Deaf Jewish cultural identity helped spur the rise of distinctly Deaf religiosity. Albert Amateau, a Deaf Turkish Jew who became the first rabbi of a Deaf congregation, delivered signed sermons and led the ritual Passover Seder in sign (Stein 300–301). Early twentieth-century Deaf Jewish intellectual life also had a powerful impact within the wider Deaf community. Susan Burch describes the Jewish Deaf as "one of the most forceful and articulate independent Deaf periodicals," whose readership extended far beyond the Deaf Jewish community and which "became a rich site for the formulation and debate of issues germane to the deaf world" (303).

Deaf Jewish activism and communal institutions remain critical to the religious and cultural life of many Deaf Jews today. Rabbi Rebecca Dubowe, a Deaf rabbi who serves the Reform Temple Adat Elohim in Thousand Oaks, California, argues that significant barriers remain in connecting Deaf Jews with a primarily hearing Jewish world. "Many Jewish Deaf people are not associated with the Jewish community," she notes, "because of the lack of accessibility. Most Deaf people tend to be a part of the greater Deaf community, because they share a common language and there are no barriers" (Ungar-Sargon). Yet the distinctiveness of Jewish identity is not always sufficiently recognized or celebrated within the broader Deaf community. Deaf Jews and sign language interpreters have called attention to the importance of developing and promoting signs for Jewish religious life that do not adopt Christian religious paradigms or the English translations of Jewish vocabulary. As Daniel Grossman notes, "names of holidays, ritual objects, and value concepts have retained their unique vocabulary and are left intact in English, French, Russian, or any other language. . . . Rather than sign a parallel English word for a Hebrew concept, I suggest a totally new sign where possible" (Grossman 62–63). In recent decades, Israeli Sign Language has also had a powerful influence on the development of Jewish signs as more Deaf Jews visit Israel and incorporate Israeli signs into their own sign languages (Sutton-Spence and Woll 28).

Rabbi Darby Leigh, a Deaf Reconstructionist rabbi who serves Congregation Kerem Shalom in Concord, Massachusetts, highlights both the challenge and the transformative potential of developing meaningful Jewish signs in his adaptation of the Sh'ma. The Sh'ma—customarily translated "Hear, O Israel, God is our God, God is One"—posits hearing as a central religious responsibility. Rather than articulate the first word of the prayer with a sign that focuses on the ear, however, Leigh begins the Sh'ma with a sign that calls viewers to pay attention. The conventional sign for Israel denotes Israel as a place, not as a group of people, so his version of the prayer evokes "the gathering of all the people before me." His sign for God begins with "an expansive perception of God" that circles high around the signer's head but which then comes down toward the chest and into the sign for "ours." For the final word of the prayer, which signals the Jewish commitment to recognizing the unity of God, Leigh begins with the sign for "many" and then resolves the multitude into "one" (see Leigh, "Shema in ASL"). Leigh's interpretation of the Sh'ma, which has also circulated in the hearing-Jewish world, attests to the potential for Deaf interpretations of Jewish teaching to revitalize the spiritual significance of traditional Jewish prayer for Deaf and hearing Jews alike. Innovations by Deaf and disabled Jewish rabbis, teachers, and community members attest to the importance of not simply securing a place for Jews with disabilities within the tradition but also fostering communities in which Jews with disabilities can bring forward cultural and religious insights that will shape and transform Jewish life for future generations.

Disability remains a significant site of religious reflection within Jewish communities. While modern readers may regard disability as a relatively fixed and stable category, examining Judaism's engagement with people considered disabled reveals the degree to which human conceptions of disability are shaped by historical circumstance and conditioned by cultural values. Attention to disability in Jewish tradition also makes plain the striking dynamism of Jewish legal thought, which emphasizes the ongoing interpretation of biblical and rabbinic sacred texts in ways that often put traditional insights into conversation with scientific and social advances. Though certain ritual and legal prohibitions remain, most modern Jewish authorities emphasize the dignity of Jews with disabilities and seek ways to minimize the restrictions or limits placed on disabled Jews' religious practice. Deaf Jews and Jews with disabilities have also claimed their own place as interpreters of the tradition, as architects of new Jewish identities that reflect the embodied experience and particular sensibilities of Jewish disability culture.

6

Catholicism and Disability

Mary Jo Iozzio

Like other Abrahamic traditions, Catholicism is firmly rooted in the scriptural texts revered by Christians and Jews. Within these traditions, biblical exegesis and theological reflection from the hermeneutic privilege of disability have emerged only recently and have gained only intermittent attention in matters of ecclesiastical practice and church discipline. Arguably, the Roman Catholic Church and its first cousin Eastern Orthodoxy hold the claim to the eldest of Christianity's church communities;[1] as such, their liturgical practice and discipline set the prototype for development in subsequent Christian denominational branches, particularly those denominations with standardized rituals of worship. While Catholicism has been a vehicle of evangelization for two millennia and many people have received the good news from Catholic apostolates, Church practice and discipline have been ambivalent in its welcome of people with disabilities. This chapter is focused on developments that suggest concern for people with disabilities in the Western traditions of the Catholic Church.

Catholicism enjoys an ancient history that includes doctrinal consistency in reference to Christian belief concerning the Trinity, creation, the incarnation (including Mary's active cooperation with the Holy Spirit), the Eucharist (and other sacraments), resurrection, the communion of saints, and the Ecclesia. Similarly, Catholicism's liturgical worship is recognizable from its standardized texts and rubrics throughout Catholic communities and subsequently by individual Catholics as they travel the world. And, quite widely known today outside of the Church polity, Catholicism teaches and advocates for social justice by upholding moral values derived from a consistent ethic of life with an explicit interest in protecting vulnerable populations. While Catholicism raises these protections to the status of human rights, bringing its teaching on the sanctity of all life (from conception to death) to its global apostolic missions, it remains somewhat indecisive about institutionalizing practices that intentionally include people with disabilities. This indecisiveness presents a challenge to the Church, especially given the consciousness raising about people who are or have been oppressed that began as early as the nineteenth century with woman suffrage, continued with recognition of genocidal violence and war atrocities in the twentieth century, until today with the exposure of colonialist marginalizations uncovered in context-based theologies inclusive of disability studies.

Clearly, attention to the subject of disabilities is a relatively new phenomenon in the humanities and, for that matter, in public conversation. Similarly, though not as obvious, Catholicism has a long history of finding places for and reaching out to people with disabling conditions that compromise their positions in their communities, a practice which today finds vocal advocates both in the Vatican and Catholic policymakers; this history is both noteworthy and admirable. For example, in the Catholic communal monastic tradition as early as the sixth century CE, religious women and men housed and cared for the sick, poor, and infirm—code for what today, with certain caveats,[2] could be recognized as care for people with disabilities. Note, however, that monastics did not necessarily welcome persons with disabilities to join their ranks. By the time of the twelfth-century Crusades and continuing today, one development of that care expanded the monastic ministries to include hostels for pilgrim travelers on their way to the Holy Land (to trace the footsteps of Jesus as much as to reclaim the place for Christendom) or to places sanctified by an apparition of the blessed mother Mary (among the more well-known apparitions are those at Lourdes, France; Fatima, Portugal; and Tepeyac, Mexico), the place of birth, conversion, or miracle of a saint, or a place marking some other kind of supernatural event. Insofar as many pilgrims traveled to those places in the hope of a miracle, those hostels became the antecedent of hospices for people who were sick and dying. These apostolates form the basis of the hospital health-care systems that many of us utilize today. (More than 600 of 2,900 not-for-profit hospitals and 1,400 of 12,000 long-term care institutions in the United States are Catholic sponsored.)[3]

As a practicing Catholic, a woman in a Church whose clergy is gender exclusive, and a person close to those who have been marginalized on account of their having been deemed "other" by gendered, raced, and ableist dominant norms, I stand in the community as a witness to those failures as well as to the many graces the Church holds through its sacramental life, theo-ethical acumen, and social advocacy for those living in impoverished and vulnerable conditions. In this chapter I provide first a brief history of the Catholic tradition inclusive of its liturgical practices and institutional exclusivity so as to lay the foundation for both its successes and failures in reference to people with disabilities. Second, I look at the nature of the global Catholic Church through church discipline as it has been organized in the documentary tradition of canon law, the rules governing church practice. Third, I explore the historical development of theological reflection on the *imago Dei* and its effect on moral praxis. Fourth, through the hermeneutic lens of disability studies, I consider the modern Catholic social teaching tradition— starting with Pope Leo XIII's *Rerum novarum* and continuing through the Second Vatican Council's constitutions *Lumen gentium* and *Gaudium et spes*, the *Compendium of the Social Doctrine of the Church* of the Pontifical Council for Justice and Peace, and the papacy of Francis—to uncover the political start of the Church's overt advocacy for people with disabilities. Fifth, I conclude with a critique of the Church's ambivalence in reference to people with disabilities in order to reconcile its teaching with its practice in the local contexts of parish-community life.

FIRST, THE CATHOLIC TRADITION

No exact date can be claimed for the "start" of the Catholic tradition, though its connection to the apostles and especially to Peter numbers it among the oldest churches of Christendom. That said, the institutions of the Church did not begin to take shape until the original witnesses (those first converts from Judaism and state-sponsored paganism who came to belief in Jesus as the Christ and Messiah) and the next generation had died, leaving the work of evangelization to those inspired by the continuing presence of Christ in the Ecclesia and in the agape meal. From its simple beginnings as a meal surrounding the blessing, breaking, and sharing of bread, the institution of the Eucharist was likely the unifying event of the early churches—in Jerusalem and Judaea, Damascus, Antioch, Ephesus, Alexandria, Corinth, Rome, and beyond. Perhaps more than other actions, the Eucharistic commemoration is what distinguished Christians as a community of believers from their Jewish and Gentile neighbors.[4] With this institution the Ecclesia would need, as Paul himself reminds us (see 1 Cor 11),[5] an organization to both support and protect the integrity of the Lord's Supper.

As early as the turn of the second century CE, the tenets of the faith were established. Those tenets followed the kerygma Jesus announced in the synagogue of Nazareth that "in your hearing" the Lord "has sent me to proclaim release to the captives and recovery of sight to the blind, to let the oppressed go free, to proclaim the year of the Lord's favor" (Luke 4:17-21). As they remembered his words and deeds and with the conviction that Jesus—crucified, died, and buried—was raised from death and now sits in glory, the apostles and first disciples realized the fullness of the revelation. That realization included the beliefs all Christians now profess:

- Jesus as God incarnate and Mary of Nazareth his mother,
- God's manifestation through a Trinity of relations (as Father, Son, and Holy Spirit),
- The Church as a communion of saints (living and deceased),
- The forgiveness of sins,
- The resurrection of the body, and
- Life everlasting.

By the end of the apostolic period and as Christian leaders brought the kerygma throughout the world a universal Ecclesia began to form; it would be another two hundred years before the church-as-organization would institute an official clerical estate consisting of a hierarchy with bishops/patriarchs, priests/presbyters, and deacons.[6]

A single Christian church lasted through the first seven ecumenical councils: Nicaea I, 325 CE; Constantinople I, 381 CE; Ephesus, 431 CE; Chalcedon, 451 CE; Constantinople II, 553 CE; Constantinople III, 680–681 CE; Nicaea II, 787 CE (Need 41–143). While the bishop-patriarchs of the church were princes among equals, a brotherly primacy had been accorded to the See of Peter, the bishop-patriarch of Rome. That primacy and theological disputes, referable to both political and ideological concerns, became a source of contention between the Eastern/Byzantine and Western/Latin churches; in 1054 those tensions sundered the "one, holy, catholic, and apostolic church" professed in the Nicene Creed. This East–West schism revealed the all-too-fallible realities of human designs for normativity in form and in matter (institution over particularity), especially when form holds the content of the faith and matter its recalcitrant diversity.

Among other effects of the East–West schism, the office of the papacy—a uniquely Roman structure that orders the succession of Peter to this day—may be the most easily recognizable feature of Catholicism. As the successor to Peter, the Pope serves as the visible head of the Catholic Church, the servant of the servants of God and shepherd of God's people (Schimmelpfennig 260–69). The See of Peter has seen its ups and downs over the centuries, from greatness to incompetence, saintliness to competing claims for the chair, intrigue, and corruption. Despite this history, the papacy remains a revered institution and, at least since the dawn of the Information Age, the Pope himself is a man revered by all people of good will. Consider the excitement surrounding the Second Vatican Council (1962–1965) and the *aggiornamento* initiatives of John XXIII or the popularity of John Paul II. Elected by the cardinals of the Church since 1059, traditionally the Pope remains in office until death, incapacity, or resignation. As many as nine popes (out of 266) have resigned from the office, with the 2013 resignation of Pope Benedict XVI setting the modern precedent (Bornstein, "Brief History"). With the Information Age and the ubiquity of communication technologies, today the Bishop of Rome has a truly worldwide audience. Recall the elevation of Archbishop Jorge Mario Cardinal Bergoglio, S.J., now Pope Francis, to Peter's chair and the media attention to this first pope from the Western Hemisphere. Since his first tweets on @Pontifex soon after his election, Francis has enjoyed more than eight million followers. His popularity has also attracted many visits to vatican.va, both driving the spread of the gospel through social media in an unprecedented fashion and speaking of God's mercy and desires for human well-being. Francis embodies the reasons Catholics revere and love the pope, indeed!

Another unifying feature of Catholicism is its liturgical practices. The Church counts seven sacraments, celebrated with prescribed ritual actions in formal worship services on both ordinary and extraordinary occasions: baptism, confirmation, Eucharist/Communion, penance/reconciliation, anointing of the sick, holy orders, and marriage. Each of these sacraments carries graces with the power to make present what they signify: God's love for us, God's healing presence comforting us, and God's celebrating with us (Martos 19–46). That is, for Catholics, sacraments are not mere representations or symbolic gestures, they are actions that were instituted by Christ during his ministry in Palestine, continued in the period of the apostles and the post-apostolic organizing and organized Ecclesia, and administered by those ordained exclusively to do so. As Christ-instituted action, the sacraments are both the visible and tangible instruments of God's grace, meeting the needs of the faithful throughout their lives. The most regularly administered of the sacraments is the Eucharist, received in the "ordinary" celebration of the daily and Sunday Mass, the Catholic liturgical re-enactment of the Lord's Supper.

In brief, the sacraments in the Catholic tradition confer God's graces:

- In baptism, where each candidate is welcomed into the community through immersion in refreshing/cleansing waters, anointed with the sacred chrism oil, the gift of the Holy Spirit, and incorporated into the Christian community and work as priest, prophet, and king (*Catholic* 1241), and clothed with the robe of salvation (this anointing, however, presents an exclusionary contradiction insofar as only the subsequently ordained adult male can serve, liturgically, as priest).[7]

- In confirmation, following the sequence begun in baptism and strengthened further by the Holy Spirit, those to be confirmed are anointed again with the chrism oil and they commit anew—now as adults—to faith in God and in Jesus of Nazareth, the Christ.

- In Eucharist/Communion, Catholics consume the body and blood of Jesus; as noted above this communion is not merely a symbolic presence, it is the real presence of Christ confected through the transubstantiation of bread and wine that, once consumed, permeates the fiber of the individual and the community so that "the Church becomes what [it] can and ought to be" (Balthasar, "Meditation," 574).

- In penance/reconciliation, Catholics experience the forgiveness of temporal sins committed against God, self, and others by recognizing the failures to love, confessing those faults to another (a priest or bishop), and celebrating the reconciliation that accompanies being found.

- In the anointing of the sick, Catholics receive the rites ordered to the healing of life-threatening physical, mental, and spiritual illnesses. (This sacrament is often administered with the sacraments of reconciliation and communion—for those near death, this communion is a Eucharistic viaticum, "the sacrament of passing over from death to life" [*Catholic* 1524]—along with an anointing of the forehead and hands.)

- In holy orders, Catholic men—here is one of the Church's most explicitly exclusive practices—are ordained to the clerical state inclusive of the authority to administer the sacraments and to advance in the hierarchy of the Church polity.

- In marriage, Catholic couples vow fidelity to one another in the presence of the Ecclesia and God.

SECOND, CHURCH DISCIPLINE AND CANON LAW

I alluded above to church discipline and the increasing selectivity/exclusivity of those ordained to administer the sacraments; that discipline is both codified in and regulated by canon law. I raise this subject to explain the manner in which universality applies to Catholicism as well as to offer the rules that govern specific church practices, including those practices that apply to persons with disabilities in the Church. In many ways, canon law makes local churches recognizable as Roman Catholic, and it governs the worldwide witness of the organizational, hierarchical, and liturgical worship peculiar to the Catholic Ecclesia.

Before the formal development of canon law, discipline in the early Church was evidenced in the *Didache* attributed to the apostles, in the subsequent treatises over the patristic and early medieval periods, and settled, for the most part, in the ecumenical councils (Papandrea 200–227, 241–42). Canon law has its roots in the sixth century Justinian Code of Roman civil law, the 1150 *Decretum* of Gratian—the "father of canon law" (ca. eleventh century–1159)—the sixteenth through nineteenth centuries' *jus novissimum* begun at the Council of Trent (1545–1563), and the *jus codicis* beginning with the 1917 *Codex Juris Canonici* (Coriden 10–32).[8] Pope John XXIII called for the complete revision of the 1917 Code in light of the work of the Second Vatican Council; John Paul II promulgated that revision, the 1983 Code of Canon Law, that is in effect today (Canon).[9]

In addition to these ecclesial roots, the Church asserts that the origins of canon law rest in its submission to the precepts of the divine law and the natural law, as well as positive laws borrowed from local secular polities that "discipline" the Ecclesia with canons, rules, and norms. Together, these laws are designed to govern the Church as a single, universal body united in faith as well as to govern the sacramental life entrusted to the apostles and their successors by the promise Christ made to be with us always. Thus the Holy Spirit ensures both the legitimacy and authority of the rules, norms, and canons that distinguish the Roman Catholic polity from the more circumscribed institutionalization of the Orthodox and Protestant Christian churches. Further, the 1983 Code displays deliberate attention to the spirit of ecumenism animated by the reforms of the Second Vatican Council, a respect for religious and conscience freedom, and the pastoral concerns of the Christian faithful. The 1,752 canons in seven books of the 1983 Code include:

1. General norms, definitions, and clarifications regarding to whom the principles apply;
2. Institutional and organizational structures concerning the rights and responsibilities of the hierarchy (from the papacy to the curia, episcopacy, vowed religious, and local clergy) and the laity;
3. Functions of the magisterium over catechesis, communication, and mission activities;

4. The propers for the celebration of sacramental/sanctifying rites;
5. Temporal goods and property rights;
6. Sanctions for dereliction of duties and other crimes; and
7. Procedures to follow in the administration of juridical acts by the ecclesiastical courts.

As a result of canon law, the rules governing who may administer the sacraments and to whom the sacraments may be administered can be observed wherever the Church gathers. While the clerical state is gender exclusive, baptism and marriage may be and are administered by both laywomen and laymen, although marriage requires the assistance of an ordained male cleric.[10] Administration of the remaining five sacraments remains an exclusive service of the ordained male clergy, from the presbyterate to the episcopacy.[11] Moreover, candidacy for ordination has its own set of exclusions, some of them pertaining rightly to those human, moral, and spiritual qualities conducive for ministry in service to the gospel, others pertaining questionably to qualities befitting an inherited able-bodied and able-minded normativity (Canon 1029). Thus, canon law holds that a man suffering "from any form of insanity, or from any other psychological infirmity, because of which he, after experts have been consulted, is judged incapable of being able to fulfill the ministry" (Canon 1041.1). Applying a hermeneutic of suspicion, however much experts may be consulted for such a determination, the tendency by many in positions of authority to rely upon a medical model of judgment when a man with a disability presents himself as a candidate for study and subsequent orders must be interrogated. That is, these canons rely on an ableist set of norms that discriminate on the basis of criteria that have been found lacking in justice (Iozzio, "Norms"). Canon 1029 intimates the kind of normativity that admits only those candidates endowed with "physical and psychological qualities in keeping with the order to be received." These exclusions to candidacy aside, if a clergyman encounters a disabling condition post-ordination, and on account of that disability he becomes unable to perform the duties incumbent upon his ministry, his orders remain valid though he may be relieved of performing the duties belonging to those orders (Canon 689.2, 930.1, 930.2; see also Hysell 2008).

In terms of laypersons, the 1983 Code reaffirms the teaching proclaimed in the Dogmatic Constitution on the Church, *Lumen gentium*, of the Second Vatican Council:

> [The] faithful are by baptism made one body with Christ and are constituted among the People of God; they are in their own way made sharers in the

priestly, prophetical, and kingly functions of Christ. . . . But the laity, by their
very vocation, seek the kingdom of God by engaging in temporal affairs. . . .
They are called there by God that by exercising their proper function and
led by the spirit of the Gospel they may work for the sanctification of the
world from within [those secular spheres] as a leaven. (§31)

By the equality of dignity and action between them and the hierarchy, the
laity fulfill their vocations in the building up of the Body of Christ, in living
lives worthy of God's people, and in promoting the Church and its work of
salvation (Canon 208–11). That said, the sacraments are the principal means
by which the faithful—lay and ordained alike—gain the graces entrusted to
the Church and exercised in the Church's liturgical rites as help for our lives of
discipleship. Where the sacraments are withheld, interrogation of cause ought
to commence to determine if denial is attached to a recalcitrant normate presumed incapacity of one sort or another. Further, while canon law governs the
administration of the sacraments, specific rules apply to certain of the sacraments in order to maintain the integrity of the sacrament in the local and universal Church. Having considered the sacrament of holy orders above, of the
remaining six sacraments, the two most likely to be questioned for reception by
people with disabilities are the Eucharist and marriage.

As a general custom in Catholicism, the practice of infant baptism is
normative while the remaining sacraments often require instruction and
the determination of capacity considering intellectual, social, and emotional
developmental stages and maturity with the potential to bar some—mostly
persons with cognitive disabilities—from receiving the graces that the sacraments bestow.[12] Recall that the Catholic Eucharist is the real presence of Christ
in the bread broken and wine poured and the means by which the Church
becomes the one Body of Christ. The Eucharist shared and consumed is the
visible manifestation of unity among the faithful by communion with the
real, material presence of Christ. Although any baptized person not prohibited by law "must be admitted to holy communion" (Canon 912), for reasons
surrounding this mystery the sacrament is reserved ordinarily to those with
"sufficient knowledge" and able to understand "according to their capacity"
(Canon 913–14). Invoking one or another impediment, some may be denied
their share in this sacrament; in those instances disunity and injustice betray
the intentions of the Second Vatican Council in *Lumen gentium* 11 when it
names the Eucharist as the source and summit of the Christian life (Catholic
1324–25). Similarly, regarding capacity and understanding, marriage requires
"the lawfully manifested consent of persons who are legally capable" (Canon
1057). To the extent that consent is absent or other impediments—such as a

previous marriage, apostasy, or censure to validity—are known, the assistance of an ordained minister (deacon or priest) to the sacrament must be withheld (Canon 1066–71). In these ways, people with disabilities, especially people with cognitive or psychological disabilities, may be denied access to the sacraments.

THIRD, THEOLOGICAL REFLECTION ON THE *IMAGO DEI*

One of the more strident concerns of the Catholic tradition is its attention to the family as the domestic church, the first place where love is celebrated in the sacramental union of spouses and the place where children are instructed in the faith. One of the reasons for this concern rests in the Church's long-standing theological reflection on the *imago Dei*. As noted in the Genesis account of human creation, human beings have been created in God's own image and likeness. As such, Catholics hold that each human being is endowed with unparalleled dignity and entitled to the care and protection attendant to that dignity from conception to demise (Congregation).[13] So endowed, conception thus heralds another instance of the human being as *imago Dei*, which is to be protected and nurtured best in a loving family.

Discussion on the domestic church often focuses on the duties of parents toward their children and their responsibilities to provide catechetical instruction on the Catholic faith, prepare them for the sacraments, and celebrate the regular devotions of family prayer and the liturgical life of the local and global Catholic community (Gaillardetz 93–116). Like most of Catholic teaching, these responsibilities arise from the firm belief that children, no less than adults, bear in themselves the *imago Dei*. The unique nature of the family, in which all members bring their own incarnation of the *imago Dei* to the fore, may very well incarnate the family resemblance to God more than any individual Christian could. That is, as God's relationality is revealed in the doctrine of the Trinity and as relationality is necessarily present in families, then family relationality resembles God's own triune relationality: families, like the individuals that comprise them, are the image and likeness of God.

In Trinitarian doctrine, God *ad intra* (God in Godself) and God *ad extra* (God for Us) exposes the tri-relational being that distinguishes the Christian faith in the one God from the Western religious traditions of Judaism and Islam. This doctrine is not a Christian pantheism; rather, since God became incarnate in the person of Jesus of Nazareth and remains active in the world through the Holy Spirit, God's self-revelation includes a tangible manifestation of the Divinity as unity-in-diversity, as one-in-three, as the tri-relational God communicating in love as Creator, Redeemer, and Sanctifier (LaCugna

243–317). If God is tri-relational and personal love, then the Christian family is not only the domestic church but also the local and universal Church and, ideally, the location of God's revelation in the world and in creative, unitive love. The *imago Dei*, then, is present and well, enjoyed and welcomed into the world by an ever-increasing cadre of the faithful making their own promises to love one another in unique, faithful, and just ways and to be loved in return.

Promising to love and be loved, the Church, in its domestic and liturgical manifestations, vows to accept the gift of a child as the *imago Dei* comes into the world again and again. To this end, the Catholic Church is committed to the protection of the right to life of every child conceived and born until natural death.[14] This commitment extends in deliberate and overt ways to those whose presence in the world signals a disability or the threat of disability, a signal that some would prefer to be unrealized (and therefore prevented by abortion, infanticide, neglect, abuse, or euthanasia).[15] In its liturgical manifestations, Catholicism follows the tradition of infant baptism by bringing the child immediately (as soon as the parents can) into the Church politic without prejudice to disability or assessment of the ability to understand. The reception of sacraments subsequent to baptism may be limited on account of the presence of one or another disability the child may have, though rarely with the force of canon law, by a local parish priest and/or his extraordinary ministers of the Eucharist. Unfortunately and applying wrongly the canons governing reception of the Eucharist (and later commitment to marriage), many children (and adults) with disabilities, particularly with cognitive and psychological disabilities though not only these, are routinely denied all sacraments.

In respect of the teaching on *imago Dei*, Catholicism has taken a leading position in opposition to the political debates surrounding parental rights and a woman's right to procure an abortion, as well as the debates on the active euthanasia of persons deemed beyond the need of basic care provisions or those unwilling to wait the final moments of their life's breath. It is because of the teaching on the *imago Dei* that Catholics place so high a price on these lives, vulnerable as they are to their own particular health conditions and subject to the vicissitudes of powers locked into the ideologies of absolute autonomy and independence and about as far away as an ideology can be from the tri-relationality and interdependence embraced in a Trinitarian theological anthropology. Further, if what we do to the least of our brothers and sisters is what we do to Christ, then persons who are vulnerable and thereby deemed "least" by dominant norms—on account of their lack of voice (i.e., the developing fetus), their having been born with disabilities, their having acquired a disabling condition through accident or illness, or their having reached an age that includes mobility, auditory, cognitive, and other impairments (see Kristeva)[16]—may very well be the persons Jesus warned the powerful to heed (see Matt 25:37-46). To the extent that those with power ignore, overlook, or deride those who are vulnerable, on account of having hunger, thirst, sickness, confinement, or nakedness, they also and to the same extent, ignore, overlook, and deride Christ.

Theological reflection on the *imago Dei* bears on this consideration, finally, for the direction it provides on diversity. Again, I turn to the nature of Catholicism as a universal body believing in God as revealed in tri-relational diversity. Across the Catholic world, belief in the Trinity, if not fully comprehensive of tri-relational diversity in its theological traditions, extends to creation "as *imago Dei*—one image reflected in the diversity of being, including the diversity of disabilities present in humankind and in a planet subject to the forces of evolutionary and seismic change. This paradigm provides the immediacy of dependence and relationality that both defines the Triune God (as interdependent if not also dependent) and reveals the *imago Dei* in humankind as radical dependence" (Iozzio, "Norms," 98). Especially in the present age with worldwide travel and communication technologies bridging the distances between the local and universal Church, diversity becomes a signal distinction of Catholicism. This diversity is a cause to be celebrated and protected as the *imago Dei* among its least and greatest members. However, diversity has been rejected often and to often dreadful effect; too few make the connections between what the Church teaches about the *imago Dei* and the way too many treat people who do not conform to the narrow norm. Diversity in humankind includes persons with disabilities today as much as it did in centuries past. Some of these people with disabilities were welcomed to communion while others were tolerated at a distance, hidden in basements, attics, and outbuildings, or mocked—all denied relational support along with opportunities to worship.

FOURTH, CATHOLIC SOCIAL TEACHING
AND THE COMMON GOOD

The modern development of the Catholic social teaching (CST) tradition began with Pope Leo XIII in his 1891 encyclical *Rerum novarum* and continues to the present with documents inclusive of Leo's successors, Vatican offices (particularly the Pontifical Council for Justice and Peace), national bishops' conferences, theologians, and the laity. The seven themes of modern CST— life and dignity of the human person (wherein much of the discussion on the *imago Dei* is found); call to family, community, and participation; rights and responsibilities; the preferential option for the poor and vulnerable; the dignity of work and the rights of workers; solidarity; and care for creation (see Kaczor, "Seven Principles"; Byron, "Ten Building Blocks")—ground the Church's mission in respect of people who have been marginalized. Many of these teachings are rooted in liberation theologies with reflection on the common good in light of the preferential option for those who are poor and otherwise vulnerable.[17] Liberation theologies direct their attention to those who are relegated to the margins of their societies because God is attentive to them. While many people with disabilities are marginalized, they are likely also to experience poverty (worldwide and therefore what should be of imperative interest and concern among the Catholic universal church, the United Nations estimates that people with disabilities number 80 percent of the world's poorest people). Mindful of liberation theology initiatives, that poverty is to be neither romanticized nor ignored. Regarding those who are poor and vulnerable on account of disabling conditions, I do not intend to deem people with disabilities any more or less favored by God than the non-disabled except insofar as they are more likely to be disdained by an unjust or dominating, and thereby dismissive, power. The Judeo-Christian tradition has long held that God remains close to those who have been treated unfairly and are, as a result of that treatment, marginalized and oppressed.[18] In CST, the teaching witness of the Church recognizes that God makes a preferential option for those who are marginalized, as such, Catholics are called to "go and do likewise" (Luke 10:37).

Without attending to the documentary specifics, the teaching on the common good can be found within most summary iterations of the principles or themes of CST (Center). Moreover, these developments have their foundations within the tradition's historical past, articulated fairly comprehensively by two of the most prominent Catholic thinkers (both building on the Platonic/Aristotelian tradition), Augustine of Hippo and Thomas Aquinas. Augustine makes the connections between virtue, peace, and the good to which all are naturally inclined and which God makes known in the precepts of the great commandment: to love God, self, and neighbor and thereby to live according to the order God has deigned for humankind (Augustine bk. XIX, ch. 5). Aquinas considers Augustine's order as well, finding the good in the end or purpose for which any act is determined. Aquinas takes this finding further as an end for individual persons and the commons since societies, which comprises individual members, must have the same end as their members—to live according to virtue, in peace, and finally with the knowledge of the truth about God (Aquinas I.II.94.2). As Albino Barrera argues:

> The common good subsists only when it is embodied in persons. It achieves
> reality in the temporal order only as it is enjoyed by its members . . . [as]
> a perfection immanent in its members [the common good] has important
> implications for the principles of distribution and participation in the social
> order . . . [that is] the perfection and well-being of the community . . .
>
> The fundamental equality enjoyed by all, the end of the community as
> founded on the perfection of the individual, and the orientation of individu-
> als to each other all give rise to the principles of nonexclusion (solidarity, par-
> ticipation, relative equality, and preferential option for the poor). (296–97)

In many ways, the tradition of the common good encapsulates much
of CST as it pertains to both individuals and societies at large. With these
dual foci, the common good coheres with recent philosophical and economic
thinking following a capabilities approach to human flourishing. This thinking concerns ever-more equitable policies relating to national development
and the development of peoples, particularly those living at the margins of
their societies and thereby inclusive of people with disabilities (Nussbaum,
Creating Capabilities, 17–68; Sen 225–320). Together and in light of the tradition on the common good, CST and the capabilities approach provide a
formidable argument for initiatives to restore communion with those who
are marginalized by making space and realizing opportunities for people
with disabilities in the Church (Iozzio, "Solidarity"). As the Church recognizes in its Pastoral Constitution on the Church in the Modern World, *Gaudium et spes*:

> Every day human interdependence grows more tightly drawn and spreads
> by degrees over the whole world. As a result the common good, that is, the
> sum of those conditions of social life which allow social groups and their
> individual members relatively thorough and ready access to their own ful-
> fillment, today takes on an increasingly universal complexion and conse-
> quently involves rights and duties with respect to the whole human race.
> Every social group must take into account the needs and legitimate aspira-
> tions of other groups, and even of the general welfare of the entire human
> family. (Vatican §26)

With this move to the common good, some of the themes of CST anticipated
in the Second Vatican Council—here I consider the preferential option for
those who are poor or otherwise vulnerable, solidarity, and participation—are
as uniquely instructive as they are comprehensive of a Catholic appreciation for
the status of people with disabilities in the Church.

The teaching on the preferential option gained voice in the work of theologians seeing, experiencing, and then reflecting upon the plight of people barely able to live under the derelict conditions of unjust regimes in collusion with unjust socio-economic institutions. The option builds on recognition of the place Jesus Christ himself occupied in salvation history, a place that included both poverty and disability (Eiesland, *Disabled God*, 89–105), a place God apparently preferred to the halls of power and wealth. Further, the option challenges complacence in the face of oppressions and marginalizations that are contrary to God's will for humankind; such oppressions and marginalizations are contrary to the common good, which good, as noted above, ensures that every member of the community receives his or her share of the bounty present in creation and in the social order. She will neither hunger nor thirst for justice since she will enjoy successfully exercising capabilities with which she had been endowed at the start. In sharing the power and wealth ordinarily reserved to the privileged with those at the margins, those previously denied development of their basic functioning capabilities— denied, for example, of sufficient nutritious food for their bodily integrity and development, education, enfranchisement, health, housing, friendship, freedom, safety, and protection from intentional harms—will flourish as God intends, though their poverty may continue.[19] If the preferential option is to hold force for and with people with disabilities, then the Church must expose what hinders as well as take definitive action to support this development.

Although given persuasive voice in the work of Latin liberation theology and the Latin American Bishops' conference meetings at Medellín and Aparecida,[20] the teaching on solidarity gained its most winning voice from reflection at the level of the popes, reaching an apogee with John Paul II. These reflections attended specifically to the work of the faithful who recognized unjust social structures and the need to unite, in solidarity, for the cause of the common good. Leo XIII inaugurated the modern tradition of CST when he wrote on behalf of workers and their families in response to the changing, and what he recognized as unsustainable, conditions of labor. He challenged the economies that benefitted some—the new "lords" and business classes of the Industrial Revolution—in increasingly inequitable proportions compared to the centuries old agrarian commons and shared goods. Although the term "solidarity" is not found in *Rerum novarum*, Leo's defense of social organizing among workers and the right to unionize laid the foundation for development of thinking on solidarity beyond the world of compensated labor to community organizing (Leo 49, 61). This foundation, focused on behalf of those whose voices and concerns have a history of being regarded expediently, if at all, by those with power and authority, resulted in change.

On the fortieth anniversary of *Rerum novarum*, Pius XI introduced the term "social charity," defining it as a juridical and social order, giving form and shape to the economic order according to the kinds of justice outlined above regarding the common good (Pius 88). Paul VI wrote that the development of humankind demands attention to three duties: mutual solidarity between wealthier and developing nations, social justice that rectifies trade relations, and universal charity to build a more humane world community. Further, Paul VI made the connection between solidarity and relationality to find that solidarity includes the hospitable welcome of strangers although the strangers he had most in mind were migrants and refugees (Paul 44, 67). John Paul II, inspiring and inspired by the *Solidarnoś'* labor movement efforts in his native Poland, spent the better part of his encyclical *Sollicitudo rei socialis* defining and engaging the reach of solidarity. John Paul II asserted:

> Solidarity is a firm and persevering determination to commit oneself to the common good; that is to say to the good of all and of each individual, because we are all really responsible for all. . . . In the light of faith, solidarity seeks to go beyond itself, to take on the specifically Christian dimension of total gratuity, forgiveness, and reconciliation. One's neighbor is then not only a human being with his or her own rights and a fundamental equality with everyone else, but becomes the living image of God. (John Paul 38, 40)

More recently, Francis has been similarly explicit when he exhorts that solidarity "presumes the creation of a new mindset which thinks in terms of community and the priority of the life of all over the appropriation of goods by a few. . . . [Solidarity] must be lived as the decision to restore to the poor what belongs to them. These convictions and habits of solidarity, when they are put into practice, open the way to other structural transformations and make them possible" (Francis 188, 189). The habits of solidarity then instigate as well as instantiate relationships between people who struggle on account of one or more systemic or institutionalized injustices and those whose circumstances protect and privilege them. Solidarity calls all members of the community to forge relationships where distance has for too long held sway.

Finally, regarding participation, CST provides strong support for the active involvement of all members of the community, inclusive of a kind of enfranchisement in the political sense. Along with the Church's position on the family as the domestic church and as a central institution in society forming individuals for themselves and others in service, the Church recognizes the communities that support individuals and families as together they seek and work for the common good. A widely held insight maintains the truths concerning how a community and its larger society will be judged—that is, by its treatment of the most vulnerable of its members. As referred above, people with disabilities number among those who are most vulnerable to a denial of support for development of their basic functioning capabilities; that denial will be judged. The Church can reverse this trend by deliberate listening and following the desires of those who have been bowed low. Thus, the principle of participation necessarily asks: how are any of us to know the needs of our sisters and brothers except by engaging each of them in their own context? In the *Compendium of the Social Doctrine of the Church*, the Church challenges the faithful to act for the common good since we are not created by God to live alone. "Living in a community is an essential expression of who we are. But community does not just happen—it is something that men and women together must work together to develop" (PCJP 149, 150). Building on the conviction that each member is *imago Dei* (endowed with dignity and the capabilities inherent therein), comprehensive participation—for example, in cultural, economic, legal, political, and social affairs—is "a duty to be fulfilled consciously by all and with a view to the common good" (189). Such participation requires access to education, especially so that when decisions are made by or on behalf of others, from the lowest to the highest levels, those decisions will be informed with a view to the well-being of all as well as with the expectation that members from the lowest to the highest levels are present at the tables where discussions take place and decisions are made. Like the principles of solidarity and the preferential option, participation can ensure that the many different members of a community are themselves informed, listened to, and involved in the development and the subsequent exercise of the rights and responsibilities that accompany membership in the proximate, local, national, ecclesial, and global communities of which we are all a part (191).

Together, these principles of CST point to an inclusive community, a community that holds the common good as a real good belonging to every member of humankind, every instance of *imago Dei*. Happily, since 1978 the Catholic bishops of the United States have recognized that "Catholics with disabilities must be able to participate fully in the celebrations and obligations of their faith, and should be included within the total fabric of society" (NCPD). Nestled under the common good, those who are marginalized are brought to the choice seats at the Lord's banquet, joined by their sisters and brothers in the solidarity of a tri-relational love and care that meets and develops those basic human capabilities necessary for each to thrive, and welcomed to voice their perspectives, experiences, and hopes in participatory governance and multi-level decision-making.

FIFTH, FROM THEORY TO PRACTICE

Much praise can be offered to the Church for its teachings and the consistency of its message on the sanctity of all human life as well as its dependence on God's good creation (given global environmental degradation, a dependence appreciated more today than in the past). However, it wasn't until 1963 that John XXIII acknowledged people with disabilities when he wrote on the rights accorded to all people, including the right to life, education, work, shelter, and other necessary social services that may be needed on account of ill-health, disability, and loss of livelihood (John 11). With the papacy of John Paul II, explicit concern for, frequent comment about, and visits among people with disabilities and their integration into all arenas of society was raised for the Catholic faithful and all the world to observe; his successors, Benedict XVI and Francis, have noted the perseverance in the face of adversities by people with disabilities, thanked those who advocate on their behalf, and stood themselves as witnesses to encounter, solidarity, and inclusion of people with disabilities.[21]

Certainly the Church has a stake in the care of, for, and with people with disabilities as much as it has a stake in the care of, for, and with all people. More than care, the Church has suggested—almost—a theology on disabilities in its preparatory documents for the year 2000 third millennium celebration's "Jubilee Day of the Community with Persons with Disabilities." Those documents start with a treatise entitled "The Person with Disabilities: The Image of God and a Place of His Wonders." Although the language of this start strikes many, rightly, as patronizing, it concludes with the challenge to "conversion and to discernment of Gospel values" (Committee, One). Further, the Preparatory Committee asserts, "the person with disabilities is rich in humanity" (Committee, Two), "has every right to be a subject-active agent in ministry" (Committee, Three), "has every right to be a subject-receiver of evangelization and catechesis" (Committee, Four), concluding that "the person with disabilities has rights and duties like every other individual" (Committee, Five). These celebrations signaled new attention to ensuring that the Jubilee's liturgical spaces were fully accessible and that persons with disabilities were involved in those events as participants and as ministers.

Earlier, in 1978, the Catholic bishops of the United States issued a "Pastoral Statement on Persons with Disabilities," wherein they recognize the Church's obligations to safeguard the Body of Christ, particularly in the sacraments, and to build the kingdom of God's peace and love. They note:

> The Catholic Church pursues its mission by furthering the spiritual, intellectual, moral and physical development of the people it serves. As pastors of the Church in America, we are committed to working for a

deeper understanding of both the pain and the potential of our neighbors who are blind, deaf, mentally retarded,[22] emotionally impaired, who have special learning problems, or who suffer from single or multiple physical handicaps—all those whom disability may set apart. We call upon people of good will to reexamine their attitudes toward their brothers and sisters with disabilities and promote their well-being, acting with the sense of justice and the compassion that the Lord so clearly desires. (USCCB)

The bishops remain attentive to the ongoing need for actions designed intentionally to advocate for ministry to and with people with disabilities. In 1995, combining canon law, sacramental theology, their "Pastoral Statement," and insights from the corpus of John Paul II and other Vatican offices, they published "Guidelines for the Celebration of the Sacraments with Persons with Disabilities." (To the United States bishops' credit, the Vatican Committee for the Year 2000 Jubilee Day adopted these guidelines for the celebrations of mass.) The hermeneutic key for these guidelines is access to full sacramental participation by Catholic people with disabilities across the diverse instantiations of the United States Church—from urban to suburban and rural dioceses and to parishes staffed by diocesan or religious order priests. "Catholics with disabilities have a right to participate in the sacraments as full functioning members of the local ecclesial community" (USCCB, "Guidelines").

All things considered, the Catholic Church is dedicated to people with disabilities in the same ways that it is dedicated to all the faithful. Unfortunately, and a reality true for other members of the Catholic communion who continue to be marginalized by prejudices, discriminations, and ignorance, many local churches are quite inaccessible, unwelcoming, and dis-valuing of the diversity presented in the Ecclesia and expressed by people with disabilities. For example, many churches were built decades before the consciousness raising of civil rights pertaining to people with disabilities, and, as such, many include steps up to the entrance, effectively leaving people with mobility disabilities shut out of the assembly, their access to religious rites denied unless a ramp is installed as an alternative passage to the sanctuary. (As long as the entry remains inaccessible, the church is, consciously or not, indicating NO SERVICE for people with mobility disabilities.) While the architects and builders of those earlier days should not be faulted, it is disheartening that so many of these buildings have not yet been adapted to accommodate the physical structures that disable those who want to enter. Related to the physical barriers, persons who are or have become homebound as a result of debilitating conditions and who appreciate the visit of a priest or minister to their homes will miss the Sunday and other holy day gatherings of the community that is the Church. Communication technologies today could remedy some of the isolation experienced by many parishioners who would be accommodated with, for example, services of the Church gathered that could be live video-streamed between the building and their homes. Entryway stairs and homebound isolation are just two examples that recount where the local ecclesial community has failed not only the bishops' and popes' directives, but have failed also, and more importantly than Church officials, the people of God as members of the Body of Christ who desire the sacramental graces and fellowship of the universal Church. One accessible Catholic Church here or there while three, four, ten, and twenty are inaccessible—structurally, technologically, or attitudinally—do little in the way of respect for the *imago Dei* dignity of people with disabilities, justice in place of discriminatory practices, or neglect of formation in Christian discipleship. Given the imperatives of evangelization and the good news of liberation, laissez-faire approaches to this state of exclusion can only be named sin.

Alternately, the resources developed by the National Catholic Partnership on Disability with and for people with disabilities and their families are hopeful. These resources provide practical help and suggestions on a spectrum of services including advocacy initiatives for parish outreach, concerns related to ministry with and for people with specific disabilities, assistance for priests with low vision, and information on accessible design and redesign. Finally, they emphasize across-the-board collaboration and the integration of people with disabilities in the ministry whereby the Church's mission is fulfilled. They adapt the principles of universal design to a "universally designed ministry" that offers the aims of inclusion as co-terminus with the call to discipleship that characterizes the people of God (NCPD, "Accessible"). Along with others who recognize accessibility through sensory perception (Yong 193–226), the NCPD recognizes the Church's liturgical practices as strongly sensory. Thus, a universally designed ministry capitalizes on the access that incense, candle lights, bells ringing, receiving the Eucharist, and gestures such as making the sign of the cross, kneeling, sitting, standing, and processing bring to the community gathered for liturgical worship. Their *Opening Doors to Welcome and Justice to Parishioners with Disabilities* follows the theological insights on the *imago Dei*, preferential option, solidarity, and participation outlined above and recognizes the practical challenges of orchestrating any liturgical celebrations with a view to noting how such celebrations can embody the hospitable sensible reach of Jesus' own sharing of touch in the communion that is his Body, the Church (NCPD 8–11).

CONCLUDING CHALLENGES

The good news that the Catholic Church brings to the world has been one response to Jesus' prayer that all will be one. In the twenty-first century most recognize the many ways that Christian communities are divided, and much has been done to work for unity. Closer to home, the Catholic Church can do better in changing the thinking, the hearts, and the practices that have segregated Catholics with disabilities from the local parish and, perhaps, its school, social programs, faith-inspired travel (of a pilgrimage sort though not necessarily "for a cure"), and participation in the sacramental life that distinguishes the tradition across the centuries. New sensibilities have raised the consciences and the consciousness of many, and more work remains yet to be done. To continue the work of unity, the Church must confess and repair its sins—institutionally and among its ranks—in discriminating against people with disabilities.

Catholicism's nearly two millennia history of worship, evangelization, and service attest to the enduring value of its mission. Today that mission is charged with reconciling its traditions with the many people who have been marginalized by social, ideological, political, and ecclesial constructions of the other. Certainly, celebration of the Eucharist and other sacraments have the power to bring together those who have been separated; but, as long as individual priests and directors of religious initiation programs refuse to instruct people with disabilities, the sacraments will remain divisive and at complete odds with Jesus' own institution of those sacraments. Mostly contrary to these practices of refusal, canon law orders the universal liturgical practices and instructs that no Catholic is to be denied communion; yet, as long as some laws exclude the admission of women, homosexual persons, and people with disabilities to holy orders and marriage, those laws will remain unjust. Finally, the theological grounding of the *imago Dei* in the Catholic life initiatives holds every human life—from conception to death—as inviolate and worthy of nurture, protection, and respect; however, as long as that respect fails to engage solidarity with our sisters and brothers with disabilities, a preferential option for those who are marginalized, and the common good on behalf of one and all, CST will remain "a noisy gong or a clanging cymbal" (1 Cor 13:1), whereas action is what the tradition and the gospel demand.

7

Protestant Christianity and Disability

Thomas Reynolds

VULNERABLY HUMAN IN GOD'S GRACE: DISABILITY IN A PROTESTANT CHRISTIAN PERSPECTIVE

In the past several decades, disability has increasingly become an important topic in Christian churches. Of course, people with disabilities have lived among and as followers of Jesus in the three major streams of Christianity— Roman Catholicism, Eastern Orthodoxy, and Protestantism—for some two thousand years. And certainly the mandate to love one's neighbor and care for the sick, poor, and marginalized has been central to the Christian message, relating directly to disability. But the current groundswell of attention to disability in Christian circles signals important insights and developments that go beyond this and until recently were mainly implicit or peripheral concerns, now being drawn out and articulated with particular potency and transformative impact. A disability studies perspective has emerged, helping to initiate a growing shift in perceptions about disability and its relation to Christian faith. Such a shift is beginning to facilitate needed changes in attitudes and practices, dismantling barriers to access and participation, and recognizing people with disabilities as contributors to the life of faith communities.

The focus of this chapter limits itself to Protestant Christianity in relation to disability. In general terms, Protestantism is distinguished from the other two main branches of historic Christianity, Roman Catholicism and Eastern Orthodoxy, by its own particular interpretation of what it means to be a Christian. Yet it is by no means a singular tradition, comprising instead a complex array of histories and identities that resist single definitions or simple descriptions. Nonetheless, even amid such a diverse historical landscape, distinguishable features present themselves to outline broad contours initially shaped by, but not limited to, sixteenth-century European movements critical of Roman Catholicism (see McGrath and Marks, *Blackwell Companion to Protestantism*). This chapter thus presents a summary portrait and analysis of these contours, exploring ambivalences and problematic conceptions related to disability, as well as foregrounding creative possibilities that emerge within a disability studies perspective. But the particular place of disability in Protestant circles—both historical and contemporary—is complex and multifaceted, and cannot adequately be portrayed in a chapter like this only by listing references to disability (or what might be understood as "disability") among key writers, or by detailing the experience of disability among faith communities through various case studies. This study, therefore, takes a different approach, exploring leading themes in historic Protestantism and bringing them into conversation with a disability studies perspective to highlight certain perils and promises through critical observations and constructive interpretations.

The ambivalent nature of Protestant Christianity's orientation to disability is manifest in many ways. On one side, problematic examples multiply that treat disability as a curse from God or sign of sin and moral fault or, more positively but equally demeaning, that laud it as a divine blessing or opportunity for heroic overcoming and faith development. On the other, however, Protestantism contains ingredients that become subversive tools resisting and countering examples like these, opening prospects for understanding disability as a feature of vulnerable human life within the love of God and, in the process, for dismantling disparaging and restrictive attitudes and actions toward people with disabilities. For example, in a well-known conversation about a child with disabilities, Martin Luther—the so-called spark of the Protestant Reformation—advises that the child be suffocated, it being nothing more than "a mass of flesh without a soul," an instrument of the devil. His understanding of God's grace and theology of the cross also offers mitigating resources counting against his viewpoint on disability in this case (Heuser, "Human Condition"). How can such ambivalence be accounted for and reframed in positive directions? To help answer this question, the discussion will first offer a preliminary portrait of the leading themes of Protestant Christianity, taking a broadly historical approach. Second, a disability studies perspective will be employed as a lens to investigate and question problematic features of Protestant beliefs and practices. In light of this, finally, the chapter will present examples of new ways of understanding central Protestant theological themes and interpreting biblical texts with reference to disability as a productive site of communal transformation, rather than a flaw to be remedied or a problem to be contained.

MAPPING CONTOURS OF PROTESTANTISM

Originating from sixteenth-century European reforms in which figures like Martin Luther and John Calvin played important roles, Protestant Christianity currently accounts for approximately 37 percent of the 2.18 billion Christians distributed geographically across the globe (Pew Research Center). It refers to the cluster of Christian traditions descending from the sixteenth-century European Reformation (i.e., Lutheran, Anglican, Anabaptist, Presbyterian, and Reformed), others related to it that arose in seventeenth- and eighteenth-century Europe and North America (e.g., Congregationalist, Methodist, and Baptist) and subsequently spread across the world, and still others that have developed more recently (e.g., Adventist, Pentecostal, and local nondenominational churches) and are rapidly growing in the Global South (Noll 2–5). Protestantism thus comprises multiple heritages and denominations or church groupings with widely varied emphases and practices. Without a common authoritative center such as in Roman Catholicism through the Papacy and magisterium (the infallible teachings originating from the office of the pope and bishops), Protestant churches have historically lacked consensus in dealing with questions about the nature of the church and about core beliefs outlining the content and nature of faith. Yet amid this diversity, certain distinguishable contours do emerge, forming a rough coherence shared by most that count themselves in the legacy of the Reformation.

Even though Protestantism is not a single tradition, its original spirit was shaped by a common desire for change, rising in a critique of fundamental beliefs and practices in the Roman Catholic Church of late-medieval Europe. Such desire for change harnessed momentum already in play for several hundred years. There had been a flurry of devotional writings and lay movements of different kinds, which empowered people with a sense of their own connection to God outside the formal order of the Church's ordained clergy. Further, there were undertakings by figures like the English reformer John Wycliffe who resisted the Church's clericalism (formal control by the clergy), rejected Papal power over secular government, and translated the Bible into vernacular. His Czech follower Jan Hus was vocal in his criticism of corruption in the Church and was burned at the stake for it in 1415. But the real moment of clarity for what became known as the Protestant Reformation came a century later, in 1517, when the German monk Martin Luther (1483–1546) wrote his famous Ninety-Five Theses criticizing certain excesses of the Church and calling for reform. While he did not initially intend to break from the Church, his efforts caught hold of prevailing winds to inspire a series of events that eventuated in all-out protests against the Church. Indeed, the term "Protestantism" was coined as sympathetic princes in the region issued a protest dissenting from decisions made by Catholic dignitaries at the Diet of Speyer in 1529 to condemn all innovations and prohibit any further calls for reformation. The main thrust of the wave of protests centered on the charge that the Church had overextended its authority and lost its spiritual integrity, becoming corrupt. While there were many points of criticism and, in turn, varied proposals for correctives—such as those by major reformers like Luther, Ulrich Zwingli (1484–1531), and John Calvin (1509–1564)—there was also continuity on several points.[1]

For most Reformers, the Roman Catholic Church of the day had gone too far to institutionalize divine grace and make itself an arbitrator of what is rather God's free gift of love and mercy offered in Jesus Christ. Such was at stake in Luther's Ninety-Five Theses, which denounced the selling of indulgences, a custom claiming to provide special access to God's merit—not to mention being a way of increasing the Church's wealth and funding its building projects.[2] Luther questioned whether grace was a commodity to be controlled by clerical regulations and bought or earned by human effort, stressing instead that God's love toward human beings is extravagant and direct and that the forgiveness of sins is freely given in Jesus Christ and received through faith independent of human ordinances. Central to the Christian message is the claim that all people have sinned and broken relation with God and each other, the good news of the gospel being that God has reached out to humanity to bring reconciliation in Christ. For Luther, salvation is restored relation with God justified by the response of faith alone, not by earning God's good favor through certain procedures or "works."[3] Accordingly, Luther accused the Church of replacing the gospel of Christ with a bureaucratic system of bondage claiming for itself the mediating power to offer forgiveness and salvation. The catchphrase *sola fide* (by faith alone) in this way became a rallying point for the Reformation. Faith was a matter of receiving in trust God's gift of salvation. John Calvin followed Luther's lead here and stressed that faith is an assurance in God's loving disposition toward the believer.[4] Using language from the apostle Paul, he spoke of believers as "elected" by God, even "predestined" for grace by God, as a way of prioritizing divine grace over human effort.[5] It is God's grace that is first, leading to the response of faith, which becomes active in practices of compassion and kindness.

The priority of God's grace over human mechanisms that would manage to control it is a major theme in Protestantism. A second theme connects with it: a priority placed upon the Bible as the authoritative measure of Christian life, even of the Roman Catholic Church. Common among reformers since Wycliffe, the principle of *sola scriptura* (by Scripture alone) was an invitation to seek out the gospel message and discern what it means to be a follower of Christ by looking directly to the witness of early apostles recorded in the New Testament. The believer finds access to God's Word (God's holy and redemptive intention for humanity) in Scripture, which when preached or read under the guidance of the Holy Spirit makes it the chief authority on matters of salvation and direction in human life. This new stress drew both from Renaissance humanism in the air, which emphasized education and underscored study of the New Testament in its original Greek, and from the resultant increase in literacy, especially after the invention of Gutenberg's printing press (ca. 1450) would make vernacular translations of the Bible widely accessible among the public. Luther himself translated the Bible into German.

With the understanding that God's saving Word was revealed in Scripture and in principle accessible to all, the Bible was held up as judge over church tradition, the highest court of appeal over even the pope. This move conferred dignity to dissent and reinforced efforts toward reform (Soulen 254–55). Swiss reformer Ulrich Zwingli, for example, was adamant about rejecting practices not mentioned in Scripture—such as the ideal of celibacy for clergy, the veneration of saints and relics, adorning churches with images, musical instruments in worship, and performing sacraments other than baptism and the Lord's Supper, the latter understood in accordance with Scripture to be a memorial remembrance of Christ and not, as in the Catholic (and Lutheran) understanding, a literal corporeal presence of Christ. The appeal to Scripture as the primary site for adjudicating matters of belief and practice had explosive implications. Indeed, the very idea that the Bible was something Christians should take up for themselves without mediation from higher authorities placed new emphasis on the ordinary layperson and their relationship to God, undercutting the privileged position of clergy in the Roman Catholic Church.

A third main feature of Protestantism thus comes to the fore, a focus on what Luther, picking up from the apostle Paul, called the "priesthood of all believers." Insofar as this theme claimed that all persons of faith are made righteous before God in Christ and counted by God as priests capable of mediating the divine presence to others, it introduced a great equalizing force in the church that, in principle, valued the place of all persons and critiqued hierarchical schemes that positioned some over others as of more intrinsic worth to God. This did not mean that all hierarchical forms of church administration were dismantled, for reformers still employed biblical models of church organization and leadership (such as bishops and deacons) but, rather, that every individual's status before God was equal. Moreover, every believer had a vocation or "calling" by God to live responsibly in the world and carry out duties specific to their own gifts and talents, some being called to ministry of leadership in the church and others to different kinds of work, all being important in glorifying God.[6]

The term "vocation," which heretofore had been reserved for clergy and monks who renounced the world for spiritual gain and ministry, was now applied to all Christians in a wider sense to mean not renouncing but engaging the world productively as a means of sanctifying everyday life. For example, for Luther, in addition to ordained ministry, "vocation" related to economic life (such as a merchant or a servant), political life (such as a king, ruler, or soldier), and familial life (marriage itself seen as vocation). Calvin further develops this line of thinking, suggesting that God provides for and appoints duties to everyone and even humble work may be willingly done knowing the task has been given by God and will bear fruit (Calvin 3.10.6).[7] Alister McGrath sums up the point for Calvin:

> Activity within the world, motivated, informed, and sanctioned by Christian faith, was the supreme means by which the believer could demonstrate his or her commitment and thankfulness to God. To do anything for God, and to do it well, was the fundamental hallmark of authentic Christian faith. Diligence and dedication in one's everyday life are, Calvin thought, a proper response to God. (McGrath 33)

The Christian is "called" by God to service, having a vocation to glorify God that can be taken up in many stations and walks of life.

In this way, the idea of the priesthood of all believers inspired an impulse to activism, motivating reform not just in the church but also in the secular world and in personal life. Calvin promoted the ideal that society as a whole should be oriented to God, and his administrative leadership in Geneva sought to model such a conception. In his view, every action in public and private life should be slanted toward embodying faith and improving things through useful employment, diligence, thriftiness, moderation, and enterprise. Later Calvinists, such as the Puritans in England and later in North America, took this further to suggest that virtue and productivity in life was a mark of faith, a sign providing evidence that one was saved by God and among the elect. Early twentieth-century sociologist Max Weber famously used the term "Protestant work ethic" to describe the character of such an exhortation to higher standards of discipline and hard work. Weber argued that this helped pave the way for capitalism by encouraging personal prosperity and saving money for investments. Whether or not this is the case, such an ethic was clearly part of an overall Protestant aim to make over and sanctify church and society. And it was built upon the assumption that God's work could be manifest in every person of faith.[8]

Related to the two other leading themes of Protestantism—the priority of God's grace received in faith and the Bible's authority in matters of faith and living—the idea of the priesthood of all believers strongly influenced varieties of Protestant thought, both liberal and conservative, and practice up to the present. It not only raises up the value and dignity of the individual before God and underscores the related importance of personal faith but also introduces a principle of prophetic critique holding all human projects and institutions accountable to God and opening up room for creative protest and the possibility of transformation by refusing to settle on any finite agenda, belief, or practice as final and absolute, identical with the divine itself. This has sometimes been called the "Protestant principle," springing from the recognition of God's sovereignty and the living character of the gospel (Dillenberger and Welch 349–50). It undergirds the often cited motto "church reformed is always reforming" (*ecclesia reformata semper reformanda*), which suggests that Protestantism is itself subject to ongoing creative criticism and reformation. The populist and egalitarian ramifications of this have not been lost on underprivileged and marginalized populations, in the earliest days inspiring cases of peasant uprisings. Moreover, it has not only encouraged pluralism among Protestant churches, molding new forms of church association that are voluntary and self-directed, but has also grown in influence to shape broader political discourse on individual rights and representational democratic governance. It has furthermore informed various movements for equality and social justice—North American examples being the woman-suffrage and abolitionist movements of the nineteenth century, the Social Gospel movement of the early twentieth century, and the more recent civil-rights and liberationist movements (see Wogaman, "Protestantism and Politics").

As Protestantism today is represented worldwide by a diversity of peoples and innumerable groups of churches and denominations, a growing appreciation for differences and a desire to acknowledge what is shared as Christians has helped create momentum toward cooperation among churches and fostered greater activism in social justice. With roots in the 1910 World

Missionary Conference in Edinburgh (which later blossomed into the World Council of Churches founded in 1948), a spirit of ecumenism or collaboration and dialogue among churches has helped build bridges among some historically divided Protestant groups and inspire new efforts at rapprochement with Catholicism (especially since the Second Vatican Council, 1962–1965). In the context of rapid globalization, a new spirit of cooperation with non-Christian religious traditions has also emerged. Furthermore, a growing awareness of the reality of past and present injustices affecting women, racialized groups, economically underprivileged groups, LGBTQ people, and people with disabilities, coupled with a new recognition of the presence of diverse Protestant Christians from post-colonial contexts in the Global South, has uncovered fertile ground for further reform in Protestant communities. It has helped to spawn renewed focus on the biblical injunctions to love one's neighbor, show hospitality to the stranger, and live in solidarity with the marginalized and poor. It is within such larger themes that attention to disability among Protestants today takes place, not merely as a side issue but as fundamental to understanding the nature of God, human beings, and what it means to be Christian.

HARNESSING A DISABILITY STUDIES PERSPECTIVE:
ASSESSING SOME TRADITIONAL PROTESTANT
APPROACHES TO DISABILITY

The leading themes of historic Protestantism discussed so far have direct bearing on framing attention to disability for faith communities. Yet it has been only recently that new insights from disability studies have pried open pathways for changes in attitudes and practices toward people with disabilities. As taken up among Protestant communities, such insights build upon biblical ideals of love and justice to move the experience and knowledge of disability from the margins to the center of social awareness, not simply as an object of care or as something wrong but as a feature of vulnerable human life as loved by God in all its embodied diversity. In this way, giving priority to a disability perspective helps expose and critique patterns of discrimination and modes of representation that stigmatize disability as an abnormal and defective aberration in need of cure or containment. David Mitchell notes: "Nearly every culture views disability as a problem in need of a solution. . . . The necessity for developing various kinds of cultural accommodations to handle the 'problem' of corporeal difference . . . situates people with disabilities in a profoundly ambivalent relation to the cultures and stories they inhabit" (15). Protestant Christianity is no exception, often investing disability with cultural meanings propped up by problematic theological conceptions and restrictive interpretations of Scripture. Common examples include understanding disability as a sign of tragedy or deficiency—even to the point of presuming that disability equates to a lack of faith, a blameworthy moral fault, or spiritual imperfection.

These meanings reveal tensions in Protestantism that belie its positive features and which a disability studies perspective can help to foreground so as to disrupt the status quo and generate new vistas of reform, even retooling the Christian imagination. Thus, this section will outline primary components of a disability studies perspective, moving then to assess problematic features endemic to traditional Christian approaches to disability that Protestants have regularly adopted uncritically. This section paves the way for a final section that will take up the three leading themes in Protestantism (discussed above) as constructively retrieved by a handful of current (mainly Protestant) authors operating from a disability studies perspective.

One provocative means employed by disability studies to disrupt common perceptions of disability has been to relocate its subject matter. The subject of disability studies is not the individual with an impairment, such as a person who uses a wheelchair or lives with a mental illness. Rather, it is the complex set of social processes and relations within which the embodied experience and knowledge of disability becomes salient. The focus shifts away from particular bodies that have problems, which are objectified as predicaments to be remedied by medical treatment or managed by caregiving assistance, to examining the means by which disability itself becomes imagined, attributed to particular bodies, and made over into a problem. The contrast is often typified as between the "medical model" and the "social model" of disability. While the former understands disability to be an impairment of the individual with resulting personal and social consequences, the latter takes it to be a factor of the relationship between an impairment and social environment. Disability represents a diminishment relative to a social context of valuation and its conventions, a perceived lack of ability to function in ways esteemed by a group, the consequences of which lead to social restrictions, exclusion, and discrimination (see Oliver and Barnes, *New Politics*; Shakespeare, *Disability Rights*).

Disability studies thus represents a "paradigm shift" away from thinking about disability as a "personal predicament" and toward conceiving of it as a "social pathology" (Goodley xi). The problem or pathology lies not in the individual but rather in the system; society is disabling in how it erects barriers limiting the experiences of certain kinds of bodies. This insight reflects developments that took shape among activists in the 1970s and 1980s as people with disabilities and their allies joined together to resist discrimination and advocate for human rights, seeking to widen conceptions of accessibility beyond "pity" and "charity" models toward full inclusion (see Shapiro, *No Pity*; Charlton, *Nothing about Us*). Some scholars note how the social model can lead to excesses—for not all the experienced disadvantages of impairments are external—produced by and resulting from society (Shakespeare, *Disability Rights*, 38–43). Nonetheless, as Lennard J. Davis notes, disability is part of a "social process that intimately involves everyone" and is a feature of society's way of imagining and producing prototypical or normal bodies; disability and normalcy are part of the same system (Davis, *Enforcing Normalcy*, 2, 48–49).

Crucial for assessing Protestantism in relation to disability, the focus then shifts away from curative and caregiving interventions to a critical interrogation of the assumptions and conventions structuring normalcy (see Titchkosky and Michalko, "Introduction"). For disability studies calls attention "to how the discrepancies between actual bodies and expected bodies are characterized within particular cultural contexts" such as faith communities (Garland-Thomson, "Disability Studies," 917). This wider focus entails an interdisciplinary framework of reference that renders the category "disability" itself unstable, complex, and open to various religious interpretations. Not only does disability become manifest in diverse ways (e.g., physically and cognitively, as chronic pain and mental illnesses), it also intersects with other experiences of marginalization on the basis of race, gender, sexuality, and class.[9] Disability is not a natural condition or property located in individual bodies but an interactive site conditioned by varied social, cultural, political, and religious factors. Even designations of impairments are interactive in this way: what counts as an impairment is a social judgment varying according to context, and some impairments are caused and exacerbated by social arrangements (Shakespeare, *Disability Rights*, 34–35).

Accordingly, a disability perspective opens up important transformative implications, which factor in reconsidering Protestant faith in relation to disability. It reverses the stigmatizing gaze or stare away from disability and back upon the social—and religious—system as the source of stigma assignment (see Garland-Thomson, *Staring*). In this way, in Rod Michalko's terms, disability becomes like a mirror reflecting back to society its own formative biases, exposing values and ideals that work negatively to devalue and marginalize different forms of embodiment (168), which in many cases, as will be documented shortly, are given religious justification. Revealed are the cracks in society's pathological pretenses to normalcy, its preoccupation with shoring up resources against deviation by enforcing processes of normalization that regulate and come to "expect" certain kinds of "able" bodies (Davis,

Enforcing Normalcy; Reynolds, *Vulnerable Communion*, ch. 2). Additionally revealed are the ways that normalcy functions to produce and privilege what Garland-Thomson calls the "normate" figure—that is, the prototypical able or normalized ideal "by which people can represent themselves as definitive human beings" (*Extraordinary Bodies*, 8). Thus it becomes possible to explore how Protestantism and normalcy have colluded in ways that call for change.

Indeed, that normalcy is exposed as a social construction means also that it is not natural and can be deconstructed. The mirror of disability is not neutral; in reflecting back, it also sends disruptive shock waves unsettling normalcy's measure of the worthwhile and good life. For disability presents a different way of being in the world, and the reality of such difference disturbs the constraints of the ordinary and turns the status quo upside down. It provokes a confrontation with society's fears and assumptions about meaningful bodies and forces a reexamination of ableist mechanisms of exclusion and normalization. In this way, as bell hooks notes, the margins are more than sites of repression, they also can be generative sites of resistance and resilience ("Marginality," 342). From a disability studies perspective, disability acts as a kind of prophetic provocation opening alternative possibilities for reimagining living together outside normalcy and welcoming different forms of embodiment as distinctive, worthwhile, and productive means of experiencing and finding meaning in the world (Garland-Thomson, *Staring*; see also Straus, *Extraordinary Measures*). Rather than making over people with disabilities to fit the system—assimilating disability through normalizing rehabilitative strategies or making it altogether disappear through curative technique or exclusion/segregation—perhaps the system itself may become more flexible in valuing, expecting, and letting bodily difference be.

Such a perspective resonates with the prophetic, liberative, and redemptive heartbeat of the gospel message of love, connecting with core Protestant themes outlined above—such as God's offer of grace outside systems of ability or "works," each person equal in value and status before God, a "priest" called to contribute. It also presents a way of understanding how attitudes toward disability in Protestant communities often do operate under the sway of normalcy. Certain fears, beliefs, values, and assumptions prevail in theological and biblical understandings, acting as a distortive undertow driving practices that demean and damage from the very place of faith that otherwise intends to affirm and empower. This amounts to, in Brett Webb-Mitchell's words, "the betrayal of people with disabilities" (9). So it is important to assess—through the "mirror" of disability—how these negative means of stigmatizing disability hold power and draw from biblical and theological resources to create "folk theologies" that are inadequate and even harmful to people with disabilities but which commonly appear across Christian traditions, not only in Protestant faith communities. From here, in the final section, it will be possible to use a disability studies lens to revisit and examine some of the core elements of Protestantism (namely, the priority of God's grace, the authority of the Bible, and the "priesthood of all believers"), developing insights from current writers in the field of theology and disability in relation to these as a vehicle of ongoing reform and transformation in Protestant communities.

Common among perceptions of disability as a flaw are conceptions that associate it with divine causality. Accounting for the experience of disability via supernatural influences, the body is treated as an index of transcendent meanings—or, in more specific Christian terms, as a site for interpreting a person's status in relation to God. Disability thus has physiognomic features, that is, a deprivation that signals inner character traits and deeper spiritual or moral realities (Yong 63–64). Worst-case scenarios (such as Luther's comment about drowning a child with disabilities) perceive disability as a subhuman threat to others, the work of the devil. It was a common belief in Luther's day that the devil took on forms—sometimes attributed to misshapen human figures and diseases—that were a danger to be resisted (see Heuser, "Human Condition"). But still today, in many ways disability is interpreted in Christian terms as a physiognomic sign of God's absence, something indicating deeper disturbing and threatening meanings that must be resisted and put away. For example, well-meaning Christians have inquired about potential evil or demonic forces at work in some behaviors representative of the autistic spectrum.[10] Interpretations of certain mental illnesses and epilepsy have also drawn similar conclusions, influenced by stories from the New Testament scriptures about demonic possession. Fear of the disruption of disability, according to systems of normalcy, often ushers in a desire to account for disability by designating underlying causes—in this case, destructive spiritual forces.

That disability is perceived as a dangerous flaw, not just to the person with disabilities but to those around that person, also links up with viewpoints that consider disability a curse or the result of sin. Here, moral or spiritual meaning is given to disability by assigning blame to the individual in a kind of physiognomic chain of causation. For if God is thought to be a moral ruler and providential influence over human life and disability is assumed to be a bodily defect accompanied by suffering out of which nothing good can come, it is a short path to considering disability a product of God's intentions, the direct result of wrongdoing on the part of a person or family. Like proportionate judgment follows a crime, disability is a measureable consequence of sin, signaling a corresponding moral or spiritual blemish. The Bible contains examples of this logic, linking righteousness with blessing and sinfulness with suffering as a punishment or curse, whether this is collective—as in the case of guilt and suffering on the part of the Israelites for failing as a people to honor their covenant with God—or individual, as in Job's friends, who falsely surmise that he has brought suffering upon himself (Job 4:7-9, 8:4-7, 11:14-20), or in passages like those in Proverbs that state, "Misfortune pursues sinners, but prosperity rewards the righteous" (Prov 13:21). Jesus himself illustrates it when encountering a man he has just healed: "See, you have been made well! Sin no more, that nothing worse befall you" (John 5:14). The stigmatization of disability as a desecration or harmful flaw is thus given religious rationale.[11]

Interpretations like these, which give negative moral and spiritual meaning to disability, were common in Jesus' time and unfortunately persist today among many Protestant communities. Part of the reason for the persistence is that they, as in the examples above, are rooted in aspects of the biblical literature. Here lies a difficulty with the Protestant reliance on the Bible as the normative text in Christian life, one that continues to shape its readers' attitudes and practices. When interpreted simplistically, selectively (even literally), and without a depth of contextual and historical understanding, scriptural passages can be appropriated in ways detrimental to people with disabilities, unwittingly reproducing normalcy as a hermeneutical vantage point. Recent studies by biblical scholars and theologians alike have noted this problem.[12] Yet trends in some Protestant traditions, influenced by Fundamentalism, exacerbate the predicament by understanding the Bible to be a univocal and complete deposit of truth revealed directly by God, literally God's word (instead of a varied collection of human testimonies to God's saving presence written in specific contexts). Orientations like this can grant unqualified authority to select biblical references that depict disability as a curse. This not only overlooks the Bible's ambivalence on disability—for example, the many biblical references to disability as productive of meanings beyond flaw or curse (as in Moses' "stutter" in Exod 4:10-12, Jacob's "limp" in Gen 32:22-32, and Paul's "weakness" in 2 Cor 12:5-10, not to mention the disabling "wounds" that remain a focus of Jesus' resurrected body in the Gospel accounts)—it conceals and reaffirms ableist biases in readers, biases that operate in advance and govern the hermeneutic selection of particular texts as definitive over others, ironically making the Bible fit normalcy even while claiming "authority" as a solely scriptural account. Thus, simplistic and selective approaches to the Bible can serve circularly to justify pretensions to normalcy rather than attend to the complexity, polyphony, and ambiguity of the Bible itself as a normative collection of texts.

Evidence of this is found in many practices of faith healing. Only here, instead of stigmatizing disability as a sign of divine absence or punishment in a gesture of fatalistic resignation, the attention is focused on actively removing disability by divine intervention. Analogous to modern medical approaches that view disability as an affliction, yet with a focus on supernatural intervention and a corresponding stress on the spiritual or moral transformation of the person, healing employs divine power as a resource for restoration, "making right" what has gone wrong. Healing narratives from New Testament accounts of Jesus' ministry are key resources for this conception among Christians. These stories portray his healing powers as a demonstration that God was doing something special through him.[13] And, as Colleen Grant notes, they generally serve a twofold function in the Gospels. They either illustrate the messianic status of Jesus, focusing not on the people healed but instead on Jesus as the Christ, the Messiah, emphasizing his authority, for example, to forgive sin (which only God can do) or heal on the Sabbath (which went against Jewish law). Or, if they focus on those healed, they do so to illustrate qualities of discipleship and faith in Jesus (Grant 73–74). In the first sense, Jesus' power to forgive sins often correlates to healing people, confirming the link between sin and disability—for example, Mark 2:1-12 tells of a paralyzed man to whom Jesus communicates that his sins are forgiven as he is healed (Grant 75). In the second sense, the stories often attribute successful healing to the faith of the person, a sign of spiritual transformation for those who were healed.[14] Under the sway of normalcy, both depictions provide motivation in church communities for identifying disability as a means to demonstrate God's healing power, expecting success in its removal but attributing blame to the person—their lack of faith—when attempts to heal fail. Nancy Eiesland notes, "Failure to be healed is often assessed as a personal flaw in the individual, such as unrepentant sin or a selfish desire to remain disabled" (*Disabled God*, 117). The implication is that remaining disabled is a matter of lack of faith.

The logic here, of expectation and resultant blame, serves to objectify and demean people with disabilities. Not only does this individualize disability as a flaw, it also introduces further social burden by making people with disabilities responsible for their own condition and cure. Further, it presents people with disabilities as agents only insofar as they desire restoration, willfully seeking to become able bodied, symbols of brokenness in need of and pursuing wholeness on normalcy's terms. The Bible can be read in a way that fuels such dynamics, as people with illnesses and disabilities are largely invisible in the healing narratives except as they appear as object lessons (Carter 130–31). David Mitchell and Sharon Snyder make the point starkly: "Not only does the New Testament cultivate social contexts that expect the eradication of disability as a resolution to human-made exclusion, it does so by depicting disabled people as the agents of their own curative ambitions" (179). People with disabilities thus bear the burden of a pathology that is socially derived, compelled to internalize normalcy's stigmatizing gaze and take responsibility for their own cure. This is reinforced by the Bible's metaphorical use of blindness, deafness, paralysis, and the like to convey moral and spiritual states requiring transformation. Individual bodies become indexes of transcendent meanings that embed normalcy.

There are, however, subtle moves in the texts to undercut such simplistic interpretations, complicating overly selective appropriations of Scripture. An illustrative story from the Gospel of John adds further dimension to this discussion. John 9:1-41 references Jesus' disciples encountering a blind man about whom they ask Jesus, "Who sinned, this man or his parents, that he was born blind" (John 9:2). In a striking reply, Jesus subverts the common assumption that disability is a consequence of sin, claiming that neither the man's parents nor he had sinned to cause the disability, but rather that "the works of God may be made manifest in him" (9:3), his healing giving witness to Jesus' status as God's anointed one. The narrative also subverts the causal link between healing and faith, as the man is healed without any stated expectation and only gradually develops an articulation of faith as he confronts challengers (9:24-34). Furthermore, the blind man is not represented as one who seeks out his own healing (Grant 75–85). Even so, however, he is still portrayed as an object lesson highlighting the "works of God" through Jesus and the man's own growing discipleship. So this text is ambiguous and contains contrasting elements to the stereotypical interpretations of disability mentioned above, even as it also contains some of these residual components. The point is that this story complicates glib interpretations that would simply reassert normalcy (Yong 50–57). Addressing these and other subtleties and ambivalences in the Bible is an important and fruitful way for Protestants, who assert the authoritative import of Scripture for Christian life, to harness insights from a disability studies perspective. It critically engages and redeems biblical texts from interpretive barriers erected in the clutches of normalcy and, in so doing, continues the work of reform.

There are, however, still other demeaning depictions of disability, which although moving beyond the more overtly negative ones discussed above still remain rooted in Protestant traditions. Examples of this emerge around the meaning of care. While churches have always shown interest in caring for the sick and poor as part of Jesus' mandate to love others, conceptions of what such care involves have been distorted by understandings of disability as a deficiency demonstrative of pity and need, and so have continued to stigmatize its presence and create barriers (Eiesland, *Disabled God*, 73–74). Disability historian Henri-Jacques Stiker details how New Testament ideals motivated the development of "systems of charity" in medieval Christian Europe (65–89). Rather than abandoning people with disabilities, as was common in antiquity, care, like hospices, were established to provide sustenance and shelter as a means of showing mercy. Several things are implied here: First, disability is represented as a dreaded loss of bodily integrity, assigned with meanings equivalent to personal tragedy, an example for others of the ruinous imperilments possible for the human body. Second, disability provided Christians with the means to grow in virtue by following the example of God's mercy and care, people with disabilities functioning as "springboards for charity" (Stiker 88). Not only does such a charity model create paternalistic dynamics of unilateral giving *to* and doing *for* people with disabilities, as if disability sums up the life of a person and renders her or him a passive and helpless recipient of the gifts of others; it also instrumentalizes people with disabilities as vehicles for able-bodied persons to demonstrate goodwill and grow in faith. Deserving of pity, disability becomes an object lesson in human misfortune and Christian charity. This approach has been adopted in various ways among Protestant churches whose care practices are limited by imagining disability as a tragedy requiring assistance from and management by others as a path to salvation (see Snyder and Mitchell 51–60). It underpins attitudes of low expectations toward people with disabilities, marginalizing them as resource drains to be tolerated or given pastoral care rather than accepted as contributing participants.

Another approach common in Protestant faith communities—and not far removed from the charity model—represents disability as a test of faith, an opportunity for heroic overcoming, or an inspiration for others. These are grouped together because they each entail a physiognomic remaking of disability into something positive, something with measurable instrumental value. Often such value is demonstrated in terms associated with the Protestant work ethic and its mandate to display faithfulness and achieve blessing through diligence, service, and overcoming of adversity. This value framework buoys conceptions of normalcy in modern societies, fueling ideals of individual autonomy, efficiency, and productivity as normative for bodies (Reynolds, *Vulnerable Communion*, ch. 3). A body acquires worth and meaning within a scheme of expectation, which anticipates usefulness for the world. Yet since disability in systems of normalcy is expected to be useless, of no worldly good or service, there is either the urge to dismiss it by exclusion, eliminate it by healing, or reimagine it as useful and somehow advantageous, an example of faith for inspiring others. In this way, moving beyond charity approaches, faith communities project their own need to make meaning of disability upon people with disabilities, mapping positive value onto bodies deemed otherwise deficient. Not only are such physiognomic interpretations objectifying and instrumentalizing, and thus largely inadequate to the experience of people with disabilities (Eiesland, "Barriers and Bridges," 218; Creamer 35–36), they serve instead to fortify a community's commitment to normalcy and further entrench stigmatizing attitudes and practices of marginalization and reproduce problematic theological notions rooted in one-dimensional readings of Scripture.

There are several (sometimes subtle) ways this occurs in Christian frames of reference; disabled bodies becoming a kind of screen onto which deeper theological meanings are projected. First, in a kind of value reversal, disability is referenced as a "cross to bear," a negative affliction with positive religious value for the individual. Drawing upon the theme of redemptive suffering—that is, interpreting challenges in life as opportunities given by God for developing character and growing in faith, even a test or trial to demonstrate faith—disability becomes a vehicle for acquiring and displaying spiritual ideals and virtues (Black 25–28). Perceived as a cross to bear, disability amounts to a struggle like the cross was for Jesus, requiring an inner composition of steadfast faith, fortitude, and humble openness to the larger purposes of God. The apostle Paul's acknowledgment of his "thorn in the flesh" and "weakness" is often cited in this context as an encouragement to view suffering as a portage into deeper reliance upon God in Christ, an ironic strength through weakness: "for whenever I am weak, then I am strong"—in the power of Christ (2 Cor 12:7-10, 12:10). Yet when non-disabled persons use such conceptions to interpret the experience of disability for people with disabilities, the result romanticizes disability as a personal blessing in disguise. An expectation to suffer virtuously is placed on the individual, disability being a personal pathology to be endured and transformed internally into spiritual gain. Such practice reflects the paternalism of the charity model, and it can also encourage resignation to what is actually an unjust social imposition. As Nancy Eiesland puts it, "Similar to the practice of emphasizing self-sacrifice to women, the theology of virtuous suffering has encouraged persons with disabilities to acquiesce to social barriers as a sign of obedience to God and to internalize second-class status inside and outside the church" (*Disabled God*, 73).

Related to this are romanticized treatments of disability that focus on its social value, remaking disability as a useful means to benefit the community. This kind of "social blessing" model of disability becomes apparent in heroic tales of personal overcoming, of achieving victory despite adversity, by which people with disabilities are deployed as inspiration for others. Noteworthy is how the burden of obtaining the status of inspiration is placed onto people with disabilities, concealing the social mechanisms of normalcy at work that individualize disability. Not only do people with disabilities bear the mark of society's diminishment; they must also now overcome such diminishment themselves within an expectation of social usefulness, becoming inspirational. This double-layered pattern is hidden sometimes in references to disability as a "cross to bear," a chance to be heroic and overcome deficits. It also surfaces in interpretations of stories from the Bible about characters through whom God worked "despite" their disability to achieve great things—such as Moses with his speech impediment—the lesson being that God can make *even* disability gainful for divine purposes. The deficiency thus becomes surmounted, essentially doing away with the disability in the public imagination. Statements still heard on Sunday mornings in church worship like "overcoming depression," "conquering disability," or "God's ability through our lack of ability" testify to the prevalence of such renderings of disability.

It is important to note yet another version of the "social blessing" model, which remakes disability into a social benefit. It comes out in references that designate disability as a sign of blessing to the community, a person deemed gifted somehow because of their disability, perceived as having unusually developed spiritual sensitivities or abilities. Such physiognomy interprets disability as a gift, reversing the negative interpretation as a curse or sign of punishment. The person here becomes exceptional *because of* the disability, both summed up by the disability and blessed by it as a gift to others. This logic can be expressed in various ways: in suggestions that a person with disabilities is "special"; in statements that people with Down syndrome are uniquely spiritual; or in statements that the experience of depression is a gift leading to self-discovery. While in some cases a person's disability in one area may augment perceptions or capacities in other areas, it is not necessarily the case and assuming so generalizes about the experience of disability. Further, such depictions of disability can be romanticizing, reducing people with disabilities to spectacles put on display as "gifted" for the benefit of others. Accordingly, disability becomes redeemable for church communities insofar as it fosters assets esteemed by the group, revealing something of the divine in some way. This reveals more about normalcy's desperate discomfort with disabled bodies and the need to find value in what is otherwise deemed worthless than it does about disability. In each case here, though, the common denominator is that disability is remade in the image of something useful and palatable—an individual or social blessing.

Thus, incorporating a disability studies perspective calls into question many traditional theological conceptions and ways of interpreting biblical texts in Protestant Christianity. It fosters a hermeneutic of suspicion (a critical interpretive standpoint that does not take things at face value without questioning), interrogating common beliefs and practices from the position of disability as a marginalized human experience. This can disrupt pretensions to normalcy in faith communities that are sanctioned by Christian idioms, resisting ableist attitudes and practices that devalue people with disabilities and press them to adopt and internalize standards of normalcy. Specifically, such a standpoint exposes and critiques common portrayals of disability as an embodied deficiency with transcendent physiognomic meanings, provoking possibilities for reform by inviting constructive alternatives. This requires revisiting leading themes in Protestantism through a different means, not only avoiding the perils of normalcy, but also retrieving the subversive and liberative power of key Christian themes. The challenge, which many Protestant scholars are now taking up, is to articulate anew the gospel's power to disrupt normalcy and make possible new ways of living together in embodied differences, one in which disability is recognized as "integral to embodied experience" and people with disabilities are welcome participants in community life (Mitchell and Snyder 181).

TOWARD NEW HORIZONS IN THE THEOLOGY OF DISABILITY FOR PROTESTANTS

Recent scholarship informed by a disability studies perspective in Protestant circles suggests new ways to deepen key themes from the Protestant Reformation, steering away from problematic undertows developed by demeaning portrayals of disability. New approaches highlight that disability itself does not need to be redeemed but is an integral part of finite human limits and vulnerability (see Creamer, *Disability and Christian Theology*; Reynolds, *Vulnerable Communion*). What needs redeeming are the processes of marginalization that create barriers to fruitful participation in community life for people with disabilities, barriers that are physical/architectural, social/attitudinal, political/structural, and theological/spiritual in nature. In this way, questions of access become fundamental, as disability "mirrors" or reflects back the ways normalcy infects beliefs and practices central to Christianity, prophetically provoking transformation and opening new ways of being vulnerably human together in the grace of God. Building upon the three leading themes of Protestantism discussed earlier, this final section will discuss recent scholarship around the clusters of God's grace and human worth, approaches to the Bible pertaining to disability, and the priesthood of all believers in an effort to highlight prospects for ongoing reform in faith communities.

The priority of God's grace over human mechanisms that would control it by parsing it according to finite standards managed by a privileged group resonates with disability studies in several ways. First, as a critique of "works righteousness," it resists limiting God's love to a reward for human achievement, something bestowed according to abilities or capacities framed within normalcy and measured by criteria that favor only a select few. God is sovereign and free and from a prodigal abundance offers the gift of grace for all. The worth of human life ultimately resides in God's inestimable and gratuitous welcome, which transcends every system of normalcy (Reynolds, *Vulnerable Communion*, chs. 5–6). This radical intuition of the Reformers cuts to the core of the gospel message: the good news of Jesus Christ for Christians is that God reaches out lovingly to embrace people where they are, as they are, neither because of virtues and abilities nor because of vices or disabilities. This subverts physiognomic interpretations of disability. All people fall short of the glory of God, being sinful (Rom 3:23); and yet all are loved into being by God and accepted into the love of God and so should accept one another (Rom 15:7). Divine grace thus undercuts the ability/disability distinction as of any merit for estimating human worth and importing moral and spiritual meanings onto disabled bodies. It also undercuts the illusion of self-sufficiency and control before God, for divine grace searches out and grasps human beings prior to any effort on their part, making it a gift, not an achievement. This exposes the illusion of normalcy for what it is: a dehumanizing means of regulating bodies by deeming certain human features and abilities as normative, thus creating prejudice and erecting barriers between people. In fact, returning to the Protestant principle, normalcy is itself an idol that warrants critique because it feigns possession of packaging value and worth, when indeed only God is ultimate. God's love extravagantly transgresses human-made boundaries and barriers; even more, it relativizes and levels them, liberating all held captive by their power, those who are marginalized as well as those who marginalize, and opening all to consider each other as neighbor, loved by God.

Recently works by several authors have accented the point, stressing that the unique value of human life depends not upon calculations made in the clutches of normalcy but upon God's inestimable and unrestricted affirmation and acceptance. Ethicist and theologian Hans Reinders, for example, develops this insight with reference to people with profound intellectual disabilities. He argues that being fully human is an endowment grounded unconditionally in the love of God that is not based upon abilities or potentialities such as purposive agency or quantifiable self-awareness. The value of human life comes extrinsically; it is a divine gift of love (38–39). For Reinders, this is the basic sense behind the statement that human beings are created "in the image of God" (Gen 1:26). And it plays out further in that God, in Christ and through the Holy Spirit, has graciously chosen to be a friend of humankind, not because of its particular abilities or lack of abilities but out of love, which is an invitation for all to receive. In turn, moving beyond charity models, Reinders suggests receiving the gift of friendship means receiving others, including people with profound disabilities, as worthy gifts of a God who has chosen all people. This requires willingness to "be with" another in an acknowledging of one's own need for friendship that blurs the lines between giving and receiving; indeed, there is nothing to *give* other than what has been "graciously received," and this animates not pity but a dynamic of "paying it forward" (319). The divine gift of friendship is revealed by perceiving others in the light of God's unconditional love.

John Swinton, a practical theologian, echoes similar ideas in a somewhat different direction in his book on dementia. His concern is to avoid reducing dementia to medical definitions and neurological accounts, which proceed by way of an emphasis on defect that individualizes the narrative as one of loss—of memory and of self. Instead, in order to "redescribe" dementia in more pastoral focus, Swinton proposes a social and relational account of personhood rooted in theological understanding such that despite their loss of memories people with dementia are held close in the memories of God, their identity intact, known intimately from before time and unconditionally accepted eternally. To be a person is to be a member of the human race (156); and to be human is to be gifted and loved by God, dependent as a creature in embodied, spiritual, and relational aspects, making dementia more than merely neurological (160–85). In the end, being human is not so much a matter of human cognitive capacities, and spirituality is not so much a factor of human knowledge about and remembrance of God, all of which are lost in dementia. It is rather a matter of divine love, of being known and remembered by God: "To be human is to be held in the memory of God" (211). And ultimately, "It is not a person's memory that assures his/her identity; it is the memory of God and, by proxy, the memory of others" (212). Thus, in the arc of Swinton's "redescription," Christians are called to be present to, name, and hold persons with dementia in care as friends of time, remembering whose they are—God's—in a community where all belong. As in Reinders' work, the focus on God's grace here reorients beliefs and practices significantly beyond assumptions of normalcy where human nature is a factor of abilities or achievements and disability is a flaw detracting from an otherwise normative body.

In fact, human nature is a matter of embodied limits (Creamer 31–34, 93–96, 108–12) and vulnerability (Reynolds 104–32), neither of which should be considered a pathology or deficit but instead as neutral, intrinsic, and even valuable features of human life. For theologian Deborah Creamer, limits are not negative limitations, things defined by what they cannot do, but rather a "quality of being" with definitive boundaries that make possible certain realities and actions (93–94). The alternative, a deficit model of anthropology, begins from the positing of a normative condition and from this vantage point focuses on what is lacking, disability framed as an unusual and abnormal defect. A limits model, on the other hand, begins with disability as one of the intrinsic features of "normal" embodied existence, theologically understood as part of a good creation (94–96). Rather than being an exception to the rule, disability is a reminder of limits and how they manifest differently in human life, some being more profound than others (32). For Creamer, this challenges "binary categories of 'us' and 'them'" and invites the recognition "that it is not only those who are labeled 'disabled' that experience limits; limits are something inherent in the experience of humanity. Rather than identifying this as an inherently negative or evil characteristic, limits are understood to be part of creation" (109). Disability is about difference, not as a defect but as a manifestation of embodied limits in a good creation loved into being by God (109–11; see also Reynolds 151–68).

It is within such limits that God encounters humanity in solidarity through Jesus Christ, which, as Nancy Eiesland notes, entails a fundamental resymbolizing of God in ways that subvert dominant symbols creating barriers to participation in the church for people with disabilities. For Eiesland, the understanding of God incarnate in Jesus as the Christ means that God identifies with human bodies in a way that makes the limits and vulnerabilities of bodies "partially constitutive of God" (*Disabled God*, 99). If Jesus is Emmanuel, God with us (Matt 1:22-23), embodied interdependence is a central ingredient, not absolute power and control. God shares the divine self with humanity and also participates in humanity in all its elements, including a tragic death on the cross. In this, God reveals the divine nature as compassion not only by "undergoing" or "suffering with" human limits and vulnerability but also by raising them up into God's own being. This is what made the resurrection crucial for the disciples' understanding of who Jesus was in connection to God. Eiesland puts it eloquently:

> In the resurrected Jesus Christ, they saw not the suffering servant for whom the last and more important word was tragedy and sin, but the disabled God who embodied both impaired hands and feet and pierced side and the imago Dei. Paradoxically, in the very act commonly understood as the transcendence of physical life, God is revealed as tangible, bearing the representations of the body reshaped by injustice and sin into the fullness of the Godhead. (99–100)

The fact that Jesus' body remains scarred in the resurrection signals that God is "with us" in the fullness of embodied limits and contingencies; he is disabled.

Importantly, this does not negate limits by representing the ideal invulnerable and perfectly whole human body. Rather, it reveals that God is in solidarity with humanity, that God knows injustice and experiences vulnerability and, moreover, discloses a new humanity, one "underscoring the reality that full personhood is fully compatible with the experience of disability" (Eiesland, *Disabled God*, 100). Here, the image of God in humanity is inclusive of disability, not despite it but through it. For the image of Christ as the disabled God repudiates physiognomic interpretations that link disability with either defective or romanticized spiritual conditions. And this delegitimizes theological rationales for marginalization of disability through stigmatization. The effect is liberating, transforming biases against people with disabilities and enabling "both a struggle for justice among people with disabilities and an end to estrangement from our own bodies" (105). Though some have criticized Eiesland's liberationist, minority-group approach for representing only a small segment of the disabled population—namely, those identified as self-representing agents experiencing marginalization—thus leaving out consideration of people with profound disabilities (cf. Reinders 165–80), her analysis still connects to major themes discussed from the work of Reinders, Swinton, and Creamer. It highlights God's grace over mechanisms of human valuation, conditioned as they are by normalcy, and underscores the vulnerability and limits of embodied human life as inclusive of disability. She links the two themes brilliantly in a Christology (or conception of Jesus Christ) that resymbolizes God as disabled. God identifies with the experience of finitude and disability such that it becomes part of God's own being, so that to exclude one is to exclude the other. This challenges Protestant communities to reform on many levels.

The implications of these insights for reform play out in new approaches to the Bible that incorporate a disability studies perspective in order to rethink how disability is represented in Scripture. Two examples bear mentioning. The first concerns the healing narratives. In light of the above discussion, some scholars shift the interpretive focus away from a narrow sense of heal-ing, that of curing bodies as a restoration to normalcy, to a wider sense of healing as shalom, a transformation toward wholeness and well-being that includes restoration to communal belonging and renewed dignity in rela-tionships of mutual regard. Kathy Black argues along these lines, noting how, because people with disabilities and illnesses had been excluded from their communities, Jesus' "healing was liberating because it meant incorpo-ration back into these communities," allowing them to be "full participants" (12). This is not to say simplistically that the elimination of disability made restoration to community possible. Instead, it is saying that Jesus deliberately crossed social boundaries, which were established to control and contain dangerous and impure bodies, to offer radical acceptance and thus reconcile people to God, each other, and themselves in a way that brought well-being and that exposed and subverted structures perpetuating exclusion and mar-ginalization (50–54).

A key ramification is that healing can happen without cure, which takes the focus off people with disabilities as seeking a "fix" so as to con-form to standards of normalcy and be included. Amos Yong, drawing from the work of Mikeal Parsons, highlights the point in showing how Luke–Acts undercuts ways the dominant culture diminishes particular bodies as of lesser status through physiognomy. Here God's work of salvation included people otherwise belittled—for example, an Ethiopian eunuch (ethnograph-ically and anatomically devalued) and Zacchaeus (undesirable shortness of size or stature)—yet whose demeaning condition was not reversed but rather accepted as it was. This opens up a new focus on how God's libera-tive work exposes and undoes restrictive social barriers by actively embrac-ing different kinds of bodies, showing no partiality (Acts 10:34), and thus challenging discriminatory attitudes and policies based upon dominant soci-ety's standards of desirability (Yong 63–69). Healing then can be rethought in ways that emphasize broader personal and social transformation that takes place through Jesus' presence, recognizing people with disabilities as already part of God's beloved community prior to any physical transformation, in a process that makes whole, overcomes alienation, and builds truly inclusive community.

This focus correlates with the larger narrative plot of Jesus' ministry as depicted in the Gospel accounts. Jesus' ministry—including healing—calls attention to exclusion by constantly challenging the status quo and overturn-ing assumptions about what normal is, refocusing community away from the center toward the margins, welcoming the uninvited outcast as the honored guest, pointing toward those shunned by society as, in fact, treasured vessels of the new community of God (Reynolds 219–28). The prophetic call here is toward a new orientation with God that ushers in communal transformation and right relations between people, such that Jesus locates the redemptive work of God with the marginalized and excluded, those wrongly counted as problems. The Gospel of Luke announces such an agenda, as Jesus identifies himself with a passage he reads from the prophet Isaiah: "The Spirit of the Lord is upon me, because he has anointed me to preach good news to the poor. He has sent me to proclaim release to the captives and recovering of sight to the blind, to set at liberty those who are oppressed, to proclaim the acceptable year of the Lord" (4:18-19).

Other scholars pick up on this sociopolitical perspective and push even further, showing an anti-imperial dynamic of resistance at work in the healing stories, even as they also imitate and reinforce imperial stereotypes. Biblical scholar Warren Carter notes that the healing narratives can be read otherwise than through physiognomic frameworks of individual punishment, forgiveness, and restoration but instead as statements about disabled bodies as sites of what he calls "imperial incursions and contest" (145). In this way, the question "Who sinned?" (from John 9 discussed earlier) can be answered, at least in part, by pointing to "empire and every and any politico-economic-cultural system" that deprives people of resources, damaging bodies and disabling people (145). In a different way, Lutheran theologian Sharon Betcher picks up on this theme and goes in a constructive direction. She points out how biblical testimonies suggest that people with disabilities—a "Crip Nation"—play an important part in opening social spaces of non-domination and mutual regard, not merely as targets for healing but as bodies that "speak back," challenge, and interrupt the power of oppressive regimes (127–31). For example, she suggests that the rallying cry of miracle working (e.g., "the blind see, the lame walk, the deaf hear") used in the Gospels may not signify the curing of individual blemishes but rather announce the social reality of liberation from enslavement and captivity (ch. 7). Debt slaves and prisoners of war were often maimed by their captors to prevent them from fleeing. So, as employed in the Hebrew prophetic writings, attestations to miracle healings are perhaps ways the Gospels announce the coming of God's reign—the prisoners are being freed.

The fact that there were "rumors of miracles" was enough to set an empire on edge, kindling expectations of hope, raising excitement for an alternative social ordering. This lays the groundwork for decolonizing resistance and insurgency, a kind of anti-hegemonic discourse sparking the remaking of the world (Betcher 143). Aimed at the heart of empire, miracle stories trade on the concept of Jubilee referenced in Luke as the "acceptable year of the Lord"

(Luke 4:19), a redemptive process based on the Hebrew scriptures that aimed at canceling the burden of debt, thus restoring freedom and unburdening the land (150–51). Connected with the reign of God, it aims to awaken consciousness, not to pity the poor and disabled but "to loosen attachment to the enslaving economics that constricted Christians' own bodies, precisely because in those conditions they couldn't always feel imperial economics as a constraint" (152). For Betcher, the point comes to this: the healing stories can be understood within the larger arc of the gospel message of liberation, the release of those held captive by debilitating systems of indebtedness and dispossession. The promise is decolonization, not bodily cure; and it aspires to a new kind of community founded upon kinship and interdependence, not imperial rule.

The second main example of how a disabilities perspective can open up new insight on the Bible as a key resource for Protestants pertains to Paul's theology of "weakness," which can be problematic with reference to disability. However, many scholars have refocused attention on weakness and disability as a means of "speaking back to" and contesting social expectations, rather than as a site of deficiency. For instance, Paul himself spoke of his own "physical infirmity" (Gal 4:13) and his "thorn in the flesh" (2 Cor 12:7) as afflictions that facilitated not merely passive reliance upon God but a deeper understanding of the paradoxical power of God at work in Christ crucified, which challenges assumptions of normalcy that correlate strength and power with abilities and achievements.[15] Simon Horne notes how, for Paul, the "fulfillment of God's power and love occurred through Christ's inability—first when he laid aside his glory and abilities in being born in human form (2 Cor 8:9; Phil 2:6-8) and second in the stripping of his glory and abilities on the cross itself" (Horne 93). As God's power is revealed in weakness and inability in Christ, so it is revealed for Paul in his own experience of weakness and inability. It is not merely that God's "grace is sufficient" (encouraging acquiescence), but also that such divine "power is made perfect in weakness" (2 Cor 12:9), a dramatic reversal of normalcy that breathes new life, new creation (Horne 95–96). Martin Albl concurs, claiming therefore that "disability takes us to the very heart" of Paul's theology, where Christ crucified is "the ultimate symbol of disability, whether disability is considered as functional limitation or as social stigma" (57–58). Instead of a social stigma (disability associated with sin and blemish), disability is a site of productive divine power, speaking back provocatively to contest the status quo, allowing Paul to exclaim: "When I am weak, then I am strong" (2 Cor 12:10). Paul's thinking here supports Eiesland's notion that Christ symbolizes the disabled God, making the limits, vulnerability, and interdependence of embodied human existence cornerstones of the liberating message of the gospel (Reynolds 231–33).

This is not to say that the experience of disability therefore has extraordinary ability inherent to it or that people with disabilities therefore are more spiritual, as if to remake disability in romanticized terms and in the image of something more beneficial according to frameworks of normalcy. Rather, it names possibilities for "staring back" at stigmatizing gazes, prophetically exposing the pretentiousness of the sovereign claim to control, to be invulnerable and without limits. And it points to possibilities for living beyond normalcy, opening space for inhabiting alternative embodiments of human life as valuable and creative. Creamer echoes such insight in claiming that "disability is not something that exists solely as a negative experience of limitation but rather that it is an intrinsic, unsurprising, and valuable element of human limit-ness" (96). In concert with Creamer, and moving beyond the negative, Eiesland notes how experience of disability informs different ways of perceiving the world, which "like our bodies, are often nonconforming and disclose new categories and models of thinking and being" (*Disabled God*, 31).

Christian communities receptive to the possibilities represented by such embodied differences experience the subversive power of what Paul calls "weakness," in that marginal members "which seem to be weaker," "that we think less honorable," are actually "indispensable" and treated with greater honor and respect (1 Cor 12:22-23). The key here, as Amos Yong articulates, is the language of what *seems* to be weaker, and what *we think* is less honorable, which is an indictment of normalcy, a provocative rebuke of elitist and hierarchical attitudes that demean certain members of the community as worthless and deficient (Yong 93). For Paul, church is a body with many parts, none of which can denounce the other as inconsequential (1 Cor 12:21), as "God has so composed the body, giving greater honor to the [alleged] inferior part, that there may be no discord in the body, but that the members may have the same care for one another. If one member suffers, all suffer together; if one member is honored, all rejoice together" (1 Cor 12:24-26). The so-called weakest members are the key to community, for the church is a place where all people are members of one another (Rom 12:5), so that discrimination against one part "disables" the whole community. A disability studies perspective thus provides tools to reexamine "weakness" as a site of provocative disruption, calling for reform and transformation, and more, to reconceive what "being together" means. Building on this, Yong suggests Paul presents an "ecclesiology of weakness" that resists ableism and lays a foundation for perceiving all members, including those with disabilities, as contributors (Yong 93).

At this point, there are obvious links to the Protestant theme of the "priesthood of all believers." It is fitting to bring the discussion to crescendo with this notion, which stresses that all persons are of unique worth in the immeasurable circle of God's embrace and are called to distinctive vocations and given gifts as equal participants in the ministry of the church. As a Pentecostal theologian, Yong relies on Paul's assertion that the Spirit of God freely distributes gifts to all members for the common good (1 Cor 12:7) in claiming "that people with disabilities are just as capable—if not more capable—of contributing to the edification of the community of faith, and hence are necessary in that sense" (94; see also 70–80). The language is important: not "more capable" because of disability but because the Spirit chooses to work where it may, not according to hierarchical arrangement or calculable human standards of worth framed within normalcy. Yong seeks to avoid "either sentimentalizing or valorizing weakness or disability" as if to make spectacles of people with disabilities (96). For as empowered within the Spirit's sweep, many gifts and abilities are possible, making everyone both recipient and provider of care. This is perhaps the meaning of Paul's encouragement that all members "have the same care for one another" (1 Cor 12:25). The church is a place of interdependency, of giving and receiving by and for all, people with disabilities being contributors instead of only recipients of care. The potential of such a conception builds upon foundations laid by early Protestant reformers but avoids perils related to the "work ethic" and provides new directions for communities of faith to pursue love of neighbor, show solidarity, and offer hospitality with all.

Love of neighbor, as a principal ethic of compassion and justice in the Bible, in this way can be conceived as a process of mutual respect and hospitality, working outside paternalistic mechanisms that unilaterally "care for" or "do to" others. For, as Betcher puts it, the Spirit works not to impose homogenizing norms and routines of "wholeness" that cater to normalcy and invalidate disability but in "multiplying forms of corporeal flourishing," in recognizing and empowering "persons living the variability and vulnerabilities of bodies with real presence to life" (64, 70). Betcher affirms Spirit as the animating principle of all life, splaying out "affective energies" that surround us and bind us together in interdependent relationships of "hospitality to difference" (199). Spirit is not a curative force but a power that connects members of the community, healing by opening up creative agency in spaces of mutuality and shared resistance to marginalization (120–21). In this way, the biblical ethic of love of neighbor and hospitality are connected as central ingredients in the work of God's Spirit: all people are loved by God and, in turn, called to hold one another in loving regard such that receiving one another in care is a way of receiving God's gifts (Reynolds 239–47). The church, ideally, is then that place where the Spirit comes to hearth, a vulnerable communion of mutual gift exchange in which "dividing walls" based upon human ordinances are abolished (Eph 2:14-15). All belong. And since God's image includes disability, and this image dwells in all human beings, the church is summoned into a radical kind of belonging, opening up to different embodiments—including disability—as if welcoming each other is to host the divine in our midst.

CONCLUSION: BEGINNING AGAIN

This chapter has attempted to highlight significant themes in historic Protestantism and bring a disability studies perspective to bear on them, noting perils and promises. The discussion has not sought to be exhaustive in its account but rather to raise important concerns and problems that call for constructive possibilities, accenting recent scholarship among some Protestant scholars who incorporate a disability studies framework. This chapter has emphasized that—germane to the guiding spirit of self-criticism and ongoing reform in the Protestant principle—insights from disability studies provoke critical questions and disruptions that can galvanize transformation in Protestant communities. It is true ambivalence toward disability haunts Christianity; many beliefs and practices imitate and contribute to the encumbrance of normalcy even as they also provide resources that expose and contest it, subverting ableist principalities and powers. Protestants who wish to respond to disability and facilitate practices of hospitality and solidarity with people with disabilities will accordingly be asked to reconsider many fundamental themes in Christianity.

Yet leading currents in Protestantism, as this chapter has attempted to show, offer resources for critical responses that propel new insights and productive possibilities not only for ongoing conversations with disability studies but also for creating open and welcoming spaces in faith communities where disability is recognized as a feature of embodied human life in all its variation. As Titchkosky and Michalko note, "Disability studies requires that we ready ourselves to loosen the hold of the normative demand to fix impairments, and that we begin to learn how to notice and think about social relations we develop with bodies conceived of as different" (11). In Protestant perspective, this requires a rethinking of God's grace and human nature in its light, remapping approaches to the Bible, and wrestling anew with what it means to be together as equals who are loved by God in our differences. Being Christian is not about controlling life by a pretense to mastery, which conquers problems and repairs brokenness, but an invitation into a relational space of love—of God and neighbor—in which creaturely limits and possibilities are accepted and valued for what they are: unconditionally embraced by God. Neither paternalistic toward nor dismissive of disability, the ideal response to God's grace is that vulnerable communion of mutual regard called the church, an ongoing and never finalized task that may only be achieved together in the Spirit. And because the task is one requiring the participation of all, access—for, by, and with all—becomes a fundamental priority.

Protestant communities across the world might take up the challenge to be a church reformed, always reforming in various ways, and, in the process, join in collaborative efforts with Catholic and Orthodox traditions, harnessing ecumenical fruits generated from resources greater than any one tradition could possess. As this book suggests, the dialogue may be extended further still to an interfaith context, with traditions working together in conversation with disability studies perspectives to create spaces of wide and deep access. Certainly it is an invitation to begin again, again.

8

Islam and Disability

Vardit Rispler-Chaim

Islam is the religion of more than 1.5 billion Muslim faithful around the world. They all adhere to the Qur'an, their holy book, which they hold to be the true collection of all divine revelations received by the Prophet Muhammad through the mediation of the angel Gabriel (Jibril) between 610 and 632 CE, when Muhammad died. It is traditionally accepted that the Qur'an was collected and canonized in its current form around 650 CE, after it had been recited and transmitted orally for about twenty years. Recent scholarship suggests earlier dates for the Qur'an's canonization. Some scholars believe that the Prophet Muhammad himself was responsible for this milestone in the making of Islam.

All Muslims also adhere to the Shari'a, an all-encompassing system of Islamic law, which has been developed by jurists since the seventh century CE, through a method called *fiqh* (literally "understanding, perception") and subsuming the four main roots of Islamic law: Qur'an, Sunna, analogy, and consensus. Occasionally several additional legal tools are utilized. The Shari'a evolved in the various schools of law in accordance with the geographic location and the legal ideology at any given age. While the Qur'an is believed to be the word of God to the Prophet Muhammad and from him to all humankind—so its content may never be contested—the Shari'a is "made" by jurists building on certain axioms or principles (*qawa'id*); its practical instructions (*furu'*) often manifest various levels of adaptation to the changing circumstances. The Shari'a is a general title for many legal books, each associated with a jurist whose team studied a variety of legal topics and formulated their conclusions in a legal compilation, usually organized in subject-chapters. The Islamic legal literature (Shari'a) thus reflects all the changes, accommodations, and developments in legal theory and practice from the days of nascent Islam in the seventh century till the present.

All Muslims also abide by the "five pillars of Islam," which occupy a significant part of all legal books throughout Islamic history; hence they are part of the Shari'a. The five pillars of Islam are the main practices that every Muslim is duty-bound to observe. As pillars support a building, so the five pillars of Islam support the religion. The five pillars unite all Muslims in five common activities that are essential for creating and maintaining Islamic society. "Islam has functioned socially by harmonizing people's activities" (Murata and Chittick 9). While the Qur'an as the word of God expresses the essence of belief and the ideals cherished by the Islamic religion, the pillars address the acts required of a Muslim in addition to belief.

The first pillar is the *shahada* (testimony or confession)—verbal acceptance of the uniqueness and unity of God, and the prophecy of Muhammad, his best and last messenger to humanity at large. Several times a day, in the ordained daily prayers, a Muslim attests that "there is no god but God" and that "Muhammad is God's messenger." Uttering this formula just once, with genuine intention and before witnesses, is sufficient for an individual who was not born Muslim to enter into the Islamic religion (Murata and Chittick 10–11; Braswell 59–60).

The second pillar of Islam is the *salat*. This is the prayer ritual every Muslim who reaches puberty must perform five times daily. Each prayer is combined with certain bodily movements such as standing upright, kneeling, and prostrating. These are repeated in a structured order of movements accompanied by recitations of certain Qur'anic chapters and blessings upon God and the Prophet Muhammad. To perform the prayer ritual, the worshipper must be in a state of ritual purity. Women who are menstruating, for example, are exempt from the duty due to lack of purity. Most prayers can be offered by a Muslim man or woman in private, or on their own. The Friday prayer (*salat al-jum'a*) and holidays prayers (*salat al-'id*) are communal and should be performed in the mosque unless the Muslim experiences difficulty in reaching the mosque. In that case he or she can conduct the prayer at their convenience at home, in hospital, and so forth (Murata and Chittick 11–15; Braswell 60–65).

The third pillar of Islam is almsgiving (*zakat* or *sadaqa*[1]). According to the Qur'an (9,60) *zakat* is a religious tax, a method to support the weak in society by means of the wealth of those who are above the poverty level—the middle and upper classes. The benefit for the taxpayer is that giving alms purifies the believer and reminds him or her that all the prosperity a believer enjoys is from God. In this sense paying alms is a way to thank God for his generosity and benevolence (Braswell 65–66; Murata and Chittick 16–17).

The fourth pillar is the fast during the month of Ramadan. "Fasting consists of refraining from eating, drinking, smoking and sexual activity" (Murata and Chittick 17). The purpose is purification of the soul, repentance for sins—to disregard temporarily bodily needs in favor of spiritual thoughts—and sympathy for those who endure hunger all year round, not only for one month. The fast is daily, from before sunrise until after sunset. It ends each day with the evening prayers, after which a full meal is eaten. At the end of the month all Muslims celebrate the three-festival day 'Id al-Fitr (breaking the fast). The fast is mandatory for all mature, sane, healthy Muslim men and women; children, pregnant and breastfeeding women, and ailing adults are exempt. If they are adults, the law offers them alternative means to compensate for each missed day of fasting, such as almsgiving and feeding the poor or fasting at a later date, if and when they have recovered from the medical or other problem that prevented their fasting in the first place. "Ramadan tests endurance and self-denial" (Braswell 68). This is an annual duty, but due to the Islamic lunar calendar it may fall in different seasons in the year. The long summer days are the hardest for the fasting believer.

The fifth pillar is the hajj (pilgrimage to Mecca). This is a set of rituals undertaken in Mecca and its surroundings, from the eighth day of Dhu al-Hijja—the twelfth and last month of the Islamic year—until the thirteenth day of the same month. All the rituals are a commemoration of various stages in the life of Abraham, the first monotheist, "the father of the Arabs," who founded, with his son Ishmael, the Ka'ba, the holiest shrine in Mecca. The pilgrimage is a duty incumbent on a Muslim once in a lifetime, if certain conditions related to his or her physical and mental health, financial state, and safety of the roads to and from Mecca are met. A woman must also have a legitimate companion to escort her to and from Mecca. If any conditions are not met, the duty to perform the hajj is postponed until they are. At the end of the hajj, Muslims all over the world join the pilgrims present in Mecca in the festival 'Id al-Adha (the sacrifice) from the tenth to the thirteenth of the month. This commemorates God's command to Abraham to sacrifice his son, who was substituted at the last moment by a ram (Wensinck).

THE SIXTH PILLAR?

Sometimes jihad is mentioned as the sixth pillar of Islam. In political terms jihad means a holy war, intended to spread God's word against the infidels and God's enemies, although the literal translation is "struggle, effort." In this literal sense, to perform the five daily prayers, to fast a whole month every year, and to go on hajj are strenuous tasks that require much struggle on the part of the believer. Jihad is attributed to the Prophet Muhammad, who distinguished "the lesser jihad" (the war against infidels) from "the greater jihad" (the struggle in one's heart against evil thoughts and bad intentions). Sometimes the latter is named *mujahada*, while physical combat is named "jihad," although both derive from the same Arabic root (Murata and Chittick 20–22; Peters 1).

ROOTS OF LAW

The Shari'a was constructed by jurists using the following four main roots of law (*usul al-fiqh*): the Qur'an, the Sunna, the *qiyas* (analogy), and *ijma'* (consensus).

As for the Qur'an, Muslims regard it as the word of God, therefore holy, and an uncontested source of wisdom and law; thus it is the first and chief root of law. Muslims also attribute great holiness to the Sunna, the second source of law. The Sunna, the tradition or legacy of Prophet Muhammad, is a record of the Prophet's sayings and deeds, and of acts performed in his presence without his overt or implied objection, thus suggesting that they were legitimized by him. The Prophet's Sunna (way of life, customs) was learned from thousands of short stories or reports, each called *hadith* (a saying, a piece of information), assembled in several large collections. These can be found today in printed volumes associated with the scholars who redacted and classified the vast Hadith literature between the eighth and tenth centuries CE.[2] The Qur'an and Sunna alone are text-based sources of Islamic law. The two other sources, analogy (*qiyas*) and unanimous agreement of jurists (*ijma'*), represent not only the relative freedom of thought exercised by Muslim jurists down the generations but also the diversity of jurists' opinions since factors such as time, place, and religious liberalism or conservatism have influenced them.

Added to the above four basic roots of law, sometimes public interest (*maslaha*, *istislah*), juristic preference (*istihsan*), and local custom (*'ada*) are also utilized in the creation of new laws (Hallaq, *Introduction*, 14–27). As the development of Islamic law unfolded, and with the approach of the modern era, these additional non-canonical tools became more practicable and led to the rejuvenation of Islamic law and its being rendered more welcoming to advances in science, medicine, economics, and other disciplines.

In Islamic law, attitudes to people with disabilities and to disability in general can therefore be retrieved from the Qur'an, the Sunna, and the immense knowledge accumulated in many medieval, pre-modern, and contemporary legal compilations (Shari'a). But more importantly there is also the vast *fatwa* literature (ad hoc *responsa*, jurisconsultations, and legal opinions). This is a massive body of legal consultations issued from the medieval Islamic era to the present day by respected scholars bearing the title *mufti* (jurisconsult). In the past, fatwa were published in collections, newspapers, and periodicals, always carrying the name of the scholar and the date of issue of his response. Today, fatwa are also announced on the radio, television, and internet sites belonging to different fatwa committees in the Islamic world, as well as on several sites of individual scholars (Masud, Messick, and Powers 3–32).

THE QUR'AN

In the Qur'an, *marad* (disease) is primarily something attributed to the heart and manifested as disbelief. Only in Qur'an 9:91 does *marad* denote an illness that hinders one from participating in jihad (possibly referring to a physical or a mental disability), contrary to "illness of the hearts." Qur'an 24:61 emphasizes that the disabled should not be segregated from social interactions. Those with disabilities specified in this verse are the blind, the lame, and the sick. Another adjective, *saqim* (sick), is mentioned in the Qur'an twice (37:89 and 37:145), but *marad* is the most frequent term for illness in the book. *Marad* is the opposite of *sihha* ("health, wholeness, correctness"). Health is one of the benevolences God ordered his servants to preserve, forbidding them to spoil or weaken through certain foods, beverages, alcohol, and excessive exertion. (Qur'an 5:90 and 7:157 set forth these prohibitions.) In fact, the whole of human existence is viewed as a journey back and forth between the poles of health and illness, well-being and suffering (Rispler-Chaim, *Disability*, 16). Well-being and sickness both originate from God. The reason for inflicting sickness upon humans is seldom attributed to God's wrath or punishment, and more often is seen as a means for testing belief. The prophet Job (Ayyub) is the epitome of perseverance in suffering and pain in the Qur'an. Thanks to his endurance, God healed his disease and rewarded him by restoring to him twofold his property and kin (see Johns 2003). The "test of faith" explanation for the affliction of one with disability is given by contemporary Muslim scholars as well (Ghaly 47–48).

THE HADITH

The Hadith mentions several of the Prophet's Companions (*sahaba*) who had disabilities, but their disabilities did not prevent them from holding public positions. For example, 'Abd Allah b. Umm Maktum was blind, but the Prophet nevertheless appointed him leader of the public prayer; 'Abd al-Rahman b. 'Awf was lame, but still he participated in several battles at the Prophet's side;

'Ammar b. Yasir had one ear cut off, yet he fought several early battles together with the Prophet; Ma'adh b. Jabal was lame, but the Prophet appointed him governor of Yemen and a religious teacher there. al-Mughira b. Shu'ba had lost an eye in battle, but the Caliph Umar appointed him governor of Bahrain and then of Al-Basrah; later the Umayyad Caliph Mu'awiya appointed him governor of Kufa. The second generation of religious scholars (Tabi'un) included some known to suffer from certain disabilities: Muhammad b. Sirin was deaf yet was considered an authority on fiqh (legal issues); 'Ata' b. Abi Rabah was one-eyed and one-armed, lame, then blind; for all that, he served as the mufti of Mecca in the time of the Umayyads. Sa'id b. al-Musayyab was one-eyed yet was renowned for his wide religious knowledge. There are more instances. All the disabled sahaba and *tabi'un* excelled in religious studies and ascended to the highest religious and communal positions, which attests to their meeting the challenge and not submitting to weakness, disability, or illness. They proved that their minds and stamina were strong and that they were as capable as healthy people.

The Prophet promised those who persevered against hardship (such as disability) and calamity the reward of entering Paradise; moreover, perseverance (*sabr*) is highly valued by God in the Islamic tradition as accounting for half of one's belief. At the same time, the Prophet encouraged Muslims to seek a remedy for any illness: this does not contradict full trust in God (*tawakkul*). Yet as much as a person is urged to try to cure his or her wounds and illnesses, it is emphasized that prevention is the best of treatments. The Islamic tradition contains many practical guidelines for the prevention of illnesses before their onset (Za'tari).[3]

THE SHARI'A

Separate chapters about people with disabilities under the relevant titles ("disabilities" and the like) can hardly be expected to feature in the Islamic legal literature; later I indicate a few exceptions, where the Arabic terminology denotes specific disabilities or disability in general. More often, reference to some type of disability is made randomly in various chapters among data which do not necessarily center on people with disabilities. Rather, if people with disabilities are mentioned it is often incidentally, as the offshoot of a discussion on healthy people. So to form a generalized picture, contemporary scholars must devise a meticulous research plan and study as many legal texts as they can muster. This might explain why the available academic literature on disabilities in Islamic law and society is, even today, relatively scarce.

SCHOLARLY LITERATURE ON ISLAM AND DISABILITY

The most prominent monographs that discuss the notion of disability in any Islamic context are *Disability in Islamic Law*, by Vardit Rispler-Chaim, *Islam and Disability*, by Mohammed Ghaly, and *Difference and Disability in the Medieval Islamic World: Blighted Bodies*, by Kristina L. Richardson. These recently published studies, though differing in content, try to sketch a general picture of attitudes to disability, whether through the legal literature (see Rispler-Chaim, *Disability in Islamic Law*), theology and the law (see Ghaly, *Islam and Disability*), or history (see Richardson, *Difference and Disability*). Michael Dols devoted an entire book, *Majnun*, to notions of "madness" (according to Dols, a general title for all mental health problems) in Islam, for which he perused Islamic law, literature, and theology, as did al-Issa with regard to mental health in medieval Islam.

Only in recent years have we witnessed a growing number of published studies on specific topics within the general field of disability; it may be limited to a certain disability, a particular geographic area, or a historical period. Such are the studies of Shefer on the insane in the Ottoman Empire in the fifteenth through the seventeenth centuries, of Scalenghe on the deaf in that empire in the sixteenth through the eighteenth centuries, of Shoshan on madness in medieval Islam (the Mamluk period in particular), and of Miles on the deaf in the Ottoman sultan's service. Dols published a paper on the leper, Long on the leper in early Islam, and Ener on the insane in nineteenth-century Egypt. Inhorn and Clarke, coming from anthropological backgrounds, wrote several monographs and papers on the problem of infertility and ways to circumvent it among Muslims and other religious groups in the Middle East. Saunders summarized attitudes to the hermaphrodite in Islamic law, as did Rispler-Chaim in a paper about sex-change operations and the *khuntha* (hermaphrodite) according to the muftis. This tendency to concentrate on one disability only, or on one historical period, seems to have prevailed in the last decade and has the potential of expanding our knowledge of additional aspects of disability in Islamic law and societies.

TERMINOLOGY

English

In English, several terms relate to a person who is unable to perform the normative physical and mental functions expected of a "healthy" human being.

According to the World Health Organization (WHO):

> The concept of disability is classified as one of three: *impairment, disability* or *handicap*. *Impairment* refers to the reduction or loss of normally exist-ing physical, psychological, or behavioral structures. *Disability* refers to the functional impairments resulting from primary damage, and the effect of the loss of function in daily life is thus the *handicap*. (qtd. in Lagerwall et al. 217)

According to the United Nations Declaration on the Rights of Disabled Per-sons, proclaimed by the Geneva Assembly's Resolution 3447 of December 9, 1975, the term "disabled person" means "any person unable to ensure by him-self or herself, wholly or partly, the necessities of a normal individual and/ or social life, as a result of a deficiency, either congenital or not, in his or her physical or mental capabilities" (qtd. in Gaff 6).

The International Labor Organization, on the other hand, asserts that "a disabled person means an individual whose prospects of securing, retaining and advancing in suitable employment are substantially reduced as a result of a duly recognized physical or mental impairment" (qtd. in Gaff 67, 75).

According to the Americans with Disabilities Act (ADA), signed into law in 1990, "a person with disability" is defined as:

1. Having a physical or mental impairment that substantially limits him or her in some major life activity, and
2. having experienced discrimination resulting from this physical or mental impairment. (qtd. in Hardman, Drew, and Egan 12–13)

In the traditional medical view, "the long term or permanent functional limitations produced by physical impairments are called disability" (Lia-chowitz 3, 12). A similar definition states: impairment is "lacking part or all of a limb, or having a defective limb, organ or mechanism of the body. Disablement is the loss or reduction of functional ability, and handicap is the disadvantage or restriction of activity caused by disability" (Brattgard 7–9).

According to Britain's Disability Discrimination Act of 1995, four ele-ments are required for a person to be considered "disabled":

a. There must be a physical or mental impairment.
b. The impairment must adversely affect the individual's capacity to carry out normal day-to-day activities.
c. The adverse effect must be substantial.
d. The adverse effect must be "long term." (Diesfeld 388–92)

R. B. Jones, a retired London pediatrician, challenges the usage of the three commonly applied terms: impairment, disability, and handicap (377–79). Handicap in his opinion is a discriminatory term as it derives from "cap in hand . . . implying that the disabled are expected to beg favors of the able." He assigns blame for handicap to "the response of the able community to those with impairments and disabilities." He prefers the term "disability," as adopted in a recent revision of the WHO classification, and combines the notions of disability and impairment. For Jones, handicap is the impairment in the attitude to disability which individuals in a society may have. He realizes that his view is somewhat revolutionary but believes this will lead to a holistic view of people with disabilities, rather than a stigmatized pitiful one.

Without doubt, the search for definition is primarily aimed at determining policies with regard to the "disabled." In many societies and countries today, being disabled means benefiting from social and legal relief and economic assistance from the state in the form of direct financial support or discounted services not available for "healthy" persons. The definition of "who is disabled" is also utilized by and against politicians in various political scenarios (Wendell, *Rejected Body*, 11–12). Still, the definition of disability must always remain relative. In a society where most girls are circumcised, she who is not is "disabled," while in other societies being circumcised equals being mutilated. In a society where many are undernourished, undernourishment is not considered a disability (Wendell 14). Iris Marion Young asserts that women in sexist societies are "physically handicapped," as they are expected to lack the strength, skills, and physical mobility that men are expected to have (qtd. in Wendell 15). Of the many more examples of the relativity of disability, here I will briefly mention only cultural relativism. Butler and Parr depict two major models in the perception of disability: the medical and the social. The medical model grew out of the rise of medical science. It utilizes specific bodily and sensory technologies that can improve aspects of daily life for some people with impairments. But this model, they claim, has seldom considered the complexity of disabled people's lives. The newly devised social model of disability tries to address the social issues that these people encounter and is "closely allied to political fights for anti-discrimination legislation and civil rights" (3). Following Dear et al., Butler and Parr welcome the expansion of the category of disability to include substance abuse, HIV, psychological conditions, and arthritis, as these imply that the human experiences of disability are "open to reinterpretation" (9). Butler and Parr do not see the body space as totally separate from the mind space but regard the two as interrelated and mutually important (14). They conclude that any study of disability should take a multidimensional view of it, and they would like the term "disability" as a catch-all category to be abandoned (15). As will be shown later, Islamic law, naturally unaware of contemporary social theories, seems always to address each disability in respect of a specific, recognizable human action or behavior, never as a catch-all category.

As for medical terminology, the medical textbooks contain many names for specific impairments and dysfunctions that laypersons are hardly aware or have never heard of. For our purposes I refer to disabilities as they are recognized by the general public, using "disability" for most dysfunctional problems people may experience and "impairment" for damage to an organ or a bodily mechanism that may lead to a disability.

Arabic

Turning now to examine Arabic terminology, we may often come across labels for bearers of specific disabilities. Examples are the *a'ma* (blind), the *asamm* (deaf), the *abkam* (dumb), the *akhras* (mute), the *a'raj* (lame), the *majnun* (insane), the *'aqim* (infertile), and the *khuntha* (hermaphrodite). There are also feminine forms in Arabic for the same adjectives—such as *'amya, 'arja, majnuna*, and so forth—to indicate that the disabled person is a woman.

Contrary to the Western terminology, I could not identify in classical Islamic sources any single general term that combines all people with disabilities as a group. This absence might in itself teach us something about attitudes to the disabled in Islamic societies. But I am reluctant to leap to conclusions at this early stage of the chapter. Only in contemporary literature in Arabic do we find rather generalized terms, such as *ashab al-'ahat* or *dhawu al-'ahat* (owners or bearers of impairments, defects), *mu'awwaqun* or *mu'aqun*—literally "those held back by difficulty and limitations to their mental or physical functions"—and *'ajaza* or *'ajizun*, pl. of *'ajiz* ("a weak person, unable to do things, like the old").[4]

The Arabic root *'a-j-z* was well known in early Islam and often used in the Qur'an and in medieval texts in the sense of someone who is unable or is made unable to do something (Zubaydi 4, 48–53). In a more specific usage, it denoted a man "unable to perform sexual intercourse with women" (Manzur 7, 236–240). The latter is a reference to a real handicap that men may experience. But *'ajaza* or *'ajizun* as a social classification of a group of people, which might equal today's "the disabled," cannot be found in the Qur'an or in the *fiqh*. It is worthwhile emphasizing again that terms that are more likely to appear today are *ashab al-'ahat* ("bearers of impairments"), and *mu'aqun* or *mu'awwaqun* ("those experiencing difficulties"). Seldom would severely handicapped or deformed persons be named *mushawwahun* ("deformed").

This adjective is often reserved for impaired fetuses still in the womb (*ajinna mushawwaha*) or for newborn infants who suffer severe malformation or mental retardation.

Ghaly found some more general terms, such as *ahl al-bala'* (people with affliction) and *ashab al-a'dhar* (people with excuses). For modern times he mentions also the use of *al-fi'at al-khassa* (special groups), *dhawu ihtiyajat khassa* (people with special needs), and *afrad ghayr 'adiyyin* (abnormal individuals) (Ghaly 11–13; Za'tari).

Only with regard to marriage do medieval *fiqh* scholars speak in a generalized manner of the *'uyub* (pl. of *'ayb*, translated as "impairments, defects, deformities") which interfere with the proper flow of marital life. These are meticulously listed in the legal literature and can befall the husband, the wife, or both. Separate chapters in almost all *fiqh* compilations are dedicated to these *'uyub*, adjacent to chapters on marriage and divorce.

The *'uyub* related to personal status issues are discussed at length, because they are considered impediments to contracting, consummating, or maintaining a healthy marriage. In my book *Disability in Islamic Law*, I devote a separate chapter to these *'uyub*. To my knowledge, "disabilities that interfere with marriage" are the only instance in medieval *fiqh* of a distinct grouping for several disabilities. We may note here that the *'uyub* in this group differ significantly: their nature may be mental (*majnun*), sexual (*'innin*, "impotent"; *khasiyy*, "castrated"), or dermatological (*abras* or *ajdham*, "a leper or one afflicted with elephantiasis"). Still, they are bundled together in one group in the legal literature. To the contemporary person, accustomed to classified Western medicine where diseases are usually named according to the organs they attack (heart, liver, lungs, blood, etc.), this is a completely new mode of thinking. The Western medical classification of diseases by the damaged organ is thus challenged by another perception, represented by the Islamic legal thought, which classifies at least one group of disabilities by their overall social impact (impediments to marriage).

Another term that could be considered fairly inclusive of a wide range of disabilities is *majnun* (madman) (see Dols, *Majnun*). Dols perceives *majnun* as encompassing the insane, the mentally disordered, the mentally deficient, the mentally disturbed, the mentally deranged, the lunatic, the imbecile, and the idiot. All the above disabilities belong to the range of mental health. I will return to *majnun* later.

One reservation about the above observation—that no single term in Arabic covers all persons with disabilities—must be made here. It has to do with the vagueness of the terms *marid*, pl. *marda* (in common use it implies a sick or ill person), and *marad* (disease). In the Qur'an, *marid* often serves to mark the opposite of healthy (whole) in both the physical and the mental sense. Infidels and hypocrites, for example, are described as having a disease in their hearts (Qur'an 2:10; 8:49; 9:125; 22:53; 24:50; 33:12, 32, 60; 47:20, 29; 74:31). The disease of the heart can be understood as a metaphor or as a real mental problem.

In the *fiqh* literature, the *marid* is mentioned in almost every chapter of the law; occasionally *marid* appears in the titles of subdivisions of legal chapters. We find, for example, *salat al-marid* (prayer of the *marid*), *talaq al-marid* (repudiation of the *marid*), *iqrar al-marid* (testimony of the *marid*), *sawm al-marid* (fasting of the *marid*), *hajj al-marid* (pilgrimage of the *marid*), jihad *al-marid* (holy war of the *marid*), and more. In the legal literature the question is often whether the function performed by the *marid*—such as prayer, testimony, signing a contract, and declaring a divorce—is legitimate and valid since the performers were at the time of their performance partially or fully incompetent due to their disease.

But what exactly the semantic field of the *marid* is in the *fiqh* remains obscure. It remains uncertain whether

1. It is a short-term illness or a permanent, chronic illness, hence bordering on what today would qualify as "disability."
2. It refers to a disease that is curable or to a terminal disease. The latter is sometimes specifically labeled *marad al-mawt* (literally disease of death), an incurable disease which destines the ill person for death or the state of dying.
3. The term is restricted to physical difficulties only or encompasses mental and emotional problems as well.

I find it worthwhile to raise these dilemmas, because from examining several discussions in the *fiqh* I have come to suspect that *marid* was used more in a general manner to cover the sick and the disabled alike. Certain aspects of *salat al-marid* (prayer of the sick) or *hajj al-marid* (hajj of the sick), for example, acknowledge human difficulty in bending, sitting down, standing up straight, and walking. As much as these conditions may be symptoms of a bad flu or a terminal illness, they can also be manifestations of severe spinal damage, paralysis, and so forth. In such disabling circumstances, *marad*, I suggest, could qualify as disability, impairment, and even permanent handicap. If this hypothesis is true, *marad* is the closest one can get to suggesting, within the canonical sources of Islamic law, a general term for a wide range of disabilities.

ISLAMIC LAW ON PEOPLE WITH DISABILITIES

The prevailing mood in the law regarding people with disability is that they are an integral part of society, never social outcasts. But since they are people with special needs, the law addresses them as well as the healthy. The difference between healthy and disabled persons is that the law grants the latter some relief in religious duties in consideration of their particular difficulties. Once the difficulty, mental or physical, is overcome, the law admits no further alleviations. Whether the disability has or has not been overcome is often a matter of conscience or between the human and God, and no state authority has been granted license by law to interfere with it. Responsibility for shifting from a disabled to a healthy mode of conduct remains the individual's. On the other hand, if with old age and the course of illness the difficulty becomes chronic, more alleviations apply under the Qur'anic principle that God aims at ease (*yusr*), not at hardship (*'usr*), for the believer (Qur'an 2:185) and that saving a human's life is always first priority (Qur'an 5:32).

The attitude to the disabled in Islamic law has generally been tolerant, accepting, accommodating and forgiving as to fulfillment/non-fulfillment of religious duties and in matters of criminal justice. This overall positive attitude may derive from the "no-fault" attitude in Islamic scriptures to sufferers of impairments or diseases (Dols, "Leper," 915). Since the ill are not perceived as punished people who "invited" the punishment through sins they may have committed, the disability is viewed rather as a trial by God, which the religious, namely the spiritually strong, will be able to withstand. The disabled are seen as people at a testing stage, but never as condemned or sinful. Sometimes added to this attitude is the understanding or the consolation that if one is disabled in one way, one may have been rewarded by God with extra talents and abilities in other ways. This tolerant attitude to people with disabilities and the understanding that disability is often temporary, that it is culture bound, and that everyone in his or her life will experience at least once, and probably more often, some periods of disability may be the reason for the scarcity of terms in Arabic for the group we call today "people with disability." Actually, all people occasionally qualify as "people with disability."

There is hardly a chapter in Islamic law books that does not also refer to people with disabilities when sketching the general rules of conduct expected of the "healthy." The law, immediately after phrasing the provisions on any matter, will always mention the alleviations offered to people who have any type of difficulty in fulfilling the basic religious commandments imposed on the healthy. This holds for those experiencing hardship in performing prayer, hajj, and Ramadan fasting, as they are offered alternative means of doing so or compensating for duties not carried out. Lengthy discussions are also found on how, if at all, people with disabilities are expected to enlist in jihad, express consent to marry or divorce (for example, when they are mute or deaf), stay married, and beget children (especially, but not solely, when the person or the spouse has a sexual disability). The law points to dilemmas concerning their ability to engage in social, political, and economic activities, such as leading the community (*imama* or *khilafa*) in peacetime or in war, serving as a *qadi* (judge) or a *mufti* (jurisconsult), and more. People with disabilities, as it transpires from the legal literature, are part of the general society and should never experience stigma or excommunication. The case of the hermaphrodite (*khuntha*), which poses difficulties for the larger society due to this person's lacking a distinct gender identity, is the clearest proof of this tendency (Rispler-Chaim, *Disability*, 69–74; see also Saunders, "Gendering the Ungendered Body").

A Note on the Hermaphrodite

> The only disability allotted an independent chapter in the fiqh compilations is the *khunutha* (being a hermaphrodite). *Khunutha* is a congenital impairment, in which an infant cannot be identified upon birth as male or female. The reason is that he or she has both female and male sexual organs, or has no sexual organs whatsoever. (Rispler-Chaim, *Disability*, 69)

The *khuntha*, especially the *khuntha mushkal* (a complicated case of hermaphroditism) is a person without clear sex characteristics or with sex characteristics of both a male and a female; in social and religious terms he or she poses difficulty not only to himself or herself but also to the surrounding society. Islamic law recognizes two sexes only; each is charged with almost the same duties, but not with the same manner of performing them because of the sex differences. So when a human being cannot be classified as male or female, questions such as the following may arise:

Should the *khuntha mushkal* pray with men or with women? Should this person inherit the share of a brother/son or a sister/daughter of the deceased? (Males and females with the same blood relation to the deceased—such as sons and daughters—do not inherit equal shares in Islamic law.) If the *khuntha mushkal* has a penis, who will perform circumcision on it?—a man cannot touch the body of a strange woman, and a woman cannot look at the genitals of a strange man. Another question is how long should society wait for clear sexual characteristics to show on the ungendered body if the disability was discovered at infancy and no distinct characteristics have appeared by puberty. May the hermaphrodite marry? Which gender may he or she marry? Can this person reproduce? Are the purposes of marriage as understood by Islamic law fulfilled?

Classical Islamic law has dwelt on these and other questions, often with acute sensitivity, with acceptance, and with the intention to accommodate the hermaphrodite in society to the greatest degree, and at the same time cause minimal harm to the healthy surrounding him or her, whether family members or unrelated members of society. All the most extreme medieval means to favor the hermaphrodite are mentioned in Rispler-Chaim (*Disability*, 70–72). In recent years, sex-change surgeries have proliferated, especially in Iran, with the aim of eliminating the problem by transferring the ungendered person via surgery into a male or a female.

This has become possible thanks to the relative legal independence of the Shi'a clerics of Iran, unlike their Sunni counterparts, in issuing Islamic legal decisions in the absence of explicit indications in the Shari'a. It is a sign of tolerance and a ray of hope for people imprisoned from birth in a body that hinders their religious and social involvement in the society into which they were born. Advances in medicine and surgery must also be accorded credit for enabling this innovation (see Bucar, "Bodies at the Margins"; Rispler-Chaim, "Sex Change Operations").

Physical Punishments

True, there are physical punishments for certain offenses in Islamic law, and offenders become handicapped as a result of them. But Islamic law also addresses the fate of criminals sentenced in that manner. At the same time, the fiscal compensations allotted to victims who have become disabled as a result of others' criminal actions, intentional or not, premeditated or negligent, reflect a very advanced mode of thinking; they are akin to the present system of calculating compensation for an injured person based on the assessed percentages of disability (or loss of functioning) (Rispler-Chaim, *Disability*; "Compassion").

Despite the general tolerance manifested by Islamic law toward people with disabilities, several exceptions must have existed. For example, Ghaly identified ambivalence among several medieval Shafi'i jurists regarding people with disabilities.[5] Those who held them in contempt were influenced by Greek physiognomy—that is, the belief that one's external appearance or handicaps attest to faults in one's character and religiosity. But most of them, he concludes, had no prejudice against people with disabilities, and some jurists were even disabled themselves (82). He detected the same ambivalence in the Hanbali jurisdiction. However, Hanbali jurists were less inclined to physiognomy (*firasa*) because this pursuit's status as a legitimate science was much debated among them. Also, as explained at least by the Hanbali Ibn al-Qayyim (d. 1350), even if physiognomy was acknowledged, the negative effect of appearance on one's spirit "is curable and recoverable by means of education, training, and habituation" (Ghaly 83–86).

THE REALITY

The status of people with disabilities in the course of Islamic history was not always as favorable as depicted in the legal literature and as mentioned above. There are several examples of this ambivalence.

With regard to the leper in early Islamic times, for example, we find contradictory reports. Some of the Prophet's companions allowed interaction with lepers, while others formulated measures of how to avoid them or even restrict their movement and segregate them from the rest of the Muslim community (Long, "Leprosy in Early Islam").

One example showing that the law may differ from social reality is the case of the *majnun*. Against Dols' critique of Islamic society's overall positive treatment of the mentally disabled, one characterized with tolerance and humanism, Shoshan ("State and Madness"), Shefer ("Insanity and the Insane"), and others relate that in the late Middle Ages madmen were often confined in small cells or even in cages, sometimes chained and whipped.

From medieval Arab historians such as al-Maqrizi, Ibn Iyas, and Ibn Furat, we learn that in 1265–1266, for example, the Mamluk sultan in Egypt decreed that "all invalids (*ashab al-'ahat*) in Cairo be assembled and transferred to al-Fayyum." In 1392 the Sultan decreed that no leper or invalid could remain in Cairo, and those who disobeyed must be punished (see Shoshan, "State and Madness"). Shoshan therefore argues that the social attitudes to the disabled in Islamic societies were not always tolerant and accepting but were sometimes tainted by exclusion and cruelty.

Al-Issa gives a more balanced account, stating that the patients restrained in hospitals were those who posed a danger to themselves or to others; nonviolent, mentally ill people were treated by family members in their homes. Society at large, he continues, was reluctant to send the ill off to hospitals, even though these were located in the center of the cities, frequented by visitors and relatives, and not secluded on the outskirts of town (57).

Much later, during the reign of Muhammad Ali (1769–1849), the insane were confined to special asylums when found by the police or committed by their families. This was to clear the streets of individuals who might pose a danger to society at large (Ener 43).

Both tolerant and less tolerant attitudes to the mentally ill developed in Islamic societies where Islamic law was known and applied. The explanation for the differences between tolerance and intolerance in practice should perhaps be sought in the political and social atmosphere that prevailed at a particular time or place. Each case should be examined separately.

On attitudes to "blighted bodies" in Mamluk Cairo, we have reports by Richardson that in 1265 or 1266 Baybars I ordered the transfer of *ahl al-'ahat* (people with disabilities) to Al Fayyum, where he established another residential area for them. This was an area of Christians and Christian monasteries, and the purpose of the exile might have been to expose *ahl al-'ahat* to a more tolerant and merciful environment. If this is correct, it may mean that the Islamic surroundings in those days were less tolerant than the Christian ones. In 1330 Sultan al-Nasir Muhammad ordered that all lepers be moved from Cairo to the area of Al Fayyum (Richardson 39).

The double standard in treatment of people with disabilities is further manifested. When Baybars established the Baybarsiyya, he stipulated that those holding positions of power there must have ideal bodies. Yet the institution (the Baybarsiyya) itself was known for taking good care of sick and disabled people. In 1438 Sultan Barsbay ordered healthy beggars off the streets of Cairo, allowing only "chronically ill, blind, and blighted people to beg in public" (Richardson 43). This may indicate sympathy for the disabled in a way that allowed them some sort of livelihood.

With regard to the status of the deaf in Ottoman Syria (sixteenth through the eighteenth centuries) Scalenghe concluded that "early modern Syria was relatively accommodating of the deaf" (10–25). According to biographies of people with hearing/speech impediments in that period, they could lead relatively normal lives. In fact, the lower the level of deafness, the better could those afflicted with it perform in society (15). There is no evidence that the deaf were secluded from the rest of society or, for example, forced to pray in a congregation of their own away from the hearing believers (18). We do not know whether a formal sign language was in use in Ottoman Syria, but there is evidence that the Sultan himself communicated with mute visitors to his palace using sign language. In the sources, it is indicated that sign language was accepted in Ottoman courts at least around the seventeenth century (20).

According to Miles, sign language was acceptable in Ottoman courts already between the sixteenth and the eighteenth centuries ("Signing in the Seraglio"). Hearing members of the sultan's family were taught to sign from an early age. Mutes and dwarfs were salaried employees of the sultans as housekeepers, tending to the sultan's physical needs, carrying messages, and accompanying him in hunting and field sports.

Infertility, especially of women, is viewed by Muslims as a major disability. Marcia Inhorn's attest that in present-day Egypt it is "a devastating problem for women" and little tolerance is expressed for the infertile woman (3); in one of her books she explains that this disability is threatening "to women's self-esteem and social status, to men's procreativity and lineage continuity, and to the reproduction of Egyptian society at large. . . . Therefore, women would struggle to overcome their childlessness" (37–38). Because of the importance assigned to childbearing and procreation, a childless woman is doomed to a low social status, and the future of her marriage is constantly threatened. A man is not subject to such discrimination since he has the option to marry an additional wife who may bear him children. In any event, infertility in society is often blamed on the wife, even though medical tests today can easily distinguish between male and female infertilities.

We can learn much about the importance of fertility today in Muslim societies from Morgan Clarke's book *Islam and New Kinship*. Its focus is on attitudes to contemporary reproductive technologies, especially among the Shi'ites of Lebanon, but it also provides a fair picture of other religious communities in that country, such as the Druze, the Christians, and the Sunnis. What emerges from Clarke's field research is a surprisingly positive attitude and acceptance of most of the new reproductive technologies by the Shi'a religious leaders, in and outside of Lebanon, often at the cost of overlooking religious prohibitions. This itself is also evidence that achieving the goal— producing a child—overrides other considerations. Infertility is a handicap that must be overcome or circumvented by almost any means.

CONCLUSION

It seems fair to conclude that in the Islamic legal literature tolerance for people with disabilities is the dominant trait in the sense that the jurists offer accommodations of all kinds to enable the disabled to participate with their community in religious rituals, commerce, and social life. For example, if the disabled cannot pray standing or prostrate, they may do so sitting or even lying down. If they cannot perform the hajj walking on their own feet, they may be carried by others or even someone else may perform the hajj in their stead when the funding is provided by the disabled person. But if that disabled person is poor he is not obliged to perform the hajj at all. Instances of such accommodations and alleviations in the Shari'a are numerous. By contrast, when one's disability has no impact on one's performance (e.g., lameness in respect to marrying or entering an economic transaction) the disability will be totally ignored.

In terms of actual practice, however, the picture is somewhat two-sided; at times the attitude to the disabled was tolerant, hence in line with the spirit of the law, and at other times it was tainted by stigma and discrimination. In Ottoman Damascus in the late sixteenth century a census was held which asked, among other characteristics, whether the head of the household was disabled. Four categories of disability were specified in that census: blindness, lameness, mental illness, and severe lameness approaching immobility. The purpose of identifying those afflicted with disability was apparently to exempt them from paying taxes. So while stigmatization obviously existed, the assumed purpose was to advance the welfare of those struggling with a disability (Richardson 105).

There is a lengthy debate between the schools of law about the mentally ill and whether they ought to pay *zakat* (mandatory almsgiving, one of the five pillars of Islamic doctrine). The Hanafi school of law, followed today by about half of the Sunni Muslims in the world (hence the majority of Muslims), exempts the disabled from paying *zakat*. The other legal schools maintain that the assets, not their owner, are taxable, thus the assets of a mentally ill or a disabled person are equal to those of a healthy person, therefore the guardian of the mentally ill (or the minor, for that matter) must pay *zakat* out of the latter's funds. As for physical disabilities, most schools do not exempt those with physical or even mental disabilities from paying *zakat*. Thus the Ottoman census of the late sixteenth century went beyond the requirements of the Hanafi school, which the Ottomans normally followed, and certainly beyond those of the other schools. We cannot conclude whether the reason for this consideration was compassion and sympathy for the disabled, ignorance of the specifics of the law, or something else. So much for people with disabilities as taxpayers. And with regard to prospective beneficiaries of *zakat* (charity), people with disabilities could be evaluated as entitled to them only when socially or economically classified as "poor" or "destitute" (*fuqara' wamasakin* in the Qur'anic terminology of Qur'an 9:60) but never on the basis of their disabilities alone (Rispler-Chaim, "Recent Interpretations").

While the Qur'an forbids maligning a person on account of his or her disabilities, it has been culturally acceptable throughout Islamic history to describe a notable by a physical visible defect he may have: *a'raj* (lame), *aqra'* (bald), *ahwal* (cross-eyed), *a'ma* (blind), and so forth. But drawing the line between intentional defamation and a supposedly innocent depiction is a tricky business (Richardson 110–22).[6]

Finally, did the law concerning people with disabilities influence reality, or was reality reflected in the law? Either way the answer must remain
"partially." Only one side of reality is reflected in Islamic law, and at the
same time, it should be noted that Islamic law itself was only partially implemented in various Islamic societies. This has been the case since at least the
tenth century CE when local, sometimes more secularized, legal traditions
were activated parallel to the Shariʿa and eventually replaced most of it. Also,
in the past two centuries, colonialism, represented by European countries,
introduced various Western legal systems into Islamic and Arab lands; this
ousted the Shariʿa in most of them or narrowed its applicability to a few fields
of law only, namely, personal status, inheritance, and *waqf* (endowments)
(Hallaq, *Introduction*, 115).

The "no-fault" attitude emerging from the Qurʾan and the Sunna to
people with disabilities, the alleviations granted to them by the Shariʿa, and
the theological understanding that there is a divine purpose in the existence
of people with disabilities in any human society all culminate in what we may
reasonably describe as an anti-eugenic Islamic *weltanschauung*. That is, any
human society, the Islamic included, is made of various types of people, and
people with disabilities are only one component of the larger picture. The
existence of disability in mankind should serve as a warning that this world
is not eternal and that there is a better world in the hereafter free of opposites
such as sickness and health, poverty and riches. All humans must remember
that we owe the proper functioning of our organs to God's power and will.
Moreover, God is perfect despite the existence of sickness and disability in his
world (Ghaly 51–53).

Regardless of the theological explanation one favors as to why disabilities exist, pragmatism is the key to understanding Islamic legal attitudes to
people afflicted with them (or, for that matter, to grasping Islamic law on
bioethical issues at large) (Rispler-Chaim, *Ethics*, 141–47). Accordingly, we
may find fierce juristic debates against the legitimacy of aborting a sick or
deformed fetus, supported mainly by theological concerns for the holiness of
human life and how early this life is believed to begin; yet at the same time
we encounter exceptional tolerance for sex-change surgeries (in particular
for hermaphrodites) (Rispler-Chaim, "Sex Change"; Bucar, "Bodies at the
Margins").[7]

Both streams, the tolerant and the conservative, find grounds in the
same Shariʿa but differ on how it is to be interpreted. Practical solutions of
the Shariʿa on bioethical issues in general, and on difficulties created by disability in particular, often rely on one of the two following legal principles:
weighing the lesser of two harms/evils (*akhaff al-dararayn*) on the one hand

and deciding when necessity renders the prohibited permissible (*al-darurat tubih al-mahzurat*) on the other. These two guidelines ensure that human life should not be tainted with hardship, as proclaimed by Qur'an 2:185: "God intends every facility for you; He does not want to put you to difficulties."

Coming to the present, the study of disability is inseparable from the human rights debate. The International Covenant on Economic, Social, and Cultural Rights (ICESCR), which came into force on January 3, 1976, under the auspices of the UN, was ratified in December 2002 by 146 states, including 41 out of 57 members of the Organization of the Islamic Conference (OIC). In Article 12 of the Covenant, consideration is given to people who suffer illness or disability. It is argued that attaining the highest level of physical and mental health is a basic human right and that maintaining an individual's good state of health also contributes to the maintenance of good public health. These perceptions can be shown to exist already in early Islamic teachings. Since the Prophet Muhammad is reported to have said that there is a cure for every disease and that any disease inflicted on mankind was already accompanied by its cure, it remains the duty of humankind to seek this cure. This is a call to promote the right to health, including the duty of states to provide good medical education, hence good medical services, to their citizens (Baderin 205–9). The treatment of physical and mental disabilities in the various kinds of Islamic literature, which was often marked by tolerance and compassion, as well as constructive guidelines for inclusion, rather than stigmatization, as has been shown above, proves that awareness of human rights existed in Islamic societies and thought before human rights became a focus of international standards and covenants.

Indigenous Traditions in the Western Hemisphere and Disability

Lavonna Lovern

The function of this chapter is to introduce issues involving disability in Indigenous cultures. Historically, examinations of Indigenous cultures have overlooked the significance and complexity involved in Indigenous cultural paradigms. This chapter will address these historic deficits by exploring some foundational knowledge claims in order to increase cultural competencies pertaining to Indigenous cultures. The chapter begins with a set of definitions designed to introduce the reader to a few concepts needed to understand how Indigenous cultures approach wellness. These definitions establish a foundation for a brief discussion of Indigenous cosmologies. The final section brings together both definitions and cosmological concepts in a discussion of health and disability in Indigenous cultures.

INTRODUCTION

When beginning a study of Native American and Alaskan Native communities, it is important to understand that there is no universal way of being. There are over five hundred federally recognized tribes and nations in the United States alone. This does not account for the recognized tribes in Canada and Central and South America. Nor does it take into account Indigenous communities in these countries that do not identify themselves as Native American or Alaskan Native. In addition to the federally recognized tribes in the United States, there exist a number of state-recognized tribes and communities as well as communities that are not officially recognized at all but claim Native American or Alaskan Native heritage. The traditions and histories of each community are unique as are their languages, community structures, and spiritualities. While some similarities may exist and allow for discussions such as the one here, it is important to recognize that the differences can be significant and should not be overlooked in order to obtain a simplified version of what it is to be Native American or Alaskan Native. Throughout this chapter, the reader should remember that any generalizations are just that and should not be applied universally to Native American or Alaskan Native tribes, nations, and communities. Neither should the generalizations be applied universally to all individuals of Native American or Alaskan Native heritage. Within any given community, individual differences create differing perspectives and should be recognized as important in order to fully understand the diversity. In the case of Native American and Alaskan Native individuals and communities, there is the additional complexity of being a colonized people. Colonization and post-colonization issues extend the complexity by bringing forth issues involving assimilation levels, on- and off-reservation differences, and differences involving the physical division of tribes or nations such as between the Eastern and Western Cherokee or the White Mountain and Mescalero Apache. The historical remnants of colonization further established issues of poverty, healthcare inequities, educational deficiencies, and discrimination, which continue to impact the Native American and Alaskan Native populations. While none of these factors can be separated from the discussion of Native American and Alaskan Native spirituality and wellness, the focus of this chapter is to give a foundation that will allow the reader to begin a more advanced set of studies that would include an understanding of these components.

Before turning to the heart of this discussion, it is important to establish some terminological contexts. First, the term used to denote the first people of the Americas represents one involving context issues. Words carry with them ideas, histories, and politics. The terms "Native American," "Alaskan Native," "American Indian," "Indian," "Indigenous," "Aboriginal," "First Nations," and many additional terms carry culturally specific positive and negative imagery. There is no one accepted term for those who first occupied the Western Hemisphere, and it should be recognized that there are concerns philosophically, socially, and politically involving the use of each of the above terms. Moreover, the above terms may not be used at all, but instead specific community designators such as Mvskoke, Dine, or Yaqui may be employed by community members. However, the specific tribal designators may be unfamiliar to individuals outside the given community. Communication among people, as well as the discussion of important topics, is hindered by a lack of well-defined and useful terminology. Given the limitations of terminology, and with an understanding of problematic terminological designators, this chapter will use "Native American," "Alaskan Native," "American Indian," "Aboriginal," and "First Nations" when they are used by sources or informants. However, in order to attempt inclusion, the term "Indigenous" will be the primary designator for those who first occupied the Western hemisphere. Additionally, as the areas of Hawaii, the Caribbean, and the Polar regions are intricately interwoven into the fabric of North, Central, and South America, the term "Indigenous" will include these communities as well. The scope, therefore, of this chapter is more properly focused on similarities in Indigenous religious/spiritual communities in the Western hemisphere as these apply to the concepts of disability.

Additionally, terms such as "primitive," "primal," "developing," and "third world" will not be used in referencing Indigenous cultures as these terms carry with them the negative and demeaning historical and political ideals that result in the promotion of discriminatory academic and social practices toward these communities. These terms carry with them images of unsophisticated individuals and communities based not in research or fact but on historical misinterpretation and prejudice. Indigenous knowledge theories, while often not taking the form of European theories, display a level of sophistication and intellectual advancement that is easily equated to those in European and Western theories. The continued use of these derogatory terms allows non-Indigenous individuals and communities to dismiss Indigenous knowledge claims without proper research.

Next, the terms "nation" and "tribe" are used by different communities according to their own standards. While these terms may have affiliation with concepts of "self-determination" in US Native American history, they often are a result of size designations. The designation may also come from older associations historically referred to as "confederacies" such as the Mvskoke or Iroquois confederacies. Each of these confederacies consisted of smaller community groupings, which may or may not have had the same cultures, religions, or languages.

A terminological definition must be clarified in terms of "belonging." This issue concerns designation of individuals "belonging to" the Indigenous category. It is not the purpose of this chapter to delve into the issues of blood quantum or tribal/nation membership. These issues are best left to other discussions and to the Indigenous communities themselves. For the purpose of this chapter, the Indigenous communities will be self-identified as such and will involve communities generally recognized among Indigenous populations. Any specific informants will be those designated by these communities as having authority to represent the ideas and traditions of a given community.

A final terminological issue that needs clarification involves the terms "religion" and "spirituality." Again, each of these terms carries with it ideas, histories, and politics both positive and negative involving differing cultural contexts. For this discussion, "religion" and "spirituality" will be used together in order to remind the reader that there is a larger academic debate involving the definition of these terms. It is not the purpose of this work to engage in a lengthy discussion of that debate or to decide on the "appropriate" definition for these terms. However, it should be noted that Indigenous communities and individuals do not often use these terms to describe their experience of Creator, spirits, rituals, or the sacred. Furthermore, where non-Indigenous definitions of these terms often are placed against the secular components of life, Indigenous definitions do not establish this dichotomous paradigm. As will be discussed later, Indigenous communities generally do not separate "sacred" and "secular" aspects of existence. So the designation that part of one's life is "religious" or "spiritual" and part of one's life is not does not adhere to Indigenous cosmologies. When the term "religious" or "spiritual" is used in this chapter, it should be understood as an attempt to make the discussion accessible to non-Indigenous individuals, not as an indicator of Indigenous beliefs or traditions.

ORAL TRADITION

Historically and currently, European American and Western communities emphasize written traditions in the transference of knowledge. It is not that these communities do not transfer information using oral tradition; it is simply that they have come to place greater levels of accuracy and legitimacy on written rather than oral tradition. Conversely, Indigenous communities have placed more emphasis on oral rather than on written transmission of knowledge regarding accuracy and legitimacy. While the historic debate as to which method is superior has been stacked in favor of the written tradition, current research has begun to reassess this stacking as no more than cultural bias. Research has revealed that oral tradition requires advanced memory skills and intensive training. While storytelling is only one type of oral tradition, it too requires that the individual be able to impart knowledge with high levels of competency (Beck, Walters, and Francisco 57). In many cases, the information must be repeated with an accuracy that requires knowledge of exact wording and exact breathing techniques. Additionally, the time required to impart this information may take several days or nights to complete. The individual responsible for the telling must train for the intensity of such sessions as these events often include stories, songs, and legends (59).

It should also be noted that the reliance on oral tradition among Indigenous communities does not necessitate a complete lack of written tradition. Many Indigenous communities acknowledge written languages existing before contact but also acknowledge that these languages did not resemble those of Europeans. The difference in appearance may have exacerbated European dismissal. Regardless of whether or not the academic community or the larger Western community accepts that written traditions occurred in Indigenous communities before contact, the issue at hand is the legitimacy and accuracy of oral tradition as a means of transferring knowledge. The common mistake made in discussions of oral tradition is that it equates this means of information transference with the child's game of "telephone." In this game, children whisper a phrase or story to each other and enjoy the change of information from the first person to the last. Equating oral tradition with this children's game has resulted in the illegitimate dismissal of vast bodies of Indigenous knowledge. Unfamiliar audiences find flaws with oral tradition and knowledge because they fail to understand the process (McIsaac 93). Indeed, the use of the term "oral tradition" carries so many negative stereotypes it may be preferable to use the term "oral literature" (Couture 162). Gregory Cajete, writing in *Native Science*, explains that oral tradition requires an understanding of Indigenous information transference as "symbolic" (metaphorical) (28–31; 94). Therefore, the practice of oral literature requires one to think on multiple levels and in multiple dimensions at the same time. Given Cajete's analysis, the amount of information transmitted through oral literature is comparable in accuracy and legitimacy to Western written literature but differs in the memory capacity needed to store the information. Canada has recently begun to recognize oral literature as both accurate and legitimate in court cases as is documented in Bruce Miller's work *Oral History on Trial*. Miller expresses the importance of allowing Aboriginal individuals and communities to express their own histories, traditions, and stories in the manner appropriate to their cultures.

It is interesting that storytelling is the perceived standard of all information passed in Indigenous communities. Such stereotyping gives the impression that Indigenous people communicate only through storytelling and that no other form of knowledge transmission occurs. In point of fact, there are as many forms of oral information transference in Indigenous communities as can be found in Western written traditions. However, it may help to understand the metaphoric aspect of knowledge transference to examine storytelling as a mode of knowledge transference. Indigenous storytelling is considered a highly specialized skill that takes years if not a lifetime to master. The stories that are told must be learned with precision. Additionally, the storyteller must be skilled at reading the audience and delivering the information in a way so as to not be harmful to anyone in the audience. Keith Basso offers a discussion on language and storytelling among the Western Apache. His account of the intricacies and skills necessary to deliver information is useful in coming to understand oral literature in Indigenous communities. Basso further explains the importance of silence, timing, humor, and the thought processes that go into oral communication. Because great skill is required in proper oral literature, often only the elder population is given the authority to transmit certain information (105–49).

Within Indigenous traditions, "knowledge comes first from the family" but "may include prayer, prescience, dreams, and messages from the dead" (Holmes 37). The beginning of storytelling works first to teach and later to "remind us of who we are" in relation to family, community, and cosmology (Kovach 94). Storytelling as a method of transferring knowledge begins at a young age and includes the explanation of belonging, social organization, and ethics. As Cajete indicates, the beginning may involve what appears to be a very simple story, but as an individual grows physically and intellectually, layers of knowledge are added to the initial understanding (*Native*, 13–55). The result is a lifetime of "coming to understand" the multiple layers of information transmitted by a story, which may require simply the mention of the story name to trigger that understanding (Cajete, *Native*, 28–31; Basso 71–104). Winona LaDuke summarizes the significance of oral literature by stating that "our language, our teachings, and our cultural practices are one" ("People," 24). How the knowledge is imparted is an intricate part of the knowledge given. The process is inseparable from the social constructs that form the communities. The intricacies of language and knowledge transmission require not only great skill in the telling, but equal skill in the receiving. Indeed, the *Handbook of Critical and Indigenous Methodologies* offers a discussion of science and its transmission of stories as a method for greater cosmological understanding (Cajete 487–96).

The use of oral literature in connecting "teachings and cultural practices" allows for the Indigenous inclusion of spirit as a significant component of cosmological knowledge (LaDuke, "People," 24). While aspects of spirit exist in Western cosmological traditions, these are often relegated to specific realms of knowledge and, in some cases, discounted as possible valid knowledge claims, allowing them only a status of "faith." Indigenous knowledge allows for spirit as part of, and inseparable from, all forms of cosmological knowledge. Indeed, "knowledge that endures is spirit driven" (Meyer 218). Additionally, the "truth value" involved in Indigenous knowledge claims is derived from cosmological connections, one of which is spirit (Holmes 42).

COSMOLOGY

Historically, discussions of cosmology have included aspects of both philosophy and religion. However, more recent academic specialization has resulted in deferring the term "cosmology" to scientific disciplines. In searching for academic discussions of cosmology, one is overwhelmed with scientific discussions of the topic. Attempts to find works devoted to the whole of cosmology, including the philosophical and religious aspects, seem relegated to texts archived in ancient and medieval studies. The division of disciplines has often denied the place of philosophical and religious studies in scientific arenas, relegating ethics, deities, and spirituality to the humanities. Indigenous cultures, however, do not segregate knowledge into disciplinary structures except in the abstract sense. It is understood that the philosophical and religious/spiritual aspects of existence are essential to any discussion of cosmology. One could talk about, for example, rock formations using only scientific knowledge, but to do so would be to have only a partial discussion. For a complete discussion to take place, one must include the philosophical and the religious/spiritual components.

According to Cajete, "cosmology is a culture's guiding story, and that story reflects on ways of relating and understanding themselves in natural community" ("Seven," 495). From this perspective, a culture's cosmology gives insight into the whole of that community. The inclusion or exclusion of specific aspects pertaining to human experience boasts no objective truth but instead discloses the values, truths, organization, and relations of the given community. Additionally, cosmologies represent a community's answers to questions such as how life began, the function of life, and how objects are related in the universe. The Western scientific origin story—while still somewhat up for debate given the lack of consensus concerning dark matter and string theory—largely ascribes to some form of scientific orientation. This origin story is often not referred to as such because it falls academically into science rather than into religion, but it serves the same function as all origin stories in terms of answering questions pertaining to how and why life began. Belief or faith in a given origin story depends on the cultural upbringing of the individual. Given logical and postmodern theories of truth and knowledge, neither scientific nor religious/spiritual creation stories can be "proven" absolutely, or in many cases even beyond a reasonable doubt, and so the acceptance of each story requires a certain level of faith.

Members of Western cultures may be a bit taken aback at this point in finding themselves to be in a "faith" relationship when it comes to science, but Western logic dictates that such an understanding be employed. Science involves "facts," and facts are by logical definition contingent. Logical contingency states that things that are contingent may or may not be the case depending upon what exists in the world, but contingent things are not "necessary." Necessity, being a matter of things which cannot be other than what they are, allows for few objects or ideas to participate in the "necessary" realm. Logical discussions, of facts as contingent, then allows for limited levels of "truth" or "proof" at best. Absolute truth or proof ends up representing a small, if at all existent, population of objects or ideas. That being said, theories, which are created from facts, tend to be, at best, verifiable or justifiable but not absolute or proven. Given Western logical foundations, it makes little sense to discuss origin theories or even cosmologies in terms of necessary or absolute truth. At best the theories are justifiable or potentially verifiable. Potential verification comes from the idea that it might be possible at some point to verify things such as string theory, dark matter, or quantum gravitation. By the same token Spider Woman, spiritual realms, and life after death are also potentially verifiable. For this chapter, judgments as to whose creation story and whose cosmology is "correct" will not be considered. As postmodern theories disallow the idea that total objectivity can exist in making such judgments, it is understood that individuals and communities fall subjectively within their paradigms and so hold to the truths and cosmologies justified within those paradigms. Instead, respect for all paradigms and theories will be assumed as dictated by moral tenets within Indigenous cosmological paradigms.

THE GREAT MYSTERY

It may be best to begin a discussion of Indigenous cosmologies with a brief examination of the Great Mystery. This term was chosen from the many terms such as Creator, Great Spirit, or other designators for two reasons. First, each community and language has a different term for what may be considered the ultimate being of the universe, and this chapter does not intend to limit the discussion to one designator. Second, these terms are already compromised in the discussion because they have been translated into English and so carry with them contexts associated with the English-language paradigms rather than Indigenous-language paradigms. The use of the Great Mystery was chosen to expresses an Indigenous commonality referring to "that which is beyond human understanding." Indigenous cultures tend to allow for knowledge that is, and will always be, beyond human understanding. There is an aspect of Indigenous cosmologies that will always be a mystery and that fact is both acceptable and comfortable for members of these paradigms. Not all things require explanation or exploration. Furthermore, the use of the Great

Mystery indicates an understanding that the character of the Creator and the exact method of creation are not necessarily required in order to understand other aspects of existence. For many Indigenous communities it is enough to say things were created and then to focus on what follows from the fact that existence occurs. For these reasons, exacting descriptions of creation, events in existence, and life after existence are often left vague. Indeed, the allowance of mystery and the unexplainable is one of the many differences between Indigenous cosmologies and Western scientific cosmologies.

Considering the allowance of mystery and the metaphorical nature of knowledge as described by Cajete, it is understandable that the discussion of origin stories, nature, and relations often comes in the oral form of storytelling.

Before there were people on the earth, the Chief of the Sky spirits grew tired of his home in the Above World, because the air was always brittle with an icy cold. So he carved a hole in the sky with a stone and pushed all the snow and ice down below until he made a great mound that reached from the earth almost to the sky. Today it is known as Mount Shasta.

Then the Sky Spirit took his walking stick, stepped from a cloud to the peak, and walked down to the mountain. When he was about halfway to the valley below, he began to put his finger to the ground here and there, here and there. Wherever his finger touched, a tree grew. The snow melted in his footsteps, and the water ran down in the rivers.

The Sky Spirit broke off the small end of his giant stick and threw the pieces into the rivers. The longer pieces turned into beaver and otter; the smaller pieces became fish. When the leaves dropped from the trees, he picked them up, blew upon them, and so made the birds. Then he took the big end of his giant stick and made all the animals that walked on the earth, the biggest of which were the grizzly bears. (Modoc—Reported by Ella Clark in 1953) (Erdoes 85–86)

How water came to be, nobody knows. Where Old Man Coyote came from, nobody knows. But he was, he lived. Old Man Coyote spoke: "It is bad that I am alone. I should have someone to talk to. It is bad that there is only water and nothing else." Old Man Coyote walked around. Then he saw some who were living—two ducks with red eyes.

"Younger brothers," he said, "is there anything in this world but water and still more water? What do you think?"

"Why," said the ducks, "we think there might be something deep down below the water. In our hearts we believe this."

"Well, younger brothers, go and dive. Find out if there is something, Go!" One of the ducks dove down. He stayed under water for a long time. . . .

> At last the first duck came to the surface. "What our hearts told us was right," he said. "There is something down there, because my head bumped into it." . . .
>
> The duck went down a third time. This time he came up with a small lump of soft earth in his bill. Old Man Coyote examined it. "Ah, my younger brother, this is what I wanted. This I will make big. This I will spread around. This little handful of mud shall be our home." (Crow) (Erdoes 88)

These stories have multiple layers of meaning and offer specific knowledge within the communities to which they belong. Indeed, complete understanding requires one to have intricate familiarity with the community paradigm in which the story occurs. It is also understood that some information is lost, not only because these stories have been translated into English but also because they have lost the significance imparted by being orally given rather than written. Being written, much is lost involving relation, interaction, and the breath that brings knowledge into existence. These written versions have a tendency to mimic the Western models of scientific transferences of knowledge, which eliminates the relational and spiritual aspects involved in oral literature. The elements of ethics, relationship, and interconnectivity of the cosmos are essential in the focuses of oral literature and are often viewed as brought about through breath.

SPIRIT

For Indigenous communities, spirit "is a life force connected to all other life forces" (Meyer 218). Nothing is without spirit and all things relate through spirit. For those uncomfortable with the term "spirit" because of Western religious connotations or because of an alignment with Western scientific cosmologies, it may be easier to think of "spirit" in the Indigenous context of "energy." Energy runs through all matter and all non-matter; it connects all beings and allows those beings to interact.

Vine Deloria Jr. offers a discussion of spirit/energy in *The World We Used to Live In* that may clarify the Indigenous concept. According to Deloria Jr., the universal energy is that which stands beyond the limits of science. Western reductionist concepts of materialism involve concerns as to the ultimate "stuff" of the universe and what lies beyond that. If one continues on the reductionist model to the "smallest" or "ultimate" component of the universe, one is often plagued with the question of whether or not there is something "beyond" or more "ultimate" (193–214). Deloria Jr. offers the prospect that what lies beyond is "a similar LOGOS" or, in Indigenous ideology, "Spirit" (196). Spirit further denies the Western mind–body dichotomy and introduces the "energetic mind" (195–97). It is then the "spiritual nature [that] enhances the physical" aspects of the universe (201). Because spirit/ energy stands in a position of primacy and enhances the physical, Indigenous paradigms place spirit in a position of primary concern when considering the interaction of beings and issues of disability. According to Cajete, "The spirit and the spiritual were at the center of each human being and all that made up the universe" ("Seven," 490). For these reasons, Indigenous knowledge transmission tends to focus on the spirit/energy metaphorical level of given "stories."

The cosmological structure of spirit/energy allows for the relation and communication of all elements of existence. Communication is not restricted to physical communication but is allowed spirit to spirit. Humans can therefore communicate not only physically by mouth, ear, eyes, and hands but also spiritually with each other, which would eliminate the need to focus on sight or auditory "disabilities." Additionally, spirits of various beings can communicate including humans and animals, or humans and plants. It should be noted that communication spirit to spirit need not be considered the same as that from human to human in a physical manner. In Indigenous understanding, there is a communication that is possible beyond the physical that is part of the mystery (spirit) of the cosmos. This communication between spirits allows for the understanding that exists in Indigenous cultures between themselves and nature and between themselves and other dimensions, including spiritual dimensions. When spirit/energy connects all existence, physical barriers no longer impede communication and opportunities for gaining knowledge through spiritual channels becomes an expected and common part of existence rather than an impossible or miraculous part. An impairment of sight or sound does not result in a designator of "disability" as the primary mode of communication, cosmologically speaking, is through spirit and this does not require physical abilities.

NATURE

Spirit in all things dictates life in all things. The Earth itself is considered to be living rather than dead matter as held in Western scientific cosmologies. Furthermore, as all beings are living, they all have value, purpose, agency, and wisdom. Nature is not passive (Forbes 107). "The visible universe is indeed, dynamic, changing, and often unpredictable, and it certainly bears little or hardly any relationship to how it was at its 'birth' or beginning (if it had a beginning)" (Forbes 107). Furthermore, value is equal among all beings and so no being has cosmological preference over any other. In this way, humans are one among many and not preferred by the Creator over other beings; nature is a whole of related beings. This can be understood as one of the metaphorical layers to the knowledge stories, which use natural elements and animals as teachers of humans. In many of these stories, humans are considered the younger siblings to minerals, plants, and animals (Montejo 177). Humans are then the ones with many lessons to be learned from the wiser and older siblings. In some stories it is the humans, being mindless and selfish, that cause not only the rise of illness and disability but also the very catastrophes that require multiple creations.

Western cosmologies often view nature as adversarial. Additionally, Western concepts of nature have become entangled in Christian ideology, which can further depict nature as a negative element in human existence (Forbes 104). Indigenous cosmologies view human–nature interactions as cooperative (Mohawk 26–28). "Nature and Nation have the same root, being derived from the Latin verb *nasci*, to be born" (Forbes 103). The Indigenous concept of "born," when applied to "nation," must include nature as that from which any nation is "born."

To understand Indigenous concepts of nature, consider the intense relationship between Indigenous individuals, communities, and the land. References to earth as Mother are not to be considered quaint or childlike. It represents a commitment to the understanding that all things arise from (or are born from) earth and return to earth. The matter that makes up bodies is none other than earth itself. While in the womb, a child is created from the body of the mother, and she creates using the food and drink consumed, all of which is earth. It is "the land to which the people belong," not the land that belongs to the people (LaDuke, "People," 23). The idea is that the land from which a person is created is the land to which the individual belongs. The relationship between land mother and child is the same as between human mother and child as elements of each went into the creation. For this and other reasons, Leslie Gray states that the entire earth is "Holy Land" while some specific spaces can be considered "sacred sites" (28–29). It is not that some land is more precious than other land but that all the earth creates individuals and communities; all the earth is alive; and all the earth has value and agency of its own. The land is " 'that which feeds,' is the everything to our sense of love, joy, and nourishment. Land is our Mother" (Meyer 219).

A long time ago there were two chiefs. One was sick. Many Indians were there with their head chief. The chief said, "I am very sick; I want to lie down in the shadow." . . . "When I am dead, I want you to make a fire and

put me in it. Take a stick and scatter my ashes when I am all burnt up." That
is what he told them when he was sick. . . .

After a while he was dead. They made a big pile of wood. . . .

They made the ground smooth where they had burned the man, and
put water on it. That is what the chief had told the Indians to do when he
was sick.

They came to the place every day to see what had happened. After some
days green things came up. They put water on these; after a time they had
corn. Ears grew on the corn and when they were ripe, they picked them.
The chief who was left said that the Hopi should take the best corn and the
Havasupai should take the little ear. Each should take one. The corn is the
dead man's heart. That is, the small corn, because Coyote ran away with the
big heart. (Tikalsky, Euler, and Nagel 71–72)

According to the *Popol Vuh*, humans were made of corn (plant life), and the
animals helped to collect the food which entered into the flesh and blood
of the first men and women. This is, then, the starting point of the contribution to life and the collective survival that must exist between humans,
plants, and animals. Humans are not separated from plants since, according
to Mayan creation myths, corn, the miraculous staple domesticated in the
New World, entered into the body and became the flesh of human beings.
This, in turn, explains the profound respect, appreciation, and compassion
that Mayans feel for the trees and animals for whom they pray during their
cyclical ceremonies of the Mayan new year. (Montejo 177–78)

ALL OUR RELATIONS

Interconnectivity and spirit communication represents a unique identity construct within Indigenous knowledge. It engenders the understanding that
beings relate to one another in an equitable fashion. The Indigenous construct
requires that nature be "an extension of society" or "extended family" and one
does not "meddl[e] in the internal affairs of the 'extended family'" (Posey 29).
The relationship between the family members may be distant but requires
that respect and thoughtfulness be employed in all interactions. This concept
helps to explain why nature and the elements of nature, such as plants and animals, are given personhood in Indigenous paradigms. Reference can be seen
in Indigenous languages to geese people or tree people as an understanding of
the cosmological position of nature (Fienup-Riordan 551). Additionally, the
oral literature often refers to "brother wolf" or "cousin crane" as indicators that
nature is not for the use of humans but has its own value and purpose. Therefore, a story explaining the negative consequences of hunting or cutting down
a tree without first gaining permission from the right spiritual agency occurs

frequently in Indigenous oral literature. The consequences almost always involve negative experiences including negative health or disability events for the perpetrators of the disrespect. As mentioned earlier, the concept of "asking permission" is not to be constructed, as it has so often been in the past by both academics and the greater Western communities, to be necessarily voice-to-ear communication. Such depictions represent an unsophisticated stereotype of the deeper spirit communication that occurs.

It is understood in Indigenous cultures that individuals will participate in ceremonies or rituals, including prayers, before hunting or taking from nature to ensure that the act is done correctly with respect and reciprocity. This is considered the hunter and prey cycle of reciprocity (Fienup-Riordan 541). The communication takes place on a spiritual level, which often requires instruction. It is also understood that participants are required to listen on a level that goes beyond the physical to the spiritual. Children within Indigenous families are instructed as to how this communication is to be obtained, which may include prayer, meditation, sitting quietly, and learning to hear or read the answers that are given. While this may seem beyond the experience of Western scientific cosmology, one must remember that the limits of one cosmology do not dictate the limits of another.

It is not expected that people using different paradigms experience the same phenomena within the cosmos or that they act toward the cosmos in the same manner. Consider John Mohawk's discussion involving a Western capitalist and a socialist as they approach a tree in opposition to that of the Indigenous individuals. For the capitalist, the consideration is how to use the tree to gain the best profit whereas the socialist considers how to use the tree for the best social benefit. Conversely, the Indigenous individuals consider first how the tree wishes to exist. The value of the tree, for the Western individuals, is determined based on how it best serves humans, but the Indigenous perspective regards the tree as having value in itself and for itself (26).

The interdependence of extended family establishes that "the power of space is one of relationships" (Deloria Jr. 202). The actions and interactions of beings, persons of all species, entail consequences for all other beings. Add into nature the multidimensional aspect of the cosmos—such as the spiritual—and one begins to understand the complexity of Indigenous daily existence. Indeed, ancestral knowledge focuses on reciprocal responsibility throughout nature (Holmes 46–47). Reciprocal responsibility extends beyond the immediate moment in time to include multiple generations on either side of current existence. In this way, no element of nature should be misused because an obligation to multiple generations of ancestors exists, regarding the maintenance of the community for multiple generations of descendants.

While this idea has been misinterpreted to mean leaving these nature communities for multiple generations of human use, that interpretation fails to recognize the Indigenous concept of nature as valuable in its own right.

ETHICS

Consideration for all relations, along with the concept involving the cycle of reciprocity, establishes the foundation for an ethical system that involves two primary components. The first component establishes the concept of non-harm, which requires that to the extent one can, one should harm none. Avoidance of harm requires one to engage in commutative practices with nature to ensure that the purpose, agency, and generations of all beings be considered and respected before action is taken. The second component requires that, to the extent one can, one should assist all beings. Again, as extended family, nature obligates one to responsibilities required in family assistance such as physical and spiritual support. Within many Indigenous communities, ceremonies are held on a regular basis designed to support nature and the cosmos. The focus of these ceremonies is to preserve nature not for the sake of humans but for the sake of nature itself.

For everything taken from nature, a reciprocal obligation is created. Add to this obligation the concept involving spirit/energy connections of all things and one understands that, for Indigenous ethics, everything one thinks, says, or does must be understood as having ramifications for all one's relations. Before acting, one must consider how one's actions could impact all of the relations, which requires appropriate time be taken for deliberation. LaDuke chronicles the negative impact involving choices of environmental harm. She focuses on the consequences of choices and the results of human failures to follow reciprocity ethics.

Ethical ramifications of choices and consequences are a common theme in much of the oral knowledge passed from generation to generation. Teaching children at a young age and then allowing them to grow to remember the lessons of choices and consequences becomes a matter of "shooting an individual with a story" (Basso 37–70). As respect for all relations is understood, it also requires that individuals, including small children, not be subjected to humiliation or embarrassing correction in public. Indeed, in many cases direct correction is not done in private either so as to avoid the negative impact of such events on the individual's physical and mental health. Instead, stories that are not specifically focused on the individual can be used to teach, or to "shoot," an individual with needed lessons (Basso 61). A story that has been experienced since a young age may only need to be mentioned for the effect to be complete. The individual will then consider the meaning of the story for his or her situation (Basso 60). The implication is that one's ethical education, along with other aspects of education, is one's own responsibility. Learning one's lessons is understood to be one of the spiritual reasons for human existence in this cosmos. In addition to the consequences of not learning specific lessons, there are consequences for ignoring the need to learn any lessons at all, both of which often result in physical illness or disability. Each individual is responsible for his or her own choices and the consequences that result from those choices.

To bring together the entirety of the above information before moving into the discussion of health, it may help to consider the following quote.

> Knowledge is intended to incite humans to act in such ways as to ensure the protection and reproduction of *all* creatures in the universe. Political and social history does not exist in a different realm from indigenous cosmology; rather, it *intersects* with that cosmology. (Holmes 37–38)

The knowledge of Indigenous cosmology then comes from "heart knowledge, blood memory, and the voice of the land" (Holmes 40). Each of these has a specific impact on the health of the individual, the community, and the earth itself. As the individual and nature are extensions one from the other, their health is interactive. The health of one depends on the health of the other. Just as an individual may become unwell, the earth can also become unwell (Spector 277).

HEALTH AND WELLNESS

> In the old days the beasts, birds, fishes, insects, and plants could all talk, and they and the people lived together in peace and friendship. But as time went on the people increased so rapidly that their settlements spread over the whole earth, and the poor animals found themselves beginning to be cramped for room. This was bad enough, but to make it worse Man invented bows, knives, blowguns, spears, and hooks, and began to slaughter the larger animals, birds, and fishes for their flesh or their skins, while the smaller creatures, such as the frogs, and worms, were crushed and trodden upon without thought, out of pure carelessness or contempt. So the animals resolved to consult upon measures for their common safety. (Mooney 250)

In this story, the decision of the animal people was to inflict the consequences of illness on the human race in order to teach the humans lessons of respect and reciprocity. "The Deer next held a council under their chief, the Little Deer, and after some talk decided to send rheumatism to every hunter who should kill one of them unless he took care to ask their pardon for the offence" (Mooney 250–51). In any situation where a hunter kills, Little Deer will appear at the scene to see if the hunter obeys the proper ceremonies and the giving of thanks. According to the stories, each animal community imposed negative consequences for acts of human disrespectful behavior. The fish and reptiles caused humans to "dream of eating raw or decaying fish, so that they would lose appetite, sicken and die" (Mooney 251).

> They began then to devise and name so many new diseases, one after the other, that had not their invention at last failed them, no one of the human race would have been able to survive. . . .
>
> When the Plants, who were friendly to Man, heard what had been done by the animals, they determined to defeat the latters' evil designs. Each Tree, Shrub, arid Herb, down even to the Grasses and Mosses, agreed to furnish a cure for some one of the diseases named, and each said: "I shall appear to help Man when he calls upon me in his need." Thus came medicine; and the plants, every one of which has its use if we only knew it. . . . Even weeds were made for some good purpose, which we must find out for ourselves. When the doctor does not know what medicine to use for a sick man the spirit of the plant tells him. (Mooney 251–52)

While the above story comes from Mooney's description of Cherokee oral knowledge, and so has been subject to some debate over the years, it acts as an example of ethical violations and consequences. The disrespect to animals, the failure to treat them as people with value, and acts of thoughtlessness, violate the ethical Indigenous constructs and result in negative consequences. Humans had forgotten the lesson of reciprocity: when one receives a gift one must return the gift appropriately. Indeed, similar stories of disregard end in the severing of the human spiritual ability to communicate with animals and plants. Further traditions often allow for the restoration of communication only if humans, individuals and communities, restore the respect and reciprocity.

According to the Pima, sickness comes in two forms: "Staying Sickness" and "Wandering Sickness" (Beck, Walters, and Francisco 129). Each type of sickness has specific causes, the former are "caused by dangerous objects" and the latter by "noxious substances" (129). Other aspects of unwellness such as "bites, infant deformities, retardation . . . are not considered sicknesses" (129).

> Of all the above categories, *only Staying Sickness is the property of Pimans alone.* They are, in other words, the only people in the world who can suffer from Staying Sickness. . . . Gregorio explains . . . a special relationship

exists between the Pimans, the rules given to the Pimans at the time of creation, and their illnesses or diseases. Illnesses or diseases, Gregorio says, were
"given to" the Pimans during their early history. The Piman people must
accept these illnesses as part of the balance of creation and life, even though
they are unpleasant and dangerous. . . . The twins agreed that though each of
these were unpleasant to *The People*, all were necessary to remind *The People*
of the right way to live a long life.

   Pimans get Ka:cim sicknesses because they have behaved improperly
towards a "dangerous object" which was given "dignity" at the time of creation. Ka:cim sicknesses are cured by rituals which "appeal to the dignity
of the offended object." Problems such as retardation and deformities cannot be cured because their source is different from ka:cim sickness. These
problems come from having made fun of such afflicted people—people or
objects that *were not given dignity* at the time of creation. (Beck, Walters, and
Francisco 129)

The designation of sickness difference allows for an understanding of causal
factors. Understanding the ramifications of one's actions is not a designation
of "guilt" or "deserve," as is often found in Western cosmologies and theories,
but an identification of possible treatment options. Failing to give others proper
dignity requires different treatment than failing to deal properly with dangerous objects. Identification of causation does not entail a necessary cultural
stigma in Indigenous practices. The notion that causal factors entail a cultural
stigma or a guilt relation is an association involved in Western theologies and
should not be read into Indigenous constructs.

   Another account of unwellness and curing ceremonies is given in the
following White Mountain Apache tradition:

> This is how ceremonies started among us for the curing of sick people.
> Long, long ago, the earth was made. Then the One Who Made the Earth
> also planned for each person to have a piece of land that he could live on and
> call his own. . . .
>
>   Then two men among them became sick and grew weaker day by day.
> The people didn't do anything for them because no one knew then about
> illnesses and how to cure them. The One Who Made the Earth said, "Why
> don't you do something for those two men? Why don't you say some words
> over them?" But the people had no knowledge of curing ceremonies.
>
>   Four men among the people happened to be standing, one to the east,
> one to the south, one to the west, and one to the north. The One Who Made
> the Earth spoke to one of these men, telling him, "Everything on earth has
> power to cause its own kind of sickness, make its own trouble. There is a
> way to cure all these things." Now this man understood that knowledge was
> available. Then those four stood there. On the first night, the one standing

on the east side began to chant a set prayer all by himself. On the second night, the one on the south started to drum and sing lightning songs. On the third night, the one on the west chanted a set prayer. On the fourth night, the one on the north began to drum and sing lightning songs. They did not conceive this pattern in their own minds; it was bestowed upon them by the One Who Made the Earth. It was as if the knowledge of what they should chant or sing had suddenly been transmitted to them from outside.

Then The One Who Made the Earth said to these four, "Why don't you go to the two sick men and say some words over them and make them well?" So those four went to where the two sick men were and worked over them, and they were cured. From that time on, we had curing ceremonies and knowledge of the different kinds of sickness that may be caused by various things. That's the way all curing ceremonies started. (—Based on a tale reported by Grenville Goodwin in 1939) (Erdoes 37–38)

These three traditions represent only a fraction of the oral literature available involving wellness and unwellness in humans. Each tradition carries multiple layers of knowledge including reciprocity, respect, dignity, interrelations, and spirituality. Many layers of knowledge may be gleaned by non-members of each community. Other layers of knowledge are both specific and private to the community to which these traditions belong. It is important to note that in many cases Indigenous communities do not believe it is appropriate for all people to have all information. Some information is not for public consumption even within a given community. Indigenous paradigms respect the privacy rights regarding certain knowledge. This is often frustrating for those outside of Indigenous communities, especially for those in Western academics. However, considering the Indigenous comfort with and respect for the Great Mystery, it is not surprising that some knowledge is considered inappropriate for some people. Additionally, some knowledge can create harm if not used or handled carefully and with respect. For example, in the wrong hands knowledge of herbs can cause great harm and so should be limited to those of great wisdom and skill.

While never the most exciting part of academics, being clear on definitions and how they fit into a given paradigm assists in a more accurate understanding. To begin, Western scientific-paradigm discussions of health and disability reflect a reductionist tendency focused on cures and the elimination of the illness or disability (Hollow 31–38). The idea of health involves the "correct" or "normal" working of the body without "illness" or "disability," which represents incorrect bodily function (Davis 23–49). Wendell discusses the Western need to envision health as the overcoming of any illness or disability. Moreover, Western concepts of health contain a component of "normal" body-mind function, with deviations from that "normal" defined as "abnormal" (Davis, *Enforcing*, 23–49; Davis, "Constructing," 3–19). Individuals then strive, with the help of medicine, to maintain or return to "normal."

Conversely, Indigenous communities construct health issues in terms of wellness and unwellness (Lovern and Locust 33–54, 83–85). These terms focus on concepts of balance and harmony, which here will be used interchangeably although a deeper discussion of the terms is important for further understanding. Rather than the elimination of body or mind differences, wellness occurs when one gains an ability of "living in total harmony with nature and having the ability to survive under exceedingly difficult circumstances" (Spector 277). A person is considered to be well if he/she is able to live in harmony with his or her illness or disability. The elimination of the illness or disability is not the focus of Indigenous healing. Granted, if the illness or disability can be eliminated, that is a positive event, but if it cannot be eliminated, then the individual must come to balance with the difference as a part of his or her whole being. Wellness then requires a balancing of mind, body, and spirit (Lovern and Locust 40–54). If one component is out of balance, there can be a negative impact on the other components of the individual resulting in illness or disability. As mentioned earlier, spirit has a primary position cosmologically and so the focus of treatment is on the spiritual aspects of the individual, not on the physical, which is secondary in treatment focus.

In many cases, the treatment of unwellness begins with an attempt to find the cause of the event. The cause may be natural or unnatural (Lovern and Locust 99–100). Causes can then include contact with dead or sick people and animals but can also include conflict, anger, disrespect, or failed reciprocity. Anger, for example, is often considered a form of mental illness and may be translated as an imbalance of the mind. Efforts to restore balance, in conflict situations involving any relation, will then require the entire community to act as mediators until the conflict is resolved (Harden 42). Attempting to determine the cause of unwellness does not involve a concern for guilt or blame but is the means for determining treatment. Illness and disability are the consequences of past or current actions and the correct ceremonies must be done to maintain or to restore harmony (Spector 278). For example, "to the Navahos the treatment of an illness . . . must be concerned with the external causative factor(s) and not with the illness or injury itself" (279). The determination of the cause may take the medicine person several days of diagnostic ceremony to determine and may require several days of treatment ceremony to assist in regaining balance (279). Ceremonies may be private or may require community, including nature elements. Furthermore, Western concepts of diagnosis tend to involve an "international standards classification system. . . . The diagnoses are based on groups of symptoms that define specific disorders, which are assumed to exist across cultures" (Roubideaux 269). Indigenous wellness and unwellness occurs in cultural context, not within international standards, and must be treated within those same contexts (Patterson 237–41).

"Everything they [Indigenous people] did, they did in prayer. . . . Healing and medicines were based on spirituality. If one was sick, one did not search for a microbe or virus to blame, one searched one's very soul. What had gone wrong in the person's life to upset the balance?" (Harden 41). Prayer and ceremony help to organize Indigenous behavior throughout existence. Therefore, individuals may participate in ceremonies on a daily basis as well as in designated community ceremonies. In point of fact, almost all ceremonies in Indigenous cultures contain a healing aspect. Ceremonies, including prayers, help to return the individual, community, or nature to a harmonious state. Traditional Indigenous medicine is a part of and uses traditional ceremonies to assist in the regaining of balance (33–34).

"To live in good health is to live in accordance with certain 'lifeways' or belief systems" (Hollow 33). There is no "normal/abnormal" construct in Indigenous traditional paradigms. So, each individual is created appropriately and intentionally. A difference in a body or mind is considered part of existence. Furthermore, as all things are in constant flux, concepts of "normal" and "correct" make little sense (Cajete, *Native*, 13–19). People, as with all things in the universe, are constantly changing. For wellness to occur, each change must be brought into balance with all aspects of the individual. Additionally, since individuals exist with all their relations, the balance must extend beyond the individual to the extended family, human and non-human alike. The community then exists to assist the individual in establishing balance and maintaining it throughout that individual's life. It is further understood that balance or harmony is not a state that once achieved can be maintained without adjustment. Balance is considered a process that requires adjustments to life changes. For this reason, individuals must be diligent in their attempts to gain balance. While each individual is responsible for his or her pursuit of balance, the community has an obligation to assist. Understood in this way, it becomes clear why Indigenous cosmologies define individuals in terms of responsibilities rather than rights. Each individual, being born into a complex of extended family relations, is born into a complex of responsibilities. Body or mind differences, therefore, become less of an issue. Instead, the emphasis involving personal definition focuses on the extent to which the individual fulfills obligations. What an individual cannot do becomes less significant than what an individual can do.

According to Posey, "Up to 80 percent of the nonindustrial world's population still relies on traditional forms of medicine" (31–32). "In 1887, the US Congress passed the Dawes' Act, making it illegal for Indians to practice TIM [Traditional Indian Medicine]. TIM was covertly practiced by Indian people from 1887 until 1978, when the Indian Religious Freedom Act made it legal for Indians to use TIM" (Hollow 31). Additional struggles for religious freedom, and the right to practice traditional medicine, are documented by Smith and Snake. Even within more assimilated communities, cultural traditions of TIM often surface. The difficulty occurs when the oral knowledge exists within a person or community but there is a lack of access to traditional healers. Attempts have been made in Canada to unite Western and TIM practices to better serve the Indigenous communities (Dudziak 234–47). The amount of assimilation may dictate the outcome of these attempts and the extent to which the combined Western and Indigenous programs succeed.

DISABILITY

Western cultures focus on practices of both exclusion and segregation of those they historically labeled as "handicapped" or "disabled" (see Davis, *Enforcing*; Foucault). Indigenous cultures viewed these individuals as important and equal members of the society (Lovern and Locust 95–110). Instead of excluding or segregating, all people historically were understood to be of value and able to assist, to some extent, the extended family. Furthermore, since all people have differences, with no "normal/abnormal" designation, the differences were often seen as highly valuable to the greater society. One who may be considered a bit "slow" mentally may have good legs that assist those unable to walk far or at all. Those who may not hear well may be of extreme value for those with bad sight and vice versa. Physical abilities can then be understood in a way similar to that involving individual talent. Some people are talented in singing, ceremony, or medicine; others may be talented in hearing, sight, and mobility, but all are integral to a well-balanced society. Therefore, those considered "disabled" in the Western sense and often marginalized are considered valued social members in Indigenous communities (Patterson 239).

Individuals of difference, even those with severe differences, are understood to have value. Often these people "may be given special status as a messenger from the spiritual world or may be viewed as having 'differing abilities'" (Patterson 239). As recorded by Patterson, Ladoux gave a presentation explaining that when a child (person) "acquires a disability or chronic illness, we believe that this child is here to remind us that something is out of balance with the universe. We must pay attention to all this child will teach us" (237). One then understands that not all spirits are able to manage a different or severely different body. It takes an extremely strong spirit to attach to such a body. While Garland-Thomson has worked to reassert the value and strength of "extraordinary bodies" in Western literature, these figures have been in place for generations in Indigenous literature and recognized as such. "Among some Southwestern tribes, for example, Kokopeli, a mythical humpbacked figure playing a flute, is an important part of tribal legends because he signifies social values such as happiness or fertility" (Joe 253–54). These beings and stories exemplify the idea that spirits remain whole and intact regardless of the body to which they are attached. Furthermore, it is common to understand that the attachment of a spirit to a body is the choice of the spirit prior to integration (Lovern and Locust 95–110). Since it is just the body that is different, or may not function well in some respects, the spirit is whole and capable of communication. In this way, medicine people are often able to communicate directly spirit to spirit with individuals unable to communicate physically.

The view of spiritual aspects as superior to physical, in the Indigenous system, explains why many families will not see children of difference as being "disabled" or recognize a child as having "limitations" (Patterson 239). If the child is functioning well in the home and able to fulfill chores and obligations, the Indigenous family may see no limitation or disability at all. When limitations are noticed, the extended family and friends tend to work together to support the child's needs. This is true for all community members of difference. It is not the understanding within Indigenous communities that the needs of people, including people of difference, are an individual's or a single family's responsibility. Cultural relationships and ethics dictate the assistance of the larger community (Red Horse 243–50).

CONCLUSION

Much can be learned in Western communities from the inclusion and respect for people of difference expressed in Indigenous paradigms. Understanding the emphasis on spiritual, rather than physical, aspects of an individual allows for a redefinition of the term "person" and eliminates the need for normal/abnormal designators. While Indigenous communities have exhibited an inclusive dynamic for centuries, Western discussions involving disability are relatively new (Davis, "Constructing," 301). Ironically, Indigenous knowledge claims and discussions involving equity, value, and reciprocity of all beings are refused legitimacy until they are located within the Western academic discussions. A similar concern is echoed in *Is Disability Studies Actually White Disability Studies* (Bell 374–81). Western cultures tend to value Indigenous knowledge only after it has been "discovered" by Western explorers or academics. The prejudice against Indigenous knowledge, oral or otherwise, remains the constant in discussions of knowledge. The inclusion of Indigenous paradigms within Western disability discussions would allow for the expansion beyond what Bell calls the "incestuous" to include a global dialogue (377). Moreover, Western disability discussions attempting to eliminate discrimination would be well served to recognize that "normalcy" issues are not universal; they tend to be Western paradigm dependent. The inclusion of non-Western scholars into the field of disability studies would work to eliminate the existing dichotomous hierarchy, which lists Western scholars as the established "normal" and non-Western scholars as "abnormal" and in need of Western acceptance before being assigned legitimacy.

In addition to increasing cultural competency involving Indigenous cultures, a study of these knowledge paradigms can be used as an argument for the cultural inclusion of individuals with mental and physical differences. Adjusting to an Indigenous paradigm of inclusion increases the dignity of all relations within a community and promotes a communal balance that fosters not only wellness in the individual but a greater cosmological wellness.

Notes

1: DONAHUE

1 According to the *Oxford English Dictionary*, first by Persians; according to Doniger, first by Herodotus (*Hindus*, 30).

2 We encountered this fourfold varna system above in our discussion of the second Rig Veda creation sūkta.

3 The term *jāti* means both "kind" in general as well as regionally specific "kinds of persons."

4 The caste system in contemporary India fuses the fourfold varna system with an array of regional *jātis*, along with European sociocultural elements. The term "caste," for instance, derives etymologically from Portuguese. In contemporary Indian culture, the word *jāti* (unlike *varna*) is often used as a synonym for "caste."

5 King Dhritarashtra's name literally means "blind king." We will discuss representations in the *Mahabharata* of Dhritarashtra and his blindness in the next section.

6 The Pandavas are jointly married to one woman, Draupadi.

7 *Purusha-uttama*, also known as Vishnu and Brahman.

2: HARRIS

1 Most of this chapter will follow the conventions of ordinary language in which impairment and disability are used as synonyms. For discussions of disability that distinguish between impairment and disability, the terminology will be adjusted accordingly. The correctness or incorrectness of any particular understanding of disability is not meant to be implied by using these terms interchangeably elsewhere.

2 For two excellent resources that provide a much more detailed introduction to Indian Buddhism, see Gethin, *Foundations*, and Williams and Tribe, *Buddhist Thought*.

3 Indian Buddhist texts have been written in many different languages, the most influential of which are Sanskrit and Pali. The Sanskrit versions of Buddhist terms are used throughout this chapter. The Buddha himself spoke a regional vernacular that was

probably descended from Sanskrit, but no Buddhist texts written in this language have come down to us.

4   Buddhist texts claim that there are three kinds of suffering: ordinary pain (*duḥkha-duḥkhatā*), which we all recognize; the suffering of change (*vipariṇāma-duḥkhatā*), which refers to the dissatisfactory nature of pleasure; and conditioned suffering (*saṃskāra-duḥkhatā*), which is the kind of unsatisfactoriness resulting from the instability of everything that depends on causes and conditions. For a brief introduction, see Gethin, *Foundations*, 60–63.

5   Buddhist texts claim it is possible to take six types of rebirth, three of which are negative and three positive. The negative rebirths are as an animal, a hell denizen, and a *preta*, a kind of ghost that haunts the invisible world, tormented by a great craving it cannot satisfy. The good rebirths are as a human, a demigod, and a deity. There are also two very subtle rebirths called the form and formless realms where beings with particularly good karma can be reborn. For an overview of the Buddhist cosmos, see Williams and Tribe, *Buddhist Thought*, 74–81.

6   Early Buddhist teachings stress the importance of escaping from the cycle of death and rebirth oneself. Later Buddhist Mahayana texts begin to emphasize the value of remaining in samsara for countless eons in order to develop the skill to lead others to liberation.

7   *Karma-phala* (the fruit of karma) refers to karma's effects. The doctrine of karma is also accepted by Hinduism and Jainism, although the Buddhist emphasis on the importance of good and bad motivations in determining karmic effects distinguishes it from some other understandings.

8   The fourth noble truth is usually identified in Buddhist texts with the noble eightfold path of right view, right intention, right speech, right action, right livelihood, right effort, right mindfulness, and right concentration. For a brief explanation, see Williams and Tribe, *Buddhist Thought*, 52–55.

9   See Aśvaghoṣa for a prominent telling of this story.

10 In many versions of the story, including Aśvaghoṣa's, the four encounters are actually with disguised messengers of the gods, sent to convince the Buddha to seek liberation.

11 Some Buddhist schools of philosophy claim nirvana is an existing entity that is permanent and does not depend on causes and conditions; see Gethin, *Foundations*, 210.

12 Buddhist texts refer to this characteristic as not-self (*anātman*), but it applies to all composite phenomena and characterizes them as dependently arisen (*pratītyasamutpāda*).

13 The Madhyamaka school of Buddhist philosophy claims that nothing exists independent of labeling by sentient beings. In contrast, many early Buddhist schools accept that partless events, called *dharmas*, exist independent of human interests, but anything composed of dharmas has no reality except as a useful way of speaking.

14 The classic Buddhist example is found in *The Questions of King Milinda* (Rhys Davids 40–45).

15 For a discussion of these cognitive mistakes that is based upon early Buddhist sources, see Hamilton, *Identity and Experience*, 55–60.

16 The names for the three models are adopted from Wasserman, although their descriptions have been simplified. For a more in-depth explanation of possible models and definitions, see Altman, "Disability Definitions."

17 For an influential development of the minority model, see Oliver, *Politics*.

18 For a critique of the minority model, see Terzi, "Social Model."

19 For a detailed explanation of the human-variation model, see Scotch and Schriner, "Human Variation."

20 Both the minority and the human-variation models distinguish between impairment and disability, with impairment often being linked to functional limitation. Disability, for the social model, is the limiting of opportunities caused by social oppression upon persons with this impairment, see Smith, "Social Justice," 18–19.

21 For useful summaries of criticisms of the conflation of disability with illness, as well as partial critiques, see Wendell, "Unhealthy Disabled," 17–19; Amundson, "Biological Normality"; and Terzi, "Social Model," 143–44.

22 As a Madhyamaka, Śāntideva holds all entities, not just the ones with parts, are unreal, but for our purposes, we can ignore this complication.

23 Since Śāntideva does not clearly distinguish between biological sex and gender, the Sanskrit terms he uses, *strī* (woman) and *pums* (man), plausibly indicate both.

24 For an argument against linking Buddhist karma theory with a negative appraisal of disability, see Bejoian.

25 On rebirth as a *preta*, see note five above.

26 The image of the turtle also appears in *The Middle Length Discourses of the Buddha* (Ñāṇamoli and Bodhi 1020–21).

27 For a good explanation of the negative qualities of rebirth as a deity, see Gampopa, *Jewel Ornament*, 60–66.

28 *Jina* (conqueror) is an epithet for the Buddha.

29 For two considerations of the possible value of painful experience resulting from disability, developed independently of Buddhist insights, see Wendell, "Feminist Theory," 250–51, and Smith, "Social Justice," 26–27.

30 Early Buddhist texts consider the Buddha to have been a bodhisattva in his previous lives, but they do not encourage ordinary persons to aim for this goal.

3: LUKEY

1 Confucius (551–497 BCE) is the Latinized name of Kong Qiu, also known as Kong Zhongni. In Chinese, he is referred to as "Master Kong" (Kongfuzi). Though it reflects the influence of Western intellectual colonialism, the name Confucius is used since it is most familiar to Western readers.

2 Also remember that, given the gerundive commitment, relations themselves are processes rather than things.

3 One of the most common but narrow translations of *zhong* is "loyalty," which expresses the idea of doing one's utmost in particular relationships with one's leaders.

4 This metaphor is also appropriate for understanding one who is adept at *ren* 仁.

5 "Person" is used as a term of moral considerability and is distinguished from the term "human being," which can be used as both a moral term and a biological term.

6 See Silvers, "Reconciling Equality," esp. p. 45. Thus "impairment" is equally appropriate for a paraplegic who lost limbs from an accident and a paraplegic who was born with little function in his legs or arms.

7 To be fair, philosophers such as McMahan are not interested in defining a notion of personhood. They focus on capacities because "personhood" and "dignity" are such vague terms and liable to unjust bias in their application.

8 I wish to thank Arindam Chakrabarti for this novel way of expressing *shu* 恕.

9   There is, however, a long-standing disagreement among Confucian lineages as to whether person-becoming was the cultivation of intrinsic roots or the effortful extirpation of human flaws; see Ivanhoe, *Confucian*.

10   It should be clear that the parents do not want others to relate to their child *as parents*; Kittay is not expecting McMahan to see Sesha as his daughter.

11   Kittay critiques Peter Singer in particular for declining her invitation to visit a living community for those with mental disabilities on account of his skepticism that he would learn anything morally relevant from such a visit ("Personal," 618).

12   In order to not interpret Confucius as simply advocating corruption, consider book 15 of the *Xiaojing* wherein Confucius is aghast at the suggestion of one of his students that being filial is merely obeying the commands of one's parents. He sharply responds that sons have a duty to remonstrate (*jian* 諫) with their parents: "Thus if confronted by reprehensible behavior on his father's part, a son has no choice but to remonstrate with his father" (Henry Rosemont Jr., and Roger T. Ames, *The Chinese Classic of Family Reverence: A Philosophical Translation of the Xiaojing* [Honolulu: University of Hawaii Press, 2009], 114).

13   It is the first half of the sentence, "a father covers for his son," that suggests such an interpretation. When a child commits a wrong, responsibility falls upon the parents to address the wrong and correct the child's behavior. The child is not allowed to get away with the crime; in many cases he is expected to answer to his parents or teachers (though the legal trend has been to criminally prosecute more instances of juvenile crime).

14   Wong indicates such an understanding of Confucian autonomy in his essay in honor of Rosemont ("If We Are Not by Ourselves," 339).

4: LAMBERT

1   "The events of the world arise from the determinate (*you* 有), and the determinate arises from the indeterminate (*wu*)" (*Daodejing*, 139; ch. 40; all quotes from the *Daodejing* are from Ames and Hall's edition).

2   "The morning mushroom knows nothing of the noontime" (*Zhuangzi* 4; 1.5; all quotes from the *Zhuangzi* are from Ziporyn's edition); also see 2.7.

3   For stories about death in the *Zhuangzi*, see Ziporyn, *Zhungzi*, 45–47, especially the death of Zhuangzi's wife in the received text (Graham 123–24).

4   There is some playful speculation about what might be behind the transformations. Zhuangzi talks in passing of the "creator of things" (*zao wu zhe*), but this appears to be a rhetorical flourish, and the question is never pursued.

5   The Chinese character *dao* 道 is composed of a head 首—i.e., a person—and a road or path 辶. The character thus suggests a person moving along a path. A third meaning of dao in the text is that of discourse or a guiding social code. In this sense, dao is used critically to refer to the Confucian fondness for fixed ritual and the upholding of normative hierarchical social roles, such as ruler-minister and father-son, but the Daoists do not reject such relationships per se. The *Zhuangzi*, for example, recognizes the father-son bond, but sees it as a natural (*tian*) phenomenon, not a relationship structured by social mores.

6   See the six *qi* 六氣 in *Zhuangzi* 1.8.

7   Techniques such as meditation, breathing exercises, and fasting are used to control *qi* (*Daodejing,* 10, 56; *Zhuangzi* 4.9).

8   Zhuangzi's many debates with the logician Huizi frequently end with this conclusion (Ziporyn 38). Also note the skeptical arguments about language in chapter 2.

9   See, for example, *Daodejing,* chs. 17, 56, 57, and passim.

10   Most famous of these is the story of Cook Ding carving an ox, and doing so with such intuitive precision that he finds the spaces between the joints and his knife has remained sharp for nineteen years (Ziporyn, *Zhuangzi*, 22).

11   A contemporary example would be the tendency to contrast healthy with unhealthy and abled with disabled, and then to unreflectively associate healthy with abled and unhealthy with disabled (Schumm and Stoltzfus, "Beyond Models," 153).

12   See *Analects* 8.3, and *The Chinese Classic of Family Reverence, The Xiaojing*, sec. 1 (Rosemont and Ames, *Xiaojing*, 105).

13   Caution is needed regarding the degree to which Daoist thinking opposed Confucian thought. It is not entirely clear how much the early Confucians were moved by social approbation. Confucius approves of his daughter marrying an ex-convict and insists that the scholar-apprentice not be afraid of poverty or anonymity. Further, retreat from a troubled world is discussed in the latter books of the *Analects*, a theme typically regarded as Daoist. Confucian and Daoist schools often present a range of opinions rather than a united front.

14   This subversion of the status of the normal human body is found in other parts of the text, and extends to the treatment of the dead body. The *Zhuangzi* mocks those who attach too much significance a lifeless form. See, for example, 6.45.

15   Similar stories of acceptance of bodily transformation include 6.27 and 6.48.

16   Talk of transformations might be thought to apply only to a limited set of physical disabilities. But while congenital disablement is less easily captured by this framework, it is not entirely excluded, as even congenital issues can have distinctive patterns or ways of unfolding not captured by common knowledge. Regardless, creatively responding to transformations of the body has meaning when the able-bodied become physically disabled.

17   Miles describes how deformed fascia and limbs, leprosy and bomb blast damage lead to people feeling unable to classify the person before them and so experiencing discomfort or even revulsion. He notes that this problem is concealed to some degree in affluent countries, where medical resources enable the restoration of a semblance of human form ("Disability on a Different Model," 92–93).

18   Another related conception of body is relevant here: the *gong* (躬) body refers to the body that participates in ritualized interactions, behaving according to precedent or social expectation and fulfilling duties attaching to roles and rituals.

19   Unity (*yi* 一), which might also be translated as one, oneness, wholeness, or singularity, is prominent in chapter 6, for example.

20   Other references to unity include 6.29: "Emulating what ties all things together, on which depends even their slightest transformation, on which depends the total mass of transformation that they are." See also *DDJ* 49 and 58.

21   When treated as a metaphysical claim, such a view might seem implausible and difficult to accept. Indeed, some early Chinese schools are skeptical about this idea of a holistic unity within an extended body. For example, in Mencius 2A2 Gongsun Chou asks Mencius whether disciples of Confucius were of one body with the sage; Mencius dismisses the thought.

22   Furthermore, as A. C. Graham notes, the *Zhuangzi* never asserts that all things are one, but only that the sage looks upon them as one (*Chuang-tzŭ*, 56).

23   Compare *Zhuangzi* 6.27: "If you hide the world in the world, so there is nowhere for anything to escape to, this is an arrangement, the vastest arrangement, that can sustain all things."

24   The idea of *yiti*, or one body or a unified whole, explains the Daoist indifference to the popular distinction between life and death, since the death of the individual physical body does not entail the end of the larger ti body. In fact, death is, in some perverse sense, part of the ti body: "Who knows the single body (yiti) formed by life and death, existence and non-existence? I will be his friend" (45); "It is not life that produces death, and it is not death that brings life. . . . Both are parts of the same body, which confers on them their unity" (91). This one body encompasses the myriad forces that produce both life and death. The final move in this logic is for the sages to forget about the earthly coil entirely and to treat their human form (*xing*) as if it was something external to themselves (36).

25   This view is reinforced by the only other use of tally in the inner chapters of the *Zhuangzi* (4.9). There, the tally refers to the rigid and fixed conceptions through which people approach the world. Such people recognize only those experiences, objects, or values that "tally" or fit with their preconceived notions. This includes conventional social norms that prized an intact body, free from brandishing, tattooing, and amputation.

26   See, for example, the stories on pages 8, 30, 31, and 32.

27   *Analects* 15.42 describes an encounter between Confucius and a blind music master. On the place of blind musicians in Chinese society, see Miles, "Disability on a Different Model," 100–101.

28   Passage 20 reads: "I alone am so impassive, revealing nothing at all. Like a babe that has yet to smile; So listless, as though nowhere to go." See also *DDJ*, 28.

29   Crane is responding here to a passage in the *Zhuangzi*: "It's sad, isn't it? We slave our lives away and never get anywhere, work ourselves ragged and never find our way home. How could it be anything but sorrow? . . . Life is total confusion. Or is it that I'm the only one that's confused?" (Crane, *Aidan's Way*, 187).

30   For an account how such projects or character are necessary to the most basic human motivations to do anything, see Williams, "Persons, Character and Morality."

31   For example, Zhuangzi famously rejects the offer of an official appointment, preferring to remain free from the burdens of government (*Zhuangzi*, ch. 17).

5: BELSER

1   I follow the conventions of capitalization commonly used in Deaf communities; the capital letter in Deaf denotes membership in a particular culture that shares broad language practices, lifeways, artistic interests, and political sensibilities. While Deaf culture is customarily rooted in the organic realities of deafness, the cultural practices of Deafness are not exclusively tied to the physical fact of non-hearing. Affiliation with Deaf community is a cultural alignment. Many people with hearing impairment do not identify with Deaf culture, while some hearing children of Deaf parents may be fully enfolded within Deaf community and be recognized as culturally Deaf (Holcomb, *Introduction to American Deaf Culture*, 38).

2   Schipper notes that in Deut 7:14-15, Moses promises that if Israel obeys the divine commandments, there will be neither male nor female infertility in their midst ("Disabling Israelite Leadership," 105).

3   The commandment has also been interpreted to forbid actions that enable or encourage another person to commit a sin (Friedman, "Place a Stumbling Block").

4   Babylonian Talmud, Pesachim 116b includes a debate over whether a person who is blind may recite the Haggadah to lead the ritual and reading for the commemoration of Passover via the Seder dinner. While the text initially excludes the blind from reciting this text, the passage goes on to challenge this ruling, citing the example of both Rav Yosef and Rav Sheshet, two blind rabbis who were known to have recited the Haggadah for their students. On biblical and Talmudic figures who were blind, see Steinberg, "Blind in the Light," 284.

5   While some halakhists have followed this ruling, it has been explicitly rejected by influential decisors such as Yosef Karo, author of Shulkhan Arukh (Nevins, "Participation of Jews," 32).

6: IOZZIO

1   Much could be written about the early Christian churches of the Latin West and the Byzantine East that I do not engage in this chapter. The history is replete with doctrinal debates, convergence, and separation co-occurring within and across the cultural divide. I limit my considerations here to the Roman Catholic tradition.

2   I am aware of the dangers surrounding the conflation of people with disabilities to the scriptural challenges regarding the sick, poor, and ill. Those dangers reduce the subject noun following the definite article to an object in place of the person who may be sick with a temporary condition, who may live with little to no means of support, or who may have a persistent condition that today would be recognized as disabling. This caveat aside, many people with disabilities do experience poverty and marginalizing stigmatization on account of their "deviance" from the normative measures of being male, heterosexual, and of able body and mind.

3   See 2014 statistics available through the American Health Care Association, www.ahca .org; and Hall, "Altar and Table."

4   See Balthasar, "Eucharistic"; Balthasar, "Mediation"; and Koerpel, Form and Drama of the Church," 70–99.

5   All Scripture references are taken from the New Revised Standard Version Bible.

6   See Brent, *Ignatius of Antioch*.

7   For the contemporary understanding of the catechumenate (particularly in light of the Rite of Christian Initiation of Adults), see Dooley, "Baptismal Catechumenate."

8   For the history of canon law, see Coriden, *Introduction*.

9   For commentary, see Spiteri, *Canon Law Explained*.

10 For the laity conferring baptism, see Catholic 903, 1256, 1284, and Canon 861. For marriage, see Catholic 1623 and Canon 1108–23.

11 "Only a baptized man can validly receive sacred ordination" (Canon 1024).

12 Unfortunately, contrary to the United States Bishops' "Pastoral Statement on Persons with Disabilities," a good deal of anecdotal evidence suggests that many persons with disabilities have been denied admission to the rites of the Eucharist/Communion. See, for example, McKew, "Confirmation for Youth with Disabilities."

13 I understand that conception occurs at the time an embryo implants successfully into the uterine wall, signifying thereby the start of a pregnancy, and which is interrupted licitly only by its failure to continue to adhere, receive nutriments, and so thrive. My understanding of conception takes into account the possibility that a fertilized ovum may fail

to implant. That said, the CDF and I recognize that a fertilized ovum is the beginning of a new life.

14 By natural death, the Church refers to death as the result of illness, age, or accident, thus excluding death-dealing acts of commission and omission (with qualifications opposing the maintenance of life by all medical or technological means, i.e., vitalism).

15 Of course, the Catholic commitment to the right to life extends also to pregnancies where no anomaly or suggestion of disability is present, every conceptus bears the *imago Dei*; it is necessary to recognize the dignity belonging to every instance of the *imago Dei* however much the conceptus remains in potentiality until birth and subsequent development through infancy, childhood, and adult life. "We believe that every person is precious, that people are more important than things, and that the measure of every institution is whether it threatens or enhances the life and dignity of the human person" (USCCB, "Life").

16 Kristeva is instructive in guarding against the charity cases of Christian humanism. "As regards the specific domain of disability, it is of note that the philosophy of privation includes [wrongly] without distinction the poor, the sick, the lepers, the drifters, and the disabled, all struck by a *lack* or a *defect*" (Kristeva, "Tragedy and a Dream," 226).

17 A good deal of contemporary Catholic social teaching follows the lead of the liberation theologies in response to the unjust social structures of dictatorships and gross economic disparities between the rich and powerful over the masses of people mired in poverty and other institutionalized structures of oppression that were and are a part of the lasting effects of Western colonialism on the Americas, Africa, Asia, and the Middle East (see Gutiérrez, *Theology of Liberation*).

18 Among other references, see Exod 22:20-26; Lev 19:9-10; Job 34:20-28; Prov 31:8-9; Isa 58:5-7.

19 What God intends specifically cannot be divined, though it is generally safe to conclude that God does not create with the expectation that what is created will wither unnaturally or prematurely. That said, and following the insights of Martha C. Nussbaum on these and other "basic human functioning capabilities," surely God would not intend the denial of the goods indicative of that kind of development ("Capabilities").

20 The Latin American Bishops' Conference, CELAM, has met five times: Rio de Janeiro, Brazil (1955); Medellín, Colombia (1968); Puebla, Mexico (1979); Santo Domingo, Dominican Republic (1992); and Aparecida, Brazil (2007). The Conference at Medellín laid the groundwork for the subsequent initiatives of a theology for the poor with the poor. For the concluding document from Medellín, see CELAM, *Medellín Conclusions*.

21 To date, the only encyclical that includes reference to people with disabilities is John Paul II's *Evangelium vitae* (63). Popes Benedict and Francis have addressed our concern by means of speeches and other forms of address.

22 As many recognize today, the use of this term has been replaced, rightly, by the terms "cognitive disabilities" and "learning disabilities."

7: REYNOLDS

1 For an excellent introduction to Protestantism by an eminent historian, see Noll, *Protestantism: A Very Short Introduction*. Other now classic accounts of the Reformation and its heritage can be found in Chadwick, *The Reformation*, Dillenberger and Welch, *Protestant Christianity Interpreted through Its Development*, and Pauck, *The Heritage of the Reformation*.

2 Indulgences were a common practice in medieval Catholic traditions in which the clergy would grant pardon or remission of punishment for sin upon payment or service. Indulgences could reduce time paying for sins in purgatory in the afterlife. While Luther's Ninety-Five Theses did not completely reject all indulgences, it was critical of the notion that purgatory could be avoided by purchasing forgiveness for oneself or a loved one, thus undermining any need for personal responsibility and penance.

3 Luther uses the language of "works" to highlight human efforts to attain the righteousness that only God can freely confer through Christ. For example: "faith . . . alone can fulfill the law and justify without works. . . . Not by the doing of works but by believing do we glorify God and acknowledge that He is truthful. Therefore faith alone is the righteousness of a Christian and the fulfilling of the commandments" (Luther, "Freedom of a Christian," 61–62).

4 See Calvin. "no [person] is truly a believer unless he [or she] be firmly persuaded, that God is a propitious and benevolent [Parent] to him [or her]" (*Institutes* 3.2.16).

5 For Calvin's understanding of election and predestination, see Calvin, *Institutes* 3.21–23.

6 Luther states: "You will ask, 'If all who are in the church are priests, how do these whom we now call priests differ from laymen?' . . . Holy Scripture makes no distinction between them, although it gives the name 'ministers,' 'servants,' 'stewards' to those who are now proudly called popes, bishops, and lords and who should according to the ministry of the word serve others and teach them of the faith of Christ and the freedom of believers. Although we are all equally priests, we cannot all publicly minister and teach" (Luther, "Freedom of a Christian," 65).

7 Calvin put it this way: "there would be no employment so mean and sordid (provided we follow our vocation) as not to appear truly respectable, and be deemed highly important in the sight of God" (*Institutes* 3.10.650).

8 This also produced a corresponding stress on personal transformation in faith and virtue. Expressions of this emerged in the Pietist movements of the late seventeenth century among Lutherans in Germany and in the rise of Methodism in the Church of England under the influence of John Wesley (1703–1791), who along with his brother Charles Wesley (1707–1788) and George Whitefield (1714–1770) helped create a rebirth of religious vitality in the colonies of North America and in England—often called the Great Awakening (Noll, *Protestantism*, 43–55; Dillenberger and Welch, *Protestant Christianity*, 111–25). For John Wesley, focus was placed on conversion and renewal through the intimate reviving power of God, experienced as an affair of the heart with emotional intensity and culminating in processes of individual perfection or sanctification. The accent on personal conversion as an emotional experience of transformation increased with further North American revivals in the nineteenth century, birthing many new denominations of Protestant churches. Thus, personal, ecclesiastical, and social transformation were intertwined correlates of a Reformation emphasis on faith as a direct relation to God.

9 See Bell, "Introducing White Disability Studies"; Crawford and Ostrove, "Representations"; Erevelles, *Disability*; Garland-Thomson, *Extraordinary Bodies*; Goodley, *Disability Studies*, ch. 3.

10 The author is drawing from personal experience as the parent of a child on the autism spectrum.

11 See Elia Shabani Mligo, *Jesus and the Stigmatized*, an excellent account of such a logic with reference to people with HIV in Tanzania.

12 See Avalos, Melcher, and Schipper, *This Abled Body*; Moss and Schipper, *Disability Studies*; Black, *Healing*; and Yong, *Bible*.

13 For examples see Mark 1:23-28, 2:1-12, 7:31-37; and John 5:1-47.

14 For examples see Matt 9:22; Mark 5:34, 10:52; and Luke 8:48, 17:19, 18:42.

15 For an excellent textual analysis of Paul on his "infirmity" and its history of reception in Christian traditions, see Collins, "Paul's Disability."

8: RISPLER-CHAIM

1 There is a scholarly debate whether the two are the same, or if one term signifies a mandatory tax and the other a voluntary donation. *Zakat* is often identified with the compulsory duty, and the sharia elaborates on the different rates to be levied on different types of goods.

2 Among these collections the most trustworthy and famous are *Sahih Muslim* (d. 875) and *Sahih Bukhari* (d. 870), but *Sunan Abi Da'ud* (d. 889), *Sunan al-Tirmidhi* (d. 892), *Sunan Ibn Majah* (d. 887), Sunan al-Nisa'i, and more are also among the ten most relied upon for legal purposes.

3 Al-Za'tari is a contemporary religious scholar from Aleppo in Syria. He was born in 1965 and holds a Ph.D. in Islamic studies. He has his own website for his articles, fatwas, etc.

4 Lane, *Arabic English Lexicon*, s.v. "'a-wa-qa" and "'a-ja-za."

5 Hanafi, Shafi'i, Maliki, and Hanbali are the names of the four main schools of law in Sunni Islam. On their origins and development, see Hallaq, *Origins*, ch. 7; Melchert, "Sunni Schools," 351–66.

6 In this chapter Richardson discusses in detail the ethical and legal scholarly debate around the book *al-Nukat al-ziraf fi man ubtuliya bi'l-'ahat min al-ashraf* [Charming anecdotes about honorable people who were afflicted with disabilities] and whether it should be judged as slander or as honest biographies. The book was published around the first part of the sixteenth century by Jar Allah Ibn Fahd (1486–1547). Because of the uproar sparked by its first version, the author had to revise it and explain that he actually composed the book to "admonish those who admonish and entertain the students," not out of malicious intent.

7 "Not only transsexuality is permissible in Iran, sexual reassignment operations are financially subsidized by the Islamic Republic, supported by a clerical interpretation of Shariah . . ."; the "Islamic republic is fast becoming the sex-change capital of the world" (Bucar, "Bodies at the Martins," 602).

Works Cited

Abrams, Judith Z. *Judaism and Disability: Portrayals in Ancient Texts from the Tanach through the Bavli.* Washington, D.C.: Gallaudet University Press, 1998.

Abrams, Judith Z., and William C. Gaventa, eds. *Jewish Perspectives on Theology and the Human Experience of Disability.* Binghamton: Haworth Pastoral, 2006.

Albl, Martin. "'For Whenever I Am Weak, Then I Am Strong': Disability in Paul's Epistles." In Avalos, Melcher, and Schipper, *This Abled Body*, 145–58.

Alexander, Elizabeth Shanks. *Gender and Timebound Commandments in Judaism.* New York: Cambridge University Press, 2013.

Ali, Abdullah Yusuf. *The Qur'an Translation.* Elmhurst: Tahrike Tarsile Qur'an, 2009.

Altman, Barbara M. "Disability Definitions, Models, Classification Schemes, and Applications." In *The Handbook of Disability Studies*, edited by Gary L. Albrecht, Katerine D. Seelman, and Michael Bury, 97–122. Thousand Oaks, Calif.: Sage, 2001.

Ames, Roger. *Confucian Role Ethics: A Vocabulary.* Honolulu: University of Hawaii Press, 2011.

Ames, Roger, and David Hall. *Dao De Jing: A Philosophical Translation.* New York: Ballantine, 2003.

———. *Focusing the Familiar: A Translation and Philosophical Interpretation of the "Zhongyong."* Honolulu: University of Hawaii Press, 2001.

Ames, Roger, and Henry Rosemont. *The Analects of Confucius: A Philosophical Translation.* New York: Ballantine, 1998.

Amundson, Ron. "Biological Normality and the ADA." In *Americans with Disabilities: Exploring Implications of the Law for Individuals and Institutions*, edited by Leslie Francis and Anita Silvers, 102–10. New York: Routledge, 2000.

———. "Disability, Handicap, and the Environment." *Journal of Social Philosophy* 23, no. 1 (1992): 105–19.

Aquinas, Thomas. *Summa Theologica*. Translated by the Fathers of the English Dominican Province. New York: Benziger Brothers, 1947. Christian Classics Ethereal Library. Accessed May 24, 2014.

Appadurai, Arjun. "Topographies of the Self: Praise and Emotion in Hindu India." In *Language and the Politics of Emotion*, edited by Catherine A. Lutz and Lila Abu-Lughod, 93–113. Cambridge: Cambridge University Press, 1990.

Asanga. *Asanga's Chapter on Ethics With the Commentary of Tsong-Kha-Pa: The Basic Path to Awakening, The Complete Bodhisattva*. Translated by Mark Tatz. Lewiston, Maine: Edwin Mellen, 1986.

Aśvaghoṣa. *Life of the Buddha*. Translated by Patrick Olivelle. New York: New York University Press, 2008.

Augustine. *City of God and Christian Doctrine*. Edited by Philip Schaff. Translated by Marcus Dods. Edinburgh: T&T Clark, 1886. Christian Classics Ethereal Library. Accessed May 24, 2014.

Aurobindo, Sri. *Bhagavad Gita and Its Message: With Text, Translation and Sri Aurobindo's Commentary*. Edited by Anilbaran Roy. Twin Lakes, Wis.: Lotus Press, 1995.

Avalos, Hector, Sarah J. Melcher, and Jeremy Schipper, eds. *This Abled Body: Rethinking Disabilities in Biblical Studies*. Atlanta: Society of Biblical Literature, 2007.

Babylonian Talmud, The. Edited by Isidore Epstein. 30 vols. London: Soncino, 1952.

Baderin, Mashood A. *International Human Rights and Islamic Law*. Oxford: Oxford University Press, 2009.

Balthasar, Hans Urs von. "The Holy Church and the Eucharistic Sacrifice." *Communio: International Catholic Review* 12, no. 2 (1985): 139–45.

———. "The Mediation of the Form." In *The Glory of the Lord: A Theological Aesthetics*, edited by Joseph Fessio and John Riches, translated by Erasmo Leiva-Merikakis, 527–604. Edinburgh: T&T Clark, 1982.

Banks, Raechel. "Reform Movement: Failure to Ratify International Disability Rights Treaty Deeply Disappointing." Religious Action Center of Reform Judaism. December 5, 2012. Accessed October 20, 2013.

Barrera, Albino. "The Common Good as Due Order and Due Proportion." In *Modern Catholic Social Documents and Political Economy*, 287–304. Washington, D.C.: Georgetown University Press, 2001.

Basso, Keith H. *Wisdom Sits in Places: Landscape and Language among the Western Apache*. Albuquerque: University of New Mexico Press, 2000.

Beauchamp, Tom, and James Childress. *Principles of Biomedical Ethics*. New York: Oxford University Press, 1983.

Beck, Peggy V., Anna Lee Walters, and Nia Francisco. *The Sacred: Ways of Knowledge, Sources of Life*. Tsaile, Ariz.: Navajo Community College Press, 1992.

Bejoian, Lynne M. "Nondualistic Paradigms in Disability Studies & Buddhism: Creating Bridges for Theoretical Practice." *Disability Studies Quarterly* 26, no. 3 (2006): 2. Accessed November 14, 2013.

Bell, C. "Introducing White Disability Studies." In Davis, *Disability Studies Reader*, 2nd ed., 275–82.

———. "Is Disability Studies Actually White Disability Studies?" In Davis, *Disability Studies Reader*, 3rd ed., 374–82.

Belser, Julia Watts. "Reading Talmudic Bodies: Disability, Narrative, and the Gaze in Rabbinic Judaism." In Schumm and Stoltzfus, *Disability in Judaism*, 5–27.

Bérubé, Michael. *Life As We Know It: A Father, a Family, and an Exceptional Child*. New York: Pantheon, 1996.

Betcher, Sharon V. *Spirit and the Politics of Disablement*. Minneapolis: Fortress, 2007.

Bhatt, Usha. *The Physically Handicapped in India (A Growing National Problem)*. Bombay: Popular Book Depot, 1963.

Biale, David. *Cultures of the Jews: A New History*. New York: Random, 2002.

———. *Not in the Heavens: The Tradition of Secular Jewish Thought*. Princeton: Princeton University Press, 2010.

Black, Kathy. *A Healing Homiletic: Preaching and Disability*. Nashville: Abingdon, 1996.

Bodhi, Bhikkhu, trans. "Arahants, Bodhisattvas, and Buddhas." Access to Insight. August 22, 2010. Accessed August 17, 2013.

———, trans. *The Connected Discourses of the Buddha (Samyutta Nikāya)*. Boston: Wisdom, 2000.

———, trans. *The Numerical Discourses of the Buddha: A Translation of the Aṅguttara Nikāya*. Boston: Wisdom, 2012.

Bogdan, Robert, and Steven Taylor. "Relationships with Severely Disabled People: The Social Construction of Humanness." *Social Problems* 36, no. 2 (1989): 135–48.

Bornstein, Daniel. "A Brief History of Papal Resignations." Religion & Politics, February 24, 2013, http://religionandpolitics.org/2013/02/24/a-brief-history-of-papal-resignations/.

Braswell, George W. *Islam: Its Prophet, Peoples, Politics, and Power*. Nashville: Broadman, 1994.

Brattgard, Sven-Olaf. "Social and Psychological Aspects of the Situation of the Disabled." In *The Handicapped Person in the Community*, edited by David M. Boswell and Janet M. Wingrove, 7–9. London: Tavistock, 1974.

Brent, Allen. *Ignatius of Antioch: A Martyr Bishop and the Origin of the Episcopacy*. Edinburgh: T&T Clark, 2009.

Bucar, Elizabeth M. "Bodies at the Margins: The Case of Transsexuality in Catholic and Shia Ethics." *Journal of Religious Ethics* 38, no. 4 (2010): 601–15.

Burch, Susan. *Signs of Resistance: American Deaf Cultural History, 1900 to World War II*. New York: New York University Press, 2004.

Butler, Ruth, and Hester Parr, eds. *Mind and Body Spaces: Geographies of Illness, Impairment and Disability*. London: Routledge, 1999.

Byron, William J. "Ten Building Blocks of Catholic Social Teaching." *America* 179, no. 13 (1998): 9–12.

Cajete, Gregory. *Native Science: Natural Laws of Interdependence*. Santa Fe, N.Mex.: Clear Light, 2000.

———. "Seven Orientations for the Development of Indigenous Science Education." In *Handbook of Critical and Indigenous Methodologies*, edited by Norman K. Denzin, Yvonna S. Lincoln, and Linda Tuhiwai Smith, 487–96. Los Angeles: Sage, 2008.

Calvin, John. *The Institutes of the Christian Religion*. Translated by Henry Beveridge. Peabody, Mass.: Hendrickson, 2008.

Canon Law Society of America. *Code of Canon Law*. Vatican City: Libreria Editrice Vaticana, 1983.

Carter, Warren. "'The blind, lame and paralyzed' (John 5:3): John's Gospel, Disability Studies, and Postcolonial Perspectives." In Moss and Schipper, *Disability Studies*, 129–50.

Catholic Church. *Catechism of the Catholic Church*. Vatican City: Libreria Editrice Vaticana, 1993.

Center of Concern. *The Principle of the Common Good*. Education for Justice, 2008. Accessed April 24, 2014.

CELAM, Conference of Latin American Bishops. *Medellín Conclusions: The Church in the Present-Day Transformation of Latin America in the Light of the Council*. Bogota: General Secretariat of CELAM, 1968. Accessed April 25, 2014.

Central Conference of American Rabbis. "A Blind Person as a Witness." *CCAR Responsa* 5759, no. 8 (1999). Accessed October 22, 2013.

Chadwick, Owen. *The Reformation*. New York: Penguin, 1972.

Charlton, James. *Nothing about Us without Us: Disability, Oppression, and Empowerment*. Berkeley: University of California Press, 1998.

Christensen, Shelly. *Jewish Community Guide to Inclusion of People with Disabilities*. Minneapolis: Jewish Family and Children's Service of Minneapolis, 2007.

Clarke, Morgan. *Islam and New Kinship, Reproductive Technology and the Shariah in Lebanon*. New York: Berghahn Books, 2009.

Cohen, Lawrence. *No Aging in India: Alzheimer's, the Bad Family, and Other Modern Things*. Berkeley: University of California Press, 1998.

Cohen, Shaye. *From the Maccabees to the Mishnah*. Westminster: John Knox, 2006.

Coleman, Lerita M. "Stigma: An Enigma Demystified." In Davis, *Disability Studies Reader*, 2nd ed., 141–52.

Collins, Adela Yarbro. "Paul's Disability: The Thorn in His Flesh." In Moss and Schipper, *Disability Studies*, 164–83.

Committee for the Jubilee Day of the Community with Persons with Disabilities. *Preparation for the Jubilee Day: Parts One–Four*. Vatican City: Liberia Editrice Vaticana. December 3, 2000. Accessed April 26, 2014.

Congregation for the Doctrine of the Faith. *Donum Vitae: Instruction on Respect for Human Life in Its Origin and on the Dignity of Procreation*. Vatican City: Libreria Editrice Vaticana, 1987. Accessed April 21, 2014.

Coriden, James A. *An Introduction to Canon Law*. Rev. ed. Mahwah, N.J.: Paulist, 2004.

Couture, Joseph. "Native Studies and the Academy." In Dei, Hall, and Rosenberg, *Indigenous Knowledges*, 157–67.

Cowell, E. B., ed. *The Jātaka: Or Stories of the Buddha's Former Births*. Vol. 1. Translated by Robert Chalmers. New York, 1895. Internet Sacred Text Archive. Accessed November 14, 2013.

Crane, Sam. *Aidan's Way: The Story of a Boy's Life and a Father's Journey*. Naperville, Ill.: Sourcebooks, 2003.

Crawford, D., and J. M. Ostrove. "Representations of Disability and the Personal Relationships of Women with Disabilities." In *Women with Visible and Invisible Disabilities: Multiple Intersections, Multiple Issues, Multiple Therapies*, edited by Martha Banks and Ellyn Kaschak, 127–44. New York: Haworth, 2003.

Creamer, Deborah Beth. *Disability and Christian Theology: Embodied Limits and Constructive Possibilities*. Oxford: Oxford University Press, 2009.

Das, Veena, and Renu Addlakha. "Disability and Domestic Citizenship: Voice, Gender, and the Making of the Subject." *Public Culture* 13, no. 3 (2001): 511–31. Accessed May 15, 2013.

Davis, Lennard J. *Bending over Backwards: Disability, Dismodernism and Other Difficult Positions.* New York: New York University Press, 2002.

———. "Constructing Normalcy." In Davis, *Disability Studies Reader*, 3rd ed., 3–19.

———, ed. *The Disability Studies Reader.* 2nd ed. New York: Routledge, 2006. 3rd ed., 2010. 4th ed., 2013.

———. "The End of Identity Politics: On Disability as an Unstable Category." In Davis, *Disability Studies Reader*, 3rd ed., 301–15.

———. *Enforcing Normalcy: Disability, Deafness, and the Body.* New York: Verso, 1995.

Deloria, Vine, Jr. *The World We Used to Live In: Remembering the Powers of the Medicine Men.* Golden: Fulcrum, 2006.

Dei, George J. Sefa, Budd L. Hall, and Dorthy Goldin Rosenberg, eds. *Indigenous Knowledges in Global Contexts: Multiple Readings of Our World.* Toronto: University of Toronto Press, 2008.

Diesfeld, Kate. "Disability Matters in Medical Law." *Journal of Medical Ethics* 27 (2001): 388–92.

Dillenberger, John, and Claude Welch. *Protestant Christianity Interpreted through Its Development.* 2nd ed. New York: Macmillan, 1988.

Dols, Michael W. "The Leper in Medieval Islamic Society." *Speculum* 58, no. 4 (1983): 891–916.

———. *Majnun: The Madman in Medieval Islamic Society.* Oxford: Clarendon, 1992.

Doniger [Doniger O'Flaherty], Wendy. *The Hindus: An Alternative History.* New York: Penguin, 2009.

———. *The Laws of Manu.* New York: Penguin, 1991.

———. *The Rig Veda: An Anthology.* New York: Penguin, 1981.

———. *Textual Sources for the Study of Hinduism.* Chicago: University of Chicago Press, 1988.

Dooley, Catherine. "Baptismal Catechumenate: Model for All Catechesis." *Louvian Studies* 23 (1998): 114–23.

Dorff, Elliot. "Judaism and the Disabled: The Need for a Copernican Revolution." In *Healing and the Jewish Imagination: Spiritual and Practical Perspectives on Judaism and Health*, edited by William Cutter, 107–20. Woodstock: Jewish Lights, 2008.

Dudziak, Suzanne. "Partnership in Practice: Some Reflections on the Aboriginal Healing and Wellness Strategy." In Dei, Hall, and Rosenberg, *Indigenous Knowledges*, 234–47.

Eiesland, Nancy. "Barriers and Bridges: Relating the Disability Rights Movement and Religious Organizations." In Eiesland and Saliers, *Human Disability*, 200–29.

————. *The Disabled God: Toward a Liberatory Theology of Disability*. Nashville: Abingdon, 1994.

Eiesland, Nancy L., and Don E. Saliers, eds. *Human Disability and the Service of God: Reassessing Religious Practice*. Nashville: Abingdon, 1998.

Ener, Mine. *Managing Egypt's Poor and the Politics of Benevolence, 1800–1952*. Princeton: Princeton University Press, 2003.

Erdoes, Richard, and Alfonso Ortiz, eds. *American Indian Myths and Legends*. New York: Pantheon, 1984.

Erevelles, Nirmella. *Disability and Difference in Global Contexts: Enabling a Transformative Body Politic*. New York: Palgrave, 2011.

Fienup-Riordan, Ann. "A Guest on the Table: Ecology from the Yup'ik Eskimo Point of View." In Grim, *Indigenous Traditions*, 541–58.

Fingarette, Herbert. *Confucius: The Secular as Sacred*. Long Grove, N.Y.: Waveland, 1972.

Forbes, Jack D. "Nature and Culture: Problematic Concepts for Native Americans." In Grim, *Indigenous Traditions*, 103–24.

Foucault, Michael. *Madness and Civilization: A History of Insanity in the Age of Reason*. Translated by Richard Howard. London: Tavistock, 1982.

Fraade, Steven D. "Concepts of Scripture in Rabbinic Judaism: Oral and Written Torah." In *Jewish Concepts of Scripture: A Comparative Introduction*, edited by Benjamin D. Sommer, 31–46. New York: New York University Press, 2011.

Francis [Pope]. *Evangelium Gaudium: Apostolic Exhortation*. Vatican City: Liberia Editrice Vaticana, 2013. Accessed April 26, 2014.

Friedman, Hershey H. "Placing a Stumbling Block Before a Blind Person: An In-Depth Analysis." Jewish Law Articles. Jewish Law Blog, 2002. Accessed October 22, 2013.

Friedner, Michele. "Identity Formation and Transnational Discourses: Thinking beyond Identity Politics." *Indian Journal of Gender Studies* 15, no. 2 (2008): 365–85.

Gaff, Angela. *The Human Rights of Persons with Disabilities*. Ramallah: Al-Haq, 1994.

Gaillardetz, Richard. *A Daring Promise: A Spirituality of Christian Marriage*. Rev. ed. Barnhart, Mo.: Liguori Publications, 2007.

Gampopa. *The Jewel Ornament of Liberation*. Translated by Khenpo Konchog Gyaltsen Rinpoche. Ithaca, N.Y.: Snow Lion, 1998.

Garland-Thomson, Rosemarie. "Disability Studies: A Field Emerged." *American Quarterly* 64, no. 4 (2013): 915–26.

————. *Extraordinary Bodies: Figuring Physical Disability in American Culture and Literature*. New York: Columbia University Press, 1997.

————. "Feminist Disability Studies." *Signs: Journal of Women in Culture and Society* 30, no. 2 (2005): 1558–87.

————. "Staring Back: Self-Representations of Disabled Performance Artists." *American Quarterly* 52, no. 2 (2000): 334–38.

————. *Staring: How We Look*. Oxford: Oxford University Press, 2009.

Gethin, Rupert. *The Foundations of Buddhism*. Oxford: Oxford University Press, 1998.

Ghaly, Mohammed. *Islam and Disability: Perspectives in Theory and Jurisprudence*. London: Routledge, 2010.

Goffman, Erving. *Stigma: Notes on the Management of Spoiled Identity*. New York: Prentice-Hall, 1963.

Goldstein, Elyse. "Ceremonials, Rites, and Worship." In Schein and Waldman, *The Deaf Jew*, 56–60.

Goodley, Dan. *Disability Studies: An Interdisciplinary Introduction*. London: Sage, 2011.

Gracer, Bonnie. "What the Rabbis Heard: Deafness in the Mishnah." *Disability Studies Quarterly* 23, no. 2 (2003): 192–205.

Graham, A. C. *Chuang-tzǔ: The Inner Chapters*. Indianapolis: Hackett, 1981.

Grant, Colleen C. "Reinterpreting the Healing Narratives." In Eiesland and Saliers, *Human Disability*, 72–87.

Gray, Leslie. "The Whole Planet Is the Holy Land." In *Paradigm Wars: Indigenous Peoples' Resistance to Globalization*, edited by Jerry Mander and Victoria Tauli-Corpuz, 28–29. San Francisco: Sierra Club, 2006.

Grim, John A., ed. *Indigenous Traditions and Ecology: The Interbeing of Cosmology and Community*. Cambridge, Mass.: Harvard University Press, 2001.

Grossman, Daniel. "Jewish Signs and Vocabulary." In Schein and Waldman, *The Deaf Jew*, 61–64.

Gutiérrez, Gustavo. *A Theology of Liberation*. Maryknoll: Orbis, 1973.

Hall, Daniel. "Altar and Table: A Phenomenology of the Surgeon-Priest." *Yale Journal of Biology and Medicine* 81, no. 4 (2008): 193–98.

Hallaq, Wael B. *An Introduction to Islamic Law*. Cambridge: Cambridge University Press, 2010.

————. *The Origins and Evolution of Islamic Law*. Cambridge: Cambridge University Press, 2005.

Hamilton, Sue. *Identity and Experience: The Constitution of the Human Being According to Early Buddhism*. London: Luzac Oriental, 1996.

Harden, M. J. *Voices of Wisdom: Hawaiian Elders Speak*. Kula: Aka Press, 1999.

Hardman, Michael L., Clifford J. Drew, and M. Winston Egan. *Human Exceptionality: Society, School, and Family*. 7th ed. Boston: Allyn, 2002.

Holcomb, Thomas. *Introduction to American Deaf Culture*. New York: Oxford University Press, 2013.

Hollow, Walter B. "Traditional Indian Medicine." In *Primary Care of Native American Patients: Diagnosis, Therapy, and Epidemiology*, edited by James M.

Galloway, Bruce W. Goldberg, and Joseph S. Alpert, 31–38. Boston: Butterworth Heinemann, 1999.

Holmes, Leilani. "Heart Knowledge, Blood Memory, and the Voice of the Land: Implications of Research among Hawaiian Elders." In Dei, Hall, and Rosenberg, *Indigenous Knowledges*, 37–53.

Holtz, Barry, ed. *Back to the Sources: Reading the Classic Jewish Texts*. New York: Simon & Schuster, 1986.

———. "Marginality as a Site of Resistance." In *Out There: Marginalization and Contemporary Cultures*, edited by Russell Ferguson, Martha Gever, Trinh T. Minh-ha, and Cornel West, 341–43. Boston: MIT Press, 1990.

Horne, Simon. "'Those Who Are Blind See': Some New Testament Uses of Impairment, Inability, and Paradox." In Eiesland and Saliers, *Human Disability*, 88–101.

Heuser, Stefan. "The Human Condition as Seen from the Cross: Luther and Disability." In *Disability in the Christian Tradition: A Reader*, edited by Brian Brock and John Swinton, 184–215. Grand Rapids: Eerdmans, 2012.

Hysell, Matthew G. "Deaf Candidates to Holy Orders: Impediment or Opportunity?" M.A. Thesis. Newman Theological College, 2008. Scribd. Accessed April 21, 2014.

Inhorn, Marcia C. *Quest for Conception*. Philadelphia: University of Pennsylvania Press, 1994.

Iozzio, Mary Jo. "Norms Matter: A Hermeneutic of Disability/A Theological Anthropology of Radical Dependence." *ET-Studies* 4, no. 1 (2013): 89–106.

———. "Solidarity: Restoring Communion with Those Who Are Disabled." *Journal of Religion, Disability & Health* 15, no. 2 (2011): 139–52.

Issa, Ihsan al-, ed. *Al-Junun: Mental Illness in the Islamic World*. Madison: International Universities, 1999.

Ivanhoe, Philip. *Confucian Moral Self Cultivation*. Indianapolis: Hackett, 2000.

Jacobs, Jill. *There Shall Be No Needy: Pursuing Social Justice through Jewish Law and Tradition*. Woodstock, N.Y.: Jewish Lights, 2009.

Joe, Jennie R. "American Indian Children with Disabilities: The Impact of Culture on Health and Education Services." *The Journal of Collaborative Family HealthCare* 15, no. 3 (1997): 251–61.

John XXIII [Pope]. *Pacem in Terris: Encyclical Letter On Establishing Universal Peace in Truth, Justice, Charity, and Liberty*. Vatican City: Liberia Editrice Vaticana, 1963. Accessed April 26, 2014.

John Paul II [Pope]. *Evangelium Vitae*. Vatican City: Liberia Editrice Vaticana, 1995. Accessed April 26, 2014.

———. *Sollicitudo Rei Socialis*. Vatican City: Liberia Editrice Vaticana, 1987. Accessed April 26, 2014.

Johns, A. H. "Job." In *Encyclopedia of the Qur'an*, vol. 3, edited by Jane Dammens McAuliffe, 50–51. Leiden: Brill, 2003.

Jones, Melinda. "Judaism, Theology, and the Human Rights of People with Disabilities." In Abrams and Gaventa, *Jewish Perspectives*, 101–46.

Jones, R. B. "Impairment, Disability and Handicap—Old Fashioned Concepts?" *Journal of Medical Ethics* 27 (2001): 377–79.

Kaczor, Christopher. "Seven Principles of Catholic Social Teaching." *Catholic Answers* 18, no. 4 (2007). Accessed April 24, 2014.

Kafer, Alison. *Feminist, Queer, Crip*. Bloomington: Indiana University Press, 2013.

———. *Not So Random Thoughts*. New York: Reconstructionist, 1966.

Kittay, Eva. *Love's Labor: Essays on Women, Equality, and Dependency*. New York: Routledge, 1999.

———. "The Personal Is Philosophical Is Political: A Philosopher and Mother of a Cognitively Disabled Person Sends Notes from the Battlefield." *Metaphilosophy* 40, nos. 3–4 (2009): 606–27.

Koerpel, Robert. "The Form and Drama of the Church: Hans Urs von Balthasar on Mary, Peter, and the Eucharist." *Logos: A Journal of Catholic Thought and Culture* 11, no. 1 (2008): 70–99.

Koosed, Jennifer L., and Darla Y. Schumm. "Out of the Darkness: Examining the Rhetoric of Blindness in the Gospel of John." In Schumm and Stoltzfus, *Disability in Judaism*, 77–92.

Kovach, Margaret. *Indigenous Methodologies: Characteristics, Conversations, and Contexts*. Toronto: University of Toronto Press, 2009.

Kristeva, Julia. "A Tragedy and a Dream: Disability Revisited." *Irish Theological Quarterly* 78, no. 3 (2013): 219–30.

LaCugna, Catherine Mowry. *God for Us*. New York: HarperCollins, 1991.

LaDuke, Winona. *All Our Relations: Native Struggles for Land and Life*. Cambridge: South End, 1999.

———. "The People Belong to the Land." In *Paradigm Wars: Indigenous Peoples' Resistance to Globalization*, edited by Jerry Mander and Victoria Taulis-Corpuz, 23–25. San Francisco: Sierra Club, 2006.

Lagerwall, T., A. Ellamaa, L. Karu, M. Muklane, and T. Talvik. *Proceedings of the International Conference on Rehabilitation of Disabled Children: Present State and Future Trends*. August 12–26, 1989, Tallin, Estonia. Estonia: Tartu University, 1991.

Landsberg, Lynne. "Tell the Senate to Ratify the UN Convention on Disability Rights." *The Jewish Week*. June 19, 2013. Accessed October 20, 2013.

Lane, Edward William. *Arabic English Lexicon*. New York: Frederick Ungar, 1956.

Leigh, Darby Jared, perf. "Shema in ASL." *Ritualwell*. Reconstructionist Rabbinical College. September 26, 2011. Accessed October 24, 2013.

Leo XIII [Pope]. *Rerum Novarum: Encyclical Letter on Capital and Labor*. Vatican City: Liberia Editrice Vaticana, 1891. Accessed April 26, 2014.

Levy, Chava Willig. "A House of Hopes." In *Total Immersion: A Mikvah Anthology*, edited by Riykah Slonim, 139–42. New York: Jason Aronson, 1996.

Liachowitz, Claire H. *Disability as a Social Construct: Legislative Roots*. Philadelphia: University of Pennsylvania Press, 1988.

Linton, Simi. *Claiming Disability: Knowledge and Identity*. New York: New York University Press, 1998.

———. *My Body Politic: A Memoir*. Ann Arbor: University of Michigan Press, 2006.

Littlejohn, Ronnie. *Confucianism*. London: I. B. Tauris, 2011.

Long, Matthew L. "Leprosy in Early Islam." In Schumm and Stoltzfus, *Disability in Judaism*, 43–61.

Lovern, Lavonna L., and Carol Locust. *Native American Communities on Health and Disability*. New York: Palgrave, 2013.

Luther, Martin. "The Freedom of a Christian." In *Martin Luther: Selections from His Writings*, edited by John Dillenberger, 52–85. New York: Doubleday, 1961.

Lysaught, M. Therese. "Respect: Or, How Respect for Persons Became Respect for Autonomy." *Journal of Medicine and Philosophy* 29, no. 6 (2004): 665–80.

Maimonides, Moses. *Mishneh Torah*. Vol. 1 of *Hilchot Yesodei HaTorah* [Laws concerning the Foundations of the Torah]. Edited by Eliyahu Touger. New York: Moznaim, 1989.

Manzur, Jamal al-Din b. Mukarram al-Ansari Ibn. *Lisan al-Arab*. Cairo: Al-Mu'assasa al-Misriyya al-'Amma lilTa'lif wal-Nashr, n.d.; Beirut: Dar Beirut lilTiba'a wal-Nashr, 1955.

Martos, Joseph. *Doors to the Sacred: A Historical Introduction to Sacraments in the Catholic Church*. Barnhart: Liguori, 2001.

Marx, Tsvi C. *Disability in Jewish Law*. New York: Routledge, 2002.

Masud, M. Khalid, Brinkley Messick, and David Powers, eds. *Islamic Legal Interpretation: Muftis and Their Fatwas*. Cambridge, Mass.: Harvard University Press, 1996.

McGrath, Alister. "Calvin and the Christian Calling." *First Things: A Monthly Journal of Religion and Public Life* 94 (1999): 31–35.

McGrath, Alister E., and Darren C. Marks, eds. *The Blackwell Companion to Protestantism*. Oxford: Blackwell, 2004.

———. "Introduction: Protestantism—The Problem of Identity." In McGrath and Marks, *Blackwell Companion*, 1–19.

McIsaac, Elizabeth. "Oral Narratives as a Site of Resistance: Indigenous Knowledge, Colonization, and Western Discourse." In Dei, Hall, and Rosenberg, *Indigenous Knowledges*, 89–101.

McKew, Maureen. "Confirmation for Youth with Disabilities." Handing on the Faith, January 9, 2013. http://blog.archny.org/faith/?p=593.

McMahan, Jeff. "Cognitive Disability, Misfortune, and Justice." *Philosophy and Public Affairs* 25, no. 1 (1996): 3–35.

Melchert, Christopher, "The Formation of the Sunni Schools of Law." In *The Formation of Islamic Law*, edited by Wael B. Hallaq, 351–66. Aldershot: Ashgate, 2004.

Meyer, Manulani Aluli. "Indigenous and Authentic: Hawaiian Epistemology and the Triangulation of Meaning." In *Handbook of Critical and Indigenous Methodologies*, edited by Norman K. Denzin, Yvonna S. Lincoln, and Linda Tuhiwai Smith, 217–32. Los Angeles: Sage, 2008.

Michalko, Rod. *The Difference That Disability Makes*. Philadelphia: Temple University Press, 2002.

Miles, M. "Community and Individual Responses to Disablement in South Asian Histories: Old Traditions, New Myths?" Independent Living Institute, 2002. http://www.independentliving.org/docs3/miles2002a.html. Accessed August 1, 2013.

———. "Disability and Deafness, in the context of Religion, Spirituality, Belief and Morality, in Middle Eastern, South Asian and East Asian Histories and Cultures: Annotated Bibliography." Independent Living Institute, 2007. http://www.independentliving.org/docs7/miles200707.html. Accessed August 1, 2013.

———. "Disability on a Different Model: Glimpses of an Asian Heritage." *Journal of Religion, Disability & Health* 6, no. 3 (2002): 89–108.

———. "Glimpses of Disability in the Literature and Cultures of East Asia, South Asia, the Middle East & Africa. A modern and historical bibliography, with some annotation." Independent Living Institute, 2008. http://www.independentliving.org/docs7/miles200807.html. Accessed August 1, 2013.

———. "Signing in the Seraglio: Mutes, Dwarfs and Gestures at the Ottoman Court 1500–1700." Independent Living Institute, 2000. http://www.independentliving.org/docs5/mmiles2.html. Accessed July 24, 2013.

Mitchell, David T. "Narrative Prosthesis and the Materiality of Metaphor." In *Disability Studies: Enabling the Humanities*, edited by Sharon L. Snyder, Brenda Jo Brueggemann, and Rosemarie Garland-Thomson, 15–30. New York: Modern Language Association, 2002.

Mitchell, David T., and Sharon Snyder. "'Jesus Throws Everything Off Balance': Disability and Redemption in Biblical Literature." In Avalos, Melcher, and Schipper, *This Abled Body*, 173–83.

Miller, Bruce Granville. *Oral History on Trial: Recognizing Aboriginal Narratives in the Courts*. Vancouver: University of British Columbia Press, 2011.

The Mishnah. Edited by Herbert Danby. New York: Oxford University Press, 1933.

Mligo, Elia Shabani. *Jesus and the Stigmatized: Reading the Gospel of John in a Context of HIV/AIDs-Related Stigma in Tanzania*. Eugene, Ore.: Wipf & Stock, 2011.

Mohawk, John. "Subsistence and Materialism." In *Paradigm Wars: Indigenous Peoples' Resistance to Globalization*, edited by Jerry Mander and Victoria Taulis-Corpuz, 26–28. San Francisco: Sierra Club, 2006.

Montejo, Victor D. "The Road to Heaven: Jakaltek Maya Beliefs, Religion, and the Ecology." In Grim, *Indigenous Traditions*, 175–95.

Mooney, James. *James Mooney's History, Myths, and Sacred Formulas of the Cherokees*. Asheville, N.C.: Historical Images, 1992.

Morris, Jenny. *Pride Against Prejudice: Transforming Attitudes to Disability*. London: The Women's Press, 1991.

Moss, Candida, and Jeremy Schipper, eds. *Disability Studies and Biblical Literature*. New York: Palgrave, 2011.

Mrozik, Susanne. *Virtuous Bodies: The Physical Dimensions of Morality in Buddhist Ethics*. Oxford: Oxford University Press, 2007.

Murata, Sachiko, and Wiliam C. Chittick, eds. *The Vision of Islam*. New York: Paragon House, 1994.

Murderball. DVD. Directed by Henry Alex Rubin and Dana Adam Shapiro. Paramount Pictures & MTV Films, 2005.

Myers, Jody. "The Midrashic Enterprise of Contemporary Jewish Women." In *Jews and Gender: The Challenge to Hierarchy*, edited by Jonathan Frankel, 119–41. New York: Oxford University Press, 2000.

Nāgārjuna. *Letter to a Friend*. Translated by Padmakara Translation Group. Ithaca, N.Y.: Snow Lion, 2005.

Ñāṇamoli, Bhikkhu, and Bhikkhu Bodhi, trans. *The Middle Length Discourses of the Buddha: A Translation of the Majjhima Nikāya*. Boston: Wisdom, 1995.

NCPD [National Catholic Partnership on Disability]. "Accessible Design." National Catholic Partnership on Disability. Accessed April 26, 2014.

———. *Opening Doors to Welcome and Justice to Parishioners with Disabilities*. Washington, D.C.: National Catholic Office for Persons with Disabilities, 2003.

———. "Our Mission, Our Goal: Full Inclusion of Persons with Disabilities—In the Church and in Society." National Catholic Partnership on Disability. Accessed April 26, 2014.

———. *Welcomed and Valued: Building Faith Communities of Support and Hope with People with Mental Illness and Their Families*. Washington, D.C.: National Catholic Partnership on Disability, 2009.

Need, Stephen W. *Truly Divine and Truly Human: The Story of Christ and the Seven Ecumenical Councils*. London: SPCK, 2008.

Nevins, Daniel. "The Participation of Jews Who Are Blind in the Torah Service." In Abrams and Gaventa, *Jewish Perspectives*, 27–52.

Noll, Mark A. *Protestantism: A Very Short Introduction*. Oxford: Oxford University Press, 2011.

Ni, Peimin. *Confucius: Making the Way Great*. Shanghai: Shanghai Translation Publishing House, 2010.

Nussbaum, Martha C. "Capabilities and Human Rights." *Fordham Law Review* 66, no. 2 (1997): 273–300.

———. *Creating Capabilities: The Human Development Approach*. Cambridge, Mass.: Harvard University Press, 2011.

O'Neil, John. "Vital Signs: The Senses; No Vision, but Better Memory." *New York Times*. June 17, 2003. Accessed September 29, 2013.

Oliver, Michael. *The Politics of Disablement: A Sociological Approach*. New York: Palgrave, 1990.

Oliver, Michael, and Colin Barnes. *The New Politics of Disablement*, 2nd rev. ed. New York: Palgrave, 2012.

Olyan, Saul. "The Ascription of Physical Disability as a Stigmatizing Strategy in Biblical Icon Polemics." In Moss and Schipper, *Disability Studies*, 89–102.

———. *Disability in the Hebrew Bible: Interpreting Mental and Physical Differences*. New York: Cambridge University Press, 2008.

———. *Rites and Rank: Hierarchy in Biblical Representations of Cult*. Princeton: Princeton University Press, 2000.

Papandrea, James L. *Reading the Early Church Fathers: From the Didache to Nicaea*. Mahwah, N.J.: Paulist, 2011.

Parsons, Mikeal C. *Body and Character in Luke and Acts: The Subversion of Physiognomy in Early Christianity*. Grand Rapids: Baker Academic, 2006.

Patterson, John M. "Meeting the Needs of Native American Families and Their Children with Chronic Health Conditions." *The Journal of Collaborative Family Healthcare* 15, no. 3 (1997): 237–41.

Pauck, Wilhelm. *The Heritage of the Reformation*. Rev. and enl. ed. Oxford: Oxford University Press, 1968.

Paul VI [Pope]. *Populorum Progressio: Encyclical Letter On the Development of Peoples*. Vatican City: Liberia Editrice Vaticana, 1967. Accessed April 26, 2014.

PCJP [Pontifical Council for Justice and Peace]. *Compendium of the Social Doctrine of the Church*. Vatican City: Liberia Editrice Vaticana, 2004. Accessed April 26, 2014.

Peters, Rudolph. *Jihad in Classical and Modern Islam*. Princeton: Max Wiener, 1996.

Pew Research Center. *Global Christianity: A Report on the Size and Distribution of the World's Christian Population*. Washington, D.C.: Pew Research Center, 2011. Accessed July 19, 2015.

Pius XI [Pope]. *Quadragesimo Anno: Encyclical Letter on Reconstruction of the Social Order*. Vatican City: Liberia Editrice Vaticana, 1931. Accessed April 26, 2014.

Plaskow, Judith. *Standing Again at Sinai*. San Francisco: Harper, 1990.

Posey, Darrell. "Indigenous Ecological Knowledge." In *Paradigm Wars: Indigenous Peoples' Resistance to Globalization*, edited by Jerry Mander and Victoria Taulis-Corpuz, 29–32. San Francisco: Sierra Club, 2006.

Post, Stephen. *The Moral Challenge of Alzheimer Disease*. Baltimore: Johns Hopkins University Press, 1995.

Pye, Michael. *Skilful Means: A Concept in Mahayana Buddhism*. 2nd ed. London: Routledge, 2005.

Ramban (Nachmanides). *Commentary on the Torah*. Translated by Charles B. Chavel. New York: Shilo, 1976.

Ramer, Andrew. *Queering the Text: Biblical, Medieval, and Modern Jewish Stories*. Maple Shade: Lethe, 2010.

Raphael, Rebecca. *Biblical Corpora: Representations of Disability in Hebrew Biblical Literature*. New York: T&T Clark, 2008.

———. "Whoring after Cripples: On the Intersection of Gender and Disability Imagery in Jeremiah." In Moss and Schipper, *Disability Studies*, 103–16.

Red Horse, John. "Traditional American Indian Family Systems." *Families, Systems, & Health* 15, no. 3 (1997): 243–50.

Reinders, Hans S. *Receiving the Gift of Friendship: Profound Disability, Theological Anthropology, and Ethics*. Grand Rapids: Eerdmans, 2008.

Reynolds, Thomas E. *Vulnerable Communion: A Theology of Disability and Hospitality*. Grand Rapids: Brazos, 2008.

Rhys Davids, T. W., trans. *The Questions of King Milinda*. Oxford: Clarendon, 1890.

Richardson, Kristina L. *Difference and Disability in the Medieval Islamic World: Blighted Bodies*. Edinburgh: Edinburgh University Press, 2012.

Rispler-Chaim, Vardit. "Compassion in the Islamic Laws of *Qisas* and *Hudud*: Discussions on the Legitimacy of the Replantation of an Amputated Limb." In *Crueldad y compasión en la literatura àrabe e Islàmica*, edited by Delfina Serrano Ruano, 327–44. Madrid: Consejo superior de investigaciones científicas servicio publicaciones de la Universidad de Córdoba, 2011.

———. *Disability in Islamic Law*. Dordrecht: Springer, 2007.

———. *Islamic Medical Ethics in the Twentieth Century*. Leiden: E. J. Brill, 1993.

————. "Recent Interpretations of the Laws of *Zakāt* with Regard to People with Disabilities: A Comparison with Classical Fiqh." *Comparative Islamic Studies* 9, no. 1 (2013): 91–112.

————. "Sex Change Operations: Between Modern Medicine and Islamic Law." In *Al-Karmil* (Arabic) 18–19 (1998): 165–78.

Rosemont, Henry Jr., and Roger T. Ames. *The Chinese Classic of Family Reverence: A Philosophical Translation of the Xiaojing*. Honolulu: University of Hawaii Press, 2009.

Roubideaux, Yvette. "Cross-Cultural Aspects of Mental Health and Culture-Bound Illnesses." In *Primary Care of Native American Patients: Diagnosis, Therapy, and Epidemiology*, edited by James M. Galloway, Bruce W. Goldberg, and Joseph S. Alpert, 269–72. Boston: Butterworth Heinemann, 1999.

Sabha Parva—The Mahabharata of Krishna-Dwaipayana Vyasa. Translated by Kisari Mohan Ganguli. N.p., 1883–1896. Internet Sacred Text Archive. Accessed August 1, 2013.

Śāntideva. *A Guide to the Bodhisattva Way of Life (Bodhicaryāvatāra)*. Translated by Vesna Wallace and Alan Wallace. Ithaca, N.Y.: Snow Lion, 1997.

Sarna, Jonathan. *American Judaism: A History*. New Haven: Yale University Press, 2004.

Satlow, Michael. *Creating Judaism: History, Tradition, Practice*. New York: Columbia University Press, 2006.

Saunders, Paula. "Gendering the Ungendered Body: Hermaphrodites in Islamic Law." In *Women in Middle Eastern History*, edited by Nikki A. Keddie and Beth Baron, 74–95. New Haven: Yale University Press, 1991.

Scalenghe, Sara. "The Deaf in Ottoman Syria, 16th–18th Centuries." *The Arab Studies Journal* 12/13, no. 2/1 (2004–2005): 10–25.

Schein, Jerome D., and Lester J. Waldman, eds. *The Deaf Jew in the Modern World*. New York: Ktav Publishing House, 1986.

Schimmelpfennig, Bernhard. *The Papacy*. New York: Columbia University Press, 1992.

Schipper, Jeremy. *Disability and Isaiah's Suffering Servant*. New York: Oxford University Press, 2011.

————. "Disabling Israelite Leadership: 2 Samuel 6:23 and Other Images of Disability in the Deuteronomistic History." In Avalos, Melcher, and Schipper, *This Abled Body*, 103–14.

Schriempf, Alexa. "(Re)fusing the Amputated Body: An Interactionist Bridge for Feminism and Disability." *Hypatia: A Journal of Feminist Philosophy* 16, no. 4 (2001): 56–72.

Schumm, Darla, and Michael Stoltzfus. "Beyond Models: Some Tentative Daoist Contributions to Disability Studies." *Disability Studies Quarterly* 31, no. 1 (2011). Accessed July 5, 2014.

————, eds. *Disability in Judaism, Christianity, and Islam: Sacred Texts, Historical Traditions, and Social Analysis.* New York: Palgrave Macmillan, 2011.

Scotch, Richard K., and Kay Schriner. "Disability as Human Variation: Implications for Policy." *The Annals of the American Academy of Political and Social Science* 549 (1997): 148–59.

Sen, Amartya. *The Idea of Justice.* Cambridge, Mass.: Belknap, 2009.

Shakespeare, Tom. *Disability Rights and Wrongs.* New York: Routledge, 2006.

————. "The Social Model of Disability." In Davis, *Disability Studies Reader*, 3rd ed., 214–21.

Shapiro, Joseph P. *No Pity: People with Disabilities Forging a New Civil Rights Movement.* New York: Times Books, 1981.

Shefer, Miri. "Insanity and the Insane in the Ottoman Empire, 15th–17th Centuries." In *Being Different: Minorities, Aliens and Outsiders in History* (Hebrew), edited by Shulamit Volkov, 191–204. Jerusalem: Zalman Shazar Center, 2000.

Silvers, Anita. "Feminist Perspectives on Disability." In *The Stanford Encyclopedia of Philosophy*, edited by Edward N. Zalta. Stanford University, August 29, 2013. Accessed November 14, 2013.

————. "Reconciling Equality to Difference: Caring (F)or Justice For People with Disabilities." *Hypatia: A Journal of Feminist Philosophy* 10, no. 1 (1995): 30–55.

Shoshan, Boaz. "The State and Madness in Medieval Islam." *International Journal of Middle East Studies* 35, no. 2 (2003): 329–40.

Smith, Huston, and Reuben Snake, eds. *One Nation Under God: The Triumph of the Native American Church.* Santa Fe, N.Mex.: Clear Light, 1996.

Smith, Steven. "Social Justice and Disability: Competing Interpretations of the Medical and Social Models." In *Arguing about Disability: Philosophical Perspectives*, edited by Kristjana Kristiansen, Simo Vehmas, and Tom Shakesphere, 15–29. New York: Routledge, 2009.

Snyder, Sharon L., and David T. Mitchell. *The Cultural Locations of Disability.* Chicago: Chicago University Press, 2006.

Sommer, Deborah. "Boundaries of the *Ti* Body." *Asia Major* 21, no. 1 (2008): 293–324.

Soulen, R. Kendall. "Protestantism and the Bible." In McGrath and Marks, *Blackwell Companion*, 251–67.

Spector, Rachel E. *Cultural Diversity in Health and Illness.* New York: Appleton-Century-Crofts, 1979.

Spiteri, Laurence John. *Canon Law Explained.* Manchester: Sophia Institute, 2013.

Stein, Sarah Abrevaya. "Deaf American Culture in Historical Perspective." *American Jewish History* 95, no. 3 (2009): 277–305.

Steinberg, Abraham. "The Blind in the Light of Jewish Thought and Law." In *Tradition and Transition: Essays Presented to Chief Rabbi Sir Immanuel Jakobovits*, edited by Jonathan Sacks, 283–93. London: Jews' College Press, 1986.

Steinberg, Naomi, and Devva Kasnitz. "Disability, Speech, and Judaism: Will You Be My Aaron?" Panel at the Society for Disability Studies Conference. San Jose, California. June 16, 2011.

Stiker, Henri-Jacques. *A History of Disability*. Translated by William Sayers. Ann Arbor: University of Michigan Press, 1999.

Strassfeld, Michael. *A Book of Life: Embracing Judaism as a Spiritual Practice*. Woodstock, N.Y.: Jewish Lights, 2006.

Straus, Joseph N. *Extraordinary Measures: Disability in Music*. New York: Oxford University Press, 2011.

Strous, Rael. "The Shoteh and Psychosis in Halakhah with Contemporary Clinical Application." *The Torah u-Madda Journal* 12 (2004): 158–78.

Sutton-Spence, Rachel, and Bernice Woll. *The Linguistics of British Sign Language: An Introduction*. New York: Cambridge University Press, 1999.

Swinton, John. *Dementia: Living in the Memories of God*. Grand Rapids: Eerdmans, 2012.

Taub, Moshe. "Deafness in Halacha: A Reappraisal." *The Journal of Halacha and Contemporary Society* 1, no. 14 (2012): 5–30.

Terzi, Lorella. "The Social Model of Disability: A Philosophical Critique." *Journal of Applied Philosophy* 21, no. 2 (2004): 141–57.

Thurman, Robert A. F., trans. *The Holy Teaching of Vimalakīrti: A Mahāyāna Scripture*. Delhi: Motilal Banarsidass, 1991.

Tikalsky, Frank D., Catherine A. Euler, and John Nagel, eds. *The Sacred Oral Tradition of the Havasupai: As Retold by Elders and Headmen Manakaja and Sinyella 1918–1921*. Albuquerque: University of New Mexico Press, 2010.

Titchkosky, Tanya, and Rod Michalko. "Introduction." In *Rethinking Normalcy: A Disability Studies Reader*, edited by Titchkosky and Michalko, 1–14. Toronto: Canadian Scholars, 2009.

Tremain, Shelley. "On the Subject of Impairment." In *Disability/Postmodernity: Embodying Disability Theory*, edited by M. Corker and T. Shakespeare, 1–24. London: Continuum, 2002.

Tsong-Kha-Pa. *The Great Treatise on the Stages of the Path to Enlightenment: Lam Rim Chen Mo*. Vol. 1. Translated by Lamrim Chenmo Translation Committee. Ithaca, N.Y.: Snow Lion, 2000.

Tu, Wei-ming. *Centrality and Commonality: An Essay on Confucian Religiousness*. Albany: State University of New York Press, 1989.

Udyoga Parva—The Mahabharata of Krishna-Dwaipayana Vyasa. Translated by Kisari Mohan Ganguli, 1883–1896. Internet Sacred Text Archive. Accessed August 1, 2013.

UN Enable. "Factsheet on Persons with Disabilities." United Nations. Accessed July 10, 2014.

Ungar-Sargon, Batya. "Deaf Rabbi Prepares to Lead a Hearing Congregation in Massachusetts." *Tablet Magazine*. July 29, 2013. Accessed October 24, 2013.

USCCB [United States Conference of Catholic Bishops]. "Guidelines for the Celebration of the Sacraments with Persons with Disabilities." National Catholic Partnership on Disability, 1995. Accessed April 28, 2014.

———. "Life and Dignity of the Human Person." United States Conference of Catholic Bishops, 2013. Accessed April 23, 2014.

———. "Pastoral Statement on People with Disabilities." National Catholic Partnership on Disability, November 16, 1978. Accessed April 21, 2014.

———. "Seven Themes of Catholic Social Teaching." usccb.org. United States Conference of Catholic Bishops, 2013. Accessed April 24, 2014.

Vana Parva—The Mahabharata. Translated by Kisari Mohan Ganguli. N.p., 1883–1896. Internet Sacred Text Archive. Web. Accessed August 1, 2013.

Vatican Council, Second. *Gaudium et Spes: Pastoral Constitution on the Church in the Modern World*. Vatican City: Liberia Editrice Vaticana, 1965. Accessed April 25, 2014.

———. *Lumen Gentium: Dogmatic Constitution on the Church*. Vatican City: Libreria Editrice Vaticana, 1964. Accessed April 21, 2014.

Wasserman, David, Adrienne Asch, Jeffrey Blustein, and Daniel Putnam. "Disability: Definitions, Models, Experience." In *The Stanford Encyclopedia of Philosophy*, edited by Edward N. Zalta. Fall 2013. Stanford University, December 16, 2011. Accessed November 14, 2013.

Watson, Burton, trans. *The Lotus Sutra*. New York: Columbia University Press, 1993.

Webb-Mitchell, Brett. *Unexpected Guests at God's Banquet: Welcoming People with Disabilities into the Church*. New York: Crossroad, 1994.

Weber, Max. *The Protestant Ethic and the Spirit of Capitalism*. Translated by Talcott Parsons. New York: Scribner, 1930.

Wendell, Susan. *The Rejected Body: Feminist Philosophical Reflections on Disability*. London: Routledge, 1996.

———. "Toward a Feminist Theory of Disability." In Davis, *Disabilities Studies Reader*, 2nd ed., 243–56.

———. "Toward a Feminist Theory of Disability." In *The Feminist Philosophy Reader*, edited by A. Bailey and C. Cuomo, 826–40. Boston: McGraw-Hill, 2008.

———. "Unhealthy Disabled: Treating Chronic Illness as Disabilities." *Hypatia: A Journal of Feminist Philosophy* 16, no. 4 (2001): 17–33.

Wensinck, A. J., and B. Lewis. "Hadjdj." In *Encyclopaedia of Islam*, edited by P. Bearman, Th. Bianquis, C. E. Bosworth, E. van Donzel, and W. P. Heinrichs. 2nd ed. Leiden: Brill, 2003.

Williams, Bernard. "Persons, Character and Morality." In *The Identities of Persons*, edited by A. Rorty, 197–216. Berkeley: University of California Press, 1976.

Williams, Paul, with Anthony Tribe. *Buddhist Thought: A Complete Introduction to the Indian Tradition*. New York: Routledge, 2000.

Wogaman, J. Philip. "Protestantism and Politics, Economics, and Sociology." In McGrath and Marks, *Blackwell Companion*, 286–97.

Wolff, Jonathan. "Cognitive Disability in a Society of Equals." *Metaphilosophy* 40, nos. 3/4 (2009): 402–15.

Wong, David. "If We Are Not by Ourselves, if We Are Not Strangers." In *Polishing the Chinese Mirror: Essays in Honor of Henry Rosemont, Jr.*, edited by Marthe Chandler and Ronnie Littlejohn, 331–49. New York: Global Scholarly, 2008.

Yong, Amos. *The Bible, Disability, and the Church: A New Vision of the People of God*. Grand Rapids: Eerdmans, 2011.

Za'tari, 'Ala al-Din al-. "Ashab al-Ihtiyajat al-Khassa fi Zill al-Islam: Ri'aya waAhkam" ["People with special needs in the light of Islam: The treatment and the law"]. Alzatari. April 22, 2013. Accessed December 23, 2015.

Ziporyn, Brook. *Zhuangzi: The Essential Writings with Selections from Traditional Commentaries*. Indianapolis: Hackett, 2009.

Zubaydi, Muhammad Murtada al- (d. 1205H/1791). *Taj al-'Arus*. Cairo, 1888; Kuwait: Matba'at al-Hukuma, 1969.

Contributors

Julia Watts Belser is Assistant Professor of Jewish Studies in the Theology Department at Georgetown University. Her research centers on rabbinic literature and late antique Jewish culture, with particular interests in gender, sexuality, and disability studies. She is the author of *Power, Ethics, and Ecology in Jewish Late Antiquity: Rabbinic Responses to Drought and Disaster* (Cambridge University Press, 2015).

Amy Donahue is Assistant Professor of Philosophy in the History and Philosophy Department at Kennesaw State University in Georgia. Her areas of specialization include Indian philosophy, feminist philosophy, epistemology, and postcolonial theory.

Stephen E. Harris is Assistant Professor (Universitair Docent 2) at Leiden University, where he teaches in the Institute for Philosophy and the International BA program. He specializes in comparative and Indian philosophy, with a particular interest in Buddhist ethical texts.

Mary Jo Iozzio is Professor of Moral Theology at Boston College School of Theology and Ministry, where she teaches social ethics, fundamental moral theology, and critiques of systemic injustice with a special interest in disability studies, anti-racism, and access to the means of human flourishing. She is the author of several books and numerous articles in the areas of moral theology, social ethics, and disability.

Andrew Lambert is Assistant Professor of Philosophy at the College of Staten Island, City University of New York. His research focuses on contemporary ethics and Confucian thought, particularly the relationship between conceptions of moral conduct and personal attachment. He has translated several works in Chinese philosophy.

Lavonna Lovern is Associate Professor of Philosophy and Religious Studies and Native American Studies at Valdosta State University in Georgia. Dr. Lovern has worked with Dr. Carol Locust, in Arizona, on issues of Native American wellness, disability, and education. Her works include books on Indigenous health and disability and education as well as articles involving Native American epistemology, disability, education, and religious diversity.

Benjamin Lukey received his doctorate in comparative philosophy from the University of Hawai'i at Mānoa. His interests in philosophy of disability, comparative philosophy, and philosophy for children (p4c) have developed from his broader goal of including more voices in philosophical discourse. Since 2007, he has been part of the p4c Hawai'i initiative at the University of Hawai'i at Mānoa, piloting and developing a philosopher in residence project at Hawaii public high schools. He is currently Associate Director for the UH Uehiro Academy for Philosophy and Ethics in Education.

Thomas Reynolds is Associate Professor of Theology at Emmanuel College, of Victoria University in the University of Toronto and the Toronto School of Theology. His Ph.D. is from Vanderbilt University (2001), and his books include *The Broken Whole: Philosophical Steps toward a Theology of Global Solidarity* (SUNY 2006) and *Vulnerable Communion: A Theology of Disability and Hospitality* (Brazos 2008).

Vardit Rispler-Chaim teaches Islamic studies at the Department of Arabic Language and Literature at the University of Haifa, Israel. Her main fields of research and publication are Islamic law, Islamic medical ethics, human rights in Islam, and Qur'an and commentaries. She has published more than thirty articles on the position of Islamic ethics on topics such as abortion, genetic engineering, postmortem examinations, the beginning of life, selecting the sex of the embryo, restoration of virginity, replantation of amputated organs, and more. She is the author of two books and the editor of two books in the areas of medical ethics and disability and Islamic law.

Darla Y. Schumm is Professor of Religious Studies at Hollins University in Roanoke, Virginia. Her current research focuses on intersections between religious studies and disability studies. She is co-editor and contributor to *Disability in Judaism, Christianity, and Islam: Sacred Texts, Historical Traditions, and Social Analysis, Disability and Religious Diversity: Cross-Cultural and Interreligious Perspectives*, and co-editor of *Chronic Illness, Spirituality, and Healing: Diverse Disciplinary, Religious, and Cultural Perspectives* (Palgrave 2011, 2013). She has also authored articles in the area of religion and disability. She received her Ph.D. from Vanderbilt University in 2002.

Michael Stoltzfus is Professor of Religious Studies at Georgia Gwinnett College near Atlanta, Georgia. He is co-editor and contributor to *Disability in Judaism, Christianity, and Islam: Sacred Texts, Historical Traditions, and Social Analysis, Disability and Religious Diversity: Cross-Cultural and Interreligious Perspectives*, and *Chronic Illness, Spirituality, and Healing: Diverse Disciplinary, Religious, and Cultural Perspectives* (Palgrave 2011, 2013). He teaches in the areas of religious ethics, religious pluralism and dialogue, religion and culture, world religions, and spirituality and health. His Ph.D. in religion, ethics, and society is from Vanderbilt University.

Index